A HISTORY OF THE CARPENTERS COMPANY

Noah building the Ark
One of four murals discovered at Carpenters Hall in
1846. Taken from a watercolour painted by F. W.
Fairholt, now in the British Museum

A HISTORY OF
THE CARPENTERS
COMPANY

B. W. E. ALFORD
Lecturer in Economic History
University of Bristol

T. C. BARKER
Professor of Economic & Social History
University of Kent at Canterbury

ARCHON BOOKS, 1969

PRINTED IN GREAT BRITAIN
in 12 on 13 pt Fournier type
BY SIMSON SHAND LTD
LONDON, HERTFORD AND HARLOW

PREFACE

MUCH that has been written about London Livery Companies has been narrow in content and limited in appeal. E. B. Jupp's *Historical Account of the Worshipful Company of Carpenters of the City of London* (1848), though a pioneer work of its kind and firmly based on the Company's records, certainly falls into this category. In writing this new history, we have done our best to take a broader view: to keep our eyes upon developments in the craft and changes in the London scene as well as upon the Company's internal affairs. We show how this particular trade organization lacked much of the control it claimed for itself over wages and apprenticeship, even though the City increased its authority, before the Great Fire of 1666, by appointing it agent for the enforcement of certain building regulations.

Until quite recent times the Carpenters Company's status was modest and its income meagre. In the nineteenth century the dilapidated old Carpenters Hall was being used first as a carpet warehouse, and later as a printing concern. The foundation of the modern Company really rests upon railway compensation and the enhancement of property values which came with economic growth in Victorian times. Not that the Company was imprudent in the management of its slender resources in earlier days. Indeed, it showed considerable enterprise in the use of 'fictitious bequests' (known as testamentary devise) to protect such properties as it had from the unscrupulous demands of Tudor and Stuart monarchs. The Company's records have, in fact, enabled us not only to question some of the existing accounts of apparent charitable activity in that period but also to document its own growing prosperity in more recent times.

We should like to express our thanks to the Master and Wardens, who commissioned this book, gave us a completely

PREFACE

free hand in the writing of it, and invited Mr Oman and Mr Nevinson to appraise the Company's plate and furniture; and to the Clerk, Captain Barstow, for his unfailing assistance. When we undertook this commission, we were both members of the staff of the London School of Economics; our moving away from London made the administrative oversight of the work much more difficult than it would otherwise have been, but Captain Barstow has always shown us the utmost courtesy, understanding and helpfulness. Commander A. W. Preston assisted us greatly with the final chapter. We should also like to acknowledge the kindness of the Beadle, Mr W. H. Hopkins; and the help of his predecessor, Mr A. W. Powell, who provided information about the Company's affairs during his long period of office. To Dr A. E. J. Holleander of Guildhall Library, who has custody of most of the Company's records, we owe a special debt of gratitude. We should also like to thank Mr P. V. McGrath for reading and commenting upon the earlier chapters and Mrs Frances Neale for paleographical and research assistance. The imperfections which remain in our text are entirely our own responsibility. Although we have commented freely on each other's sections, Dr Alford bears primary responsibility for the first six chapters and Professor Barker for the last three.

B. W. E. ALFORD
University of Bristol
T. C. BARKER
University of Kent at Canterbury

CONTENTS

PLATES

DIAGRAM

CHAPTER I

THE ORIGINS OF THE COMPANY

LONG before the sealing of the first charter of incorporation of the Carpenters Company in 1477, the carpenters of London had possessed some form of craft organization. As in the case of the older crafts, it is probable that the origins of the Company are to be found in earlier, often secret, fraternities; but these fraternities were usually much less trade associations than friendly societies operating in a religious setting. They must, therefore, inevitably remain veiled in obscurity.[1] Nevertheless, from an early date the City authorities had begun to take an interest in the building crafts,[2] and it is the records of the City which, in 1212, provide the first evidence of an attempt to lay down wage regulations relating to London carpenters as a whole.[3]

At the beginning of the thirteenth century the economic life of London was controlled by a small number of wealthy merchants, who, as aldermen, composed the City's ruling oligarchy.[4] But this control was weakening. It has been estimated that London's population grew from 20,000 people in 1200 to 40,000 a century later.[5] This resulted mainly from the increasing prosperity of the capital which attracted many newcomers from the country—who were known as 'forrens', as distinct from aliens who came from abroad. Such rapid growth generated forces capable of undermining the dictatorial authority of the aldermen. Not unnaturally in this environment, the crafts began to assert their independence openly and to demand a voice in the running of London affairs. And it is probable that one example of the effects of these pressures, as well as of the growing burden of administration on the City, was the decision made during the popular mayoralty of Walter Hervey in 1271,[6] to entrust the task of inspecting and reporting on infringements of the City's building regulations to leading masons and carpenters, who were sworn to serve the City in this capacity. Similarly, when, in 1284, a new ordinance was issued in an effort to control the wages of carpenters, masons, plasterers, daubers and tilers, it was laid down that 'in each ward there should be two good and honest men assigned to discover what masons or carpenters take wages in the City contrary to the Statute of the City'.[7] Who these 'good and honest' men were was not recorded. Indeed, we have no names of Sworn City Carpenters until the end of the thirteenth century. Then, in 1299, Robert Osekyn and John de Wrytele, master carpenters, were sworn to do their duty in all matters relating to their trade as prescribed by City ordinances.[8] In the same year the assistance of the craft trades in general was sought in an attempt to weed out criminal elements among the 'forrens'.[9]

'Whereas a great number of misdoers and disturbers of the King's peace lie hid among the good men of the City, it is ordained that the better and more discreet engaged in the several trades of the City, shall cause a register to be made of all the names of masters, their apprentices and servants, and diligently inquire among themselves as to the conduct and behaviour of all and singular so engaged. And if any be found of bad repute and behaviour, and unfit to remain in the City, they shall present such in rolls to the Warden and Aldermen at the Guildhall [sic] as often as need be, that the said Warden and Aldermen may do therein as may seem best for the welfare of the City . . .'.

In many instances, however, these 'criminal elements' represented no more than a growing spirit of association. For example, Walter de Maydenestan, carpenter, was, on January 31, 1298/9, charged by the Mayor and Aldermen, 'with gathering together a parliament of carpenters at Milehende, where they bound themselves by a corporal oath not to observe a certain ordinance or provision made by the Mayor and Aldermen touching their craft and daily wages, which was enrolled in the "paper" of the Guildhall'.[10] The defendant denied the charge and demanded a trial by jury; unfortunately, the verdict is not revealed.

The future, however, lay with the less extreme elements among the carpenters, with the kind of men who had been chosen to serve the City. Yet, there is no evidence to suggest that these men, though prominent carpenters, were among the leaders of the City crafts, or that they formed a significant number among the small independent householders. In the subsidy roll of 1292, for instance, only three carpenters were assessed, at very low rates.[11] On the other hand, over the following century, the number and nature of carpenters' wills enrolled in the Court of Husting at least indicate that the ownership of property was not altogether beyond the reach of the thrifty carpenter.[12]

Between 1309 and 1312 there was a marked rise in the enrolment of redemptioners at Guildhall, and the fact that groups enrolled together suggests strongly that they were the leading men of crafts, who were now seeking the freedom of the City as the first steps towards giving more formal status to *de facto* organizations.[13] This development was part of a more general movement, led by the large crafts, to establish wider citizenship rights and craft control; objects which were difficult to realize in the face of efforts by the King to increase his powers over the City, and the unending flow of immigrants.[14] The success of this crusade was finally embodied in the famous royal charter of 1319; from henceforth, no stranger could be admitted to citizenship unless his claim was supported by six men of the craft he wished to follow—thus citizenship and craft membership now became almost synonymous.[15] Among those seeking admission to the freedom of the City by redemption were six carpenters—John de Wymbisshe, John de Lodesworth, William de Nottele, Stephen de Redebourne, Robert de Frensshe, and John de Langgereche.[16] Possibly through decease, none of these men is among the carpenters mentioned in the subsidy rolls of 1319 and 1332; while the fact that only eleven carpenters were assessed—seven paying amounts varying between 6½d and 3s 4d, and four paying amounts between 5s and 13s 4d[17]—illustrates that as a group carpenters were still firmly among the ranks of poor craftsmen.

Although the evidence relating to this early period is slender, nevertheless it does begin to reveal a pattern which is brought into sharper relief as the century progresses. It seems probable that most members of the craft were journeymen, and that there was a much smaller number of master craftsmen, who achieved some prominence, usually as holders of the civic appointments of Sworn City Carpenters. And throughout the fourteenth century carpenters' wills were frequently enrolled in the Court of Husting, showing the continuity of this more prosperous element in the craft.[18]

As yet there have been only weak indications that the carpenters possessed any form of organization. Positive evidence in this respect does not come until 1333, when the 'Brotherhood of Carpenters of London' drew up its 'Boke of Ordinances'.[19] The extant copy of these ordinances was produced in 1388–9 to comply with a command of Richard II, who was attempting to gain greater control over City companies and crafts by means of a system of licences. This body of carpenters was described as 'a Fraternity to be [holden in the] Church of Saint Thomas of Acon beside the Conduit of London and in the Church of Saint John the Baptist at Holywell beside London'. It was ordained that brothers and sisters of the fraternity should gather at Mass on each twelfth day in the mid-winter, and again on Midsummer Day, offering a penny on each occasion; the penalty for non-attendance was the payment of one pound of wax. These ordinances were almost solely concerned with the provision of charitable aid to members of the fellowship—to 'pay to the helping of sick men which that fall in [to] disease, as by falling down of an house or hurting of any eye or other divers sicknesses, twelve pence by the year'; to provide for 'any brother or sister [who] have naught of his own to be buried, he shall be honestly buried at the cost of the Brotherhood'; and 'if any brother or sister die honest death out of London the distance of twelve miles, and he have naught whereof to be buried of his own, then shall the Wardens of the Brotherhood wend thither and bury him at the common cost of the Brotherhood'; should any fellow carpenter fall into poverty through sickness, 'he shall have ... fourteen pence a week during this poverty, after he hath lain sick for a fortnight', and if there proved to be insufficient in the common box to meet such contingencies, then it was provided that a collection should be made among the brethren. The only ordinance dealing with trade matters was one directing any member who had work available 'to work his own brother before any other', unless his 'brother' was not skilled enough to perform the work in question. Six of the sixteen articles dealt with the simple procedure for running the fraternity—quarterages were to be paid; no one was to be received into the fraternity unless it was by the unanimous consent of all its members; if any 'brother' or 'sister became of evil name', they were to be expelled; failure to answer the quarterly summons of the Masters was to entail a penalty of one pound of wax, 'but he have a very excuse [*sic*] for his absence'; four wardens were to be chosen each year to rule the fraternity; and finally, any disputes between members were to be brought first to the wardens and the fellowship.

The strong friendly society character of the fraternity which was not at all concerned about rights of citizenship, and only slightly interested in trade matters, is further emphasized by the fact that these ordinances were not submitted to Guildhall for approval. Feeling ran high, of course, against the constant stream of country carpenters who were diluting the labour force in London. In 1339, for instance, five carpenters were charged with using physical violence to prevent 'forrens' from entering the City and working for less than 6d a day.[20] Although a charge of having 'beaten and maimed' one of them could not be sustained, there was clear evidence of intimidation. Sporadic outbreaks of this nature occurred later in the century, but by then the series of visitations of plague, of which the Black Death of 1348 is the best known,[21] had brought about a sharp change in the labour supply. There was now an acute shortage of labour and those craftsmen who survived the terrible epidemics were not slow to demand higher wages. The City authorities endeavoured to keep carpenters' wages down by ordinances issued in 1350, 1360 and 1372.[22] How much assistance was received from the leading carpenters in enforcing these rates of pay is not clear. Moreover, for lack of records it is impossible to assess the effects of the new economic forces upon the Fraternity. No doubt death and disease taxed its friendly society facilities to the utmost; but in the longer run, the higher wages and greater bargaining power of individual carpenters undoubtedly strengthened their association. Besides, this accords with a recent assessment of the later Middle Ages as a period, not of decline and decay, but of growth and more evenly distributed prosperity.[23] In the country at large there was a marked buoyancy in urban affairs, and many fraternities and craft societies in the building trades sought to consolidate their corporate interests.[24]

The beginning of a continuous record of the Carpenters Company is provided by a lease dated January 22, 1428/9, recording the purchase by three carpenters of a ninety-eight-year lease of five cottages and a piece of waste land in All Hallows by London Wall, subject to an annual rental of 20s.[25] The wisdom of this decision soon became obvious, but even those who made it could not have foreseen the extent to which it would affect the future of the Company. The cottages were pulled down and 'instead thereof one Great Hall and three New Houses on the east side of the said Hall and one new house on the west was then erected and built'.[26] Among the original lessees of the Hall were John Blomvyle, Richard Bryght, and Thomas Sexton—all of whom were Sworn City Carpenters.

This identity between City and Company might be taken as evidence of the continuity of some form of organization among London carpenters stretching back to the Fraternity of 1388. Besides, the possession of a hall by any but the wealthiest companies in the early fifteenth century was unusual;[27] and by itself it is suggestive of a fairly long-standing relationship of trust between the leading carpenters in London, as well as of their confidence in their ability to establish some degree of control over the craft as a whole. More particularly, between 1389 and 1438 thirty-one wills of 'Citizens and Carpenters' were enrolled, and among this number were two which refer specifically to the 'Carpenters Company': that of William Strete in 1417 which includes a legacy to the Company, and that of William Stodeye in July 1426 which lists among his possessions 'a gown of the last Livery of the Carpenters'.[28] Persuasive though this evidence might appear, it is still too circumstantial to be conclusive. This new hall was nowhere near the churches mentioned in the 'Boke of Ordinances'; and there can be little doubt that although there might have been some continuity of organization among London carpenters, it was inevitably of a very tenuous nature. In 1376, for example, the Corporation had need to draw up a list of the leading companies and crafts in London.[29] Forty-seven trades and crafts were named—including what were then such lowly companies as those of the Joiners and the Plumbers—but the Carpenters were not important enough to be included among them. Quite apart from this, however, it will be shown in more detail in the next chapter that, even under the most favourable circumstances for the development of small craft companies, the small-scale and highly mobile nature of the carpenters' craft made it difficult to achieve strong company organization; and it was made even more difficult while the demand for crown building, with its attendant impressment of masons and carpenters, remained so preponderant in relation to the supply of building craftsmen. Moreover, in the fourteenth century the larger financial rewards went not to the carpenter but to his superior fellow craftsman, the freemason.

Under the more favourable conditions of the fifteenth century the Company flourished. The growing attention paid to the regulation of the craft is reflected in the increasing detail and comprehensiveness of the accounts, which survive from 1438.[30] At the same time, the links with the Corporation—so helpful to craft regulation—were strengthened; and the names of the leaders of the company—Blomvile, Salisbury, Goldington, Bird, Seryll, Orchard, Ray, White and others—occur frequently as signatories to the reports on building offences made to Guildhall by the City Masons and Carpenters.[31] By 1466, therefore, the Company was sufficiently well established to apply for, and obtain, a coat of arms and common seal—the craft being denoted by 'A felde silver a Chevron sable grayled iii Compass of the same'.[32] Eleven years later, in 1477, the progress of the Carpenters was crowned when they received from Edward IV their first charter of incorporation.[33] That this charter was obtained only after several years' effort is evident from the Warden's accounts. What was obviously a rough copy of the proposed charter was drawn up in 1472 at a charge of 8d.[34] Then, in 1475, the following entries occur:[35]

Itm paid to maister naylarde for the
   Copy of a corporaĉon x^s viij^d
Itm paid to John Shernall for the Armes v^s viij^d

And in 1477 it is recorded:[36]

Itm paid for a corporation   xxiiij^{li} viij^d

The industry and purpose of those who promoted this scheme, and the support that they were given by members of the craft, was similarly recorded:[37]

'And in the yere of Kyng Edward iiijth xvij was the Corporacon purchaced by ye labo^r of Thoms. perte John White Robt Crosby and Pers baily the viijth day of Auguste And these be the names of them y^t gaffe therto:—'

This is followed by a further list of those who had not yet subscribed towards the cost. And, finally, in 1478 the payment for the seal was entered:[38]

Itm. paid for the seele of the Crafte   xxviij[s].

The Charter confirmed that the control of the Company was vested in the master and wardens, who also had the right to hold any possessions for the commonalty. The Company was given power to plead in any courts, and to receive bequests and gifts of property which could be put in mortmain. The Carpenters' property was now securely held and at last they could boast the full trappings of a City Livery Company.

The most fundamental influence on the Company during this period is represented, however, not by the grant of arms, the seal, or the charter, but by the new ordinances which had been drawn up in 1455, and apparently acted on by the Carpenters from that date, although not formally enrolled at Guildhall until 1487;[39] the delay was due probably to the unsettled conditions following the Wars of the Roses and to the constant recurrence of the plague. The new ordinances were in marked contrast to those of 1333, as they were an expression of intent to control one of the main branches of the medieval building industry.

The 'Boke' of 1333 had contained only sixteen articles; that of 1455 contained thirty. Unlike the old, the new ordinances contained few provisions dealing with religious and fraternal matters; most of them dealt, either directly or indirectly, with trade questions. Moreover, whereas there had formerly been an allusion to carpenters working outside London, the purview of the Company was now limited to London and its 'suburbs'. In 1333 it was prescribed that those seeking admission to the fellowship were to be elected by the 'common consent of all its members', and this was now superseded by detailed rules of procedure. The solitary fine of one pound of wax to be paid for failure to comply with some of the early regulations was replaced by a comprehensive list of forfeits. Control over the Company was to be exercised

by a master and three wardens, who were to be elected annually—
'that the Maister Wardeyns and feolaship of the said Crafte and
their Successours yeerely fromhensforth forever in the day of
Seint Laurence the Martir may assemble togiders at ther Comon
Halle and than and there of theym self elect and chose oon
Maister and iij Wardeyns'[40]—and once elected, these officials
could appoint up to eight assistants to help them in the perfor-
mance of their duties. These assistants had either to have held
office in the Company, or were to be 'most honest psones' (men
of long standing). Together, this body was to form a Court,
which was to meet at the Hall every Friday, and to be responsible
for submitting an annual statement of accounts. The Livery, or
Clothing, of the Company was to be composed of those freemen
who were worth 20 marks or more, and it was obligatory to take
it up. Admission to the freedom by redemption [i.e. by purchase]
could only take place with the consent of the Assistants, and all
apprentices had to be presented to the Master and Wardens before
being bound. Provision was still made for unemployed members,
and this was strengthened by a clause which forbade any member
to supplant a fellow craftsman; and no apprentice or journeyman
was to be employed until he had given proof of his ability. A
number of regulations dealt with the crucial matter of controlling
the labour supply—particularly the flow of 'forrens' into the City,
which the Company sought to stem, if not dam, by a series of
licences and prohibitions.[41] At the same time, members were forbidden to undertake the work of masons, plumbers, plasterers,
and tylers, in return for reciprocal agreements with these allied
crafts.[42] In addition, the Master and Wardens were given the
authority to search for all timbers, boards, etc., which did not
comply to the standard sizes and qualities laid down by the City.
Finally, the posts of Master Carpenter of Guildhall, and of Bridge-
house, were to be held by freemen of the Company—the holders
of these offices being responsible, under the City, for supervising
all carpenters' work at Guildhall and at London Bridge. The
comprehensive nature of these ordinances meant that if they were

successfully put into operation, the Company would be possessed of considerable control over all building work in London.

Thus, firmly established as one of the 'lesser crafts', the Carpenters came forty-eighth in a list of seventy companies that subscribed to a loan of 1488.[43] Moreover, this list provides an illustration of the relative power and influence of the various City companies: for example, the Mercers subscribed £740, the Grocers £455, the Drapers £420, the Goldsmiths £280, the Skinners £150, the Haberdashers £120, the Ironmongers £80, the Butchers £50, the Stationers £20, the Plumbers £14, the Painters £12, the Carpenters £8, the Joiners £8, the Masons £4, and the Wheelwrights 20s. Another measure of difference in scale between 'greater' and 'lesser' is given by the fact that the annual income and expenditure of the Grocers varied between ten and twenty times that of the Carpenters.[44] Nevertheless, the Carpenters were sufficiently distinguished to be taken as a model for other aspiring crafts; and in 1497 the Pewterers paid 2½d to view Carpenters Hall in order to pick up ideas which might help them in the designing of a hall of their own.[45]

During the sixteenth century the Company steadily increased in strength, but this was accompanied by a growing formality in its domestic affairs. The corporate nature of the Company was gradually given greater emphasis, and the term 'Brotherhood', frequently to be found in the earlier records, gave way to 'this House'.[46] This change of character was fostered by the lengthening calendar of formal occasions. And to deal with increasing administration, in 1487 a Clerk was appointed at an annual fee of 33s 4d.[47] This official supervised the day-to-day running of the Company, aided by a Beadle, references to whom go back to the earliest extant accounts of 1438.[48] Separate minutes recording the decisions of the Court begin in 1533,[49] and these show that, although the ordinances provided for weekly meetings, this degree of regularity was never attained.[50] Between 1533 and 1573 Courts met on average twelve times a year, although this does not show the greater regularity after 1566, when the average rose to twenty-eight. This rise was maintained during the period 1573–94, when the average was twenty-five, with a peak of forty-one courts in 1573. The increase in the mid-'sixties, however, coincided with the arrival of a new Clerk, John FitzJohn, noteworthy for his exceptional diligence,[51] so the explanation of it may be simply the more careful keeping of records, which would imply that earlier figures are not a completely accurate record.

From the quarterage payments it is possible to trace the rise in the Carpenters' total membership.[52] In the late 1430s there were about forty freemen, by the mid-'fifties this had risen to nearly fifty, and then it continued at about the same level, with a tendency to fall, until 1477 when the acquisition of the charter led to a sharp increase to 106. Shortly afterwards the total fell back to just above the level of the 1430s, probably due to the severe outbreak of plague in 1479. But there was a quick recovery in the 1490s, and by 1500 the Company could boast more than 130 freemen. Unfortunately, there is a gap in the Wardens' Accounts between 1516 and 1546, so there is no record of membership for this period. Nevertheless, it would appear that the growth in numbers was maintained, because from 1546–73 membership fluctuated between 130 and 200, and from 1573 until the end of the century between 250 and 300.

Growing attention was paid to questions of procedure. The order in which the Wardens and Assistants should take their places at various functions was carefully prescribed.[53] And the original ordinance regulating the number of Livery was given a new significance, when, in 1571, it was ordained that:[54]

'. . . at the Requeste of some of the Lyverie that for the worshipp of this mysterie those that nowe are and those that hereafter shallbe called into the clothinge of this companie to be knowen from the reste of the yomanrie everie Quarterdaie when the companie dothe met ther at theyr Quartersupper By reason whereof . . . Two shillings everie May wch was towardes the buyinge and making of Fower dozen Napkins for the hole clothynge ... and everye Quarterdaie or when anie of the clothinge shall fortune to have anie Repaste in this house the Second Warden shall then deliver so manie of the said Napkins as shall then be of the Lyverie to occupie the same ...'.

Out of a total membership of between 250 and 300 no more than forty were called to the Livery, and of these on average eight formed the Court of Assistants.[55] Thus, the Carpenters now began to follow the common pattern of organization among City Livery Companies. The remainder of the freemen were known as the Yeomanry; the first mention of which occurs in 1556,[56] although as early as 1468 there is a reference to the 'young men of the Company'.[57] But, unlike some other craft organizations, the Livery were not distinguished from the Yeomanry by virtue of being the non-craft element of the Company; the distinction here was that between the relatively prosperous and the less prosperous craftsmen,[58] or, by and large, between masters and journeymen. Indeed, the lack of friction between the two elements suggests that the path from the lower to the higher level was open to those who could make it, a fact which will shortly be seen to result from new developments in the building trades.

As the leading members became wealthier, the possessions of the Company were increased. Among gifts in the later fifteenth century were two silver macers, silver spoons, a basin or ewer, two candlesticks of latten, and an iron hearth for the Hall.[59] Of outstanding importance was the bequest of property by Thomas Warham in 1481, the year of incorporation. This consisted of a messuage and four gardens in Lime Street, subject to an annual payment of 20s to the parishes of St Dionis, Backchurch, and St Andrew, Undershaft.[60] This bequest more than doubled the rent roll which up to that time had consisted solely of receipts from the Hall property.

In common with all City companies the Carpenters played their part in the pageant of State and the civic life the capital. The

Warden's accounts provide an indirect commentary on these events; a barge was hired for accompanying the Mayor to Westminster, payments were made for processional banners, expenses were incurred from the sombre occasion of the burial of Henry VII, and from the high-spirited celebration of Henry VIII's coronation. At the domestic level *esprit* was fostered by a conviviality which has always been the mark of a City Livery Company. The first mention of the 'feste day' is in 1454, although it is not until 1490 that full details of these occasions are available. After the business had been settled, the commonalty settled down to a fare which, when compared with the twentieth century, shows some striking contrasts. The fruit was limited to oranges and damsons, for instance, and the vegetables to peas, onions and parsley. On the other hand, such sixteenth-century delicacies as swan and sparrow might appeal to the modern gastronome.

By the end of the fifteenth century the Carpenters Company had firmly established itself, aided, no doubt, by its frequent use as agent for the enforcement of the City's building ordinances. Yet it was never really successful in enforcing these controls; wages continued to rise and irregularities in building continued to occur. The Company, never more than 300 strong before 1600, represented a minor fraction of the total force of carpenters at work in London. There was apparently a gulf between theory and practice which deserves further investigation.

CHAPTER II

THE COMPANY AND THE CONTROL OF THE CRAFT
1400-1600

———————

THE political climate of London during the fourteenth century made it difficult for the small crafts to break loose from their subjection to the established Companies. And with the advent of more democratic government towards the end of the century, it did not necessarily follow that each individual craft thereby became free to assert its independence.[1] The carpenters must be counted among the less fortunate in this respect.

The small-scale nature of carpenters' work inevitably made Company organization difficult. The individual craftsman had only his skill to sell; it was either financially impossible or too risky for a would-be building contractor to carry stocks and employ labour to undertake a wide variety of work, and in the case of big customers the materials would have already been purchased for him. Equally, on the demand side conditions were unfavourable.[2] The biggest customers for building were the Crown and the Church, who usually employed permanent or semi-permanent officials to control building operations. This meant that impressment of labour for Crown building was a common occurrence in the thirteenth and fourteenth centuries; for example, in 1359, a chronicler noted that Wykeham had impressed nearly every mason and carpenter in the country so that only deserters were available to work for the general public.[3] Although this was probably a somewhat exaggerated report it does, nevertheless, indicate the degree of monopoly of building labour which could be exercised by the Crown, and there are numerous other examples on a less extensive scale. Carpenters could be taken from London to far-distant Wales to work on castle building; and inevitably this meant that a nascent organization in London would be stillborn. Moreover, those who achieved eminence in these fields—as architects, designers and wood-carvers—could have had little need for the protection of a small craft company. For example, William Lyngwode gained such a reputation for his work that Bishop Woodlock, in 1308, wrote to Bishop Salmon of Norwich asking that Lyngwode be excused for a year from 'doing suit to your court'.[4] And at a lower level, the supervision of groups of carpenters or masons working on churches or castles was easily entrusted to officials who were employed permanently; and as much of the work was of a repetitive nature—so many gargoyles for facing a church, or so many wall posts for a hammer beam roof—it could be done in workshops specially constructed for the purpose. Sometimes, it is true, the keenness of the ecclesiastical and royal authorities to recruit labour was not matched by an ability to pay for it, but this provided opportunities for specialist dealers in short-term finance, not for master carpenters.

From the late fourteenth century onwards, however, the trade underwent a number of changes. There was a decline in the amount of royal building and practically a cessation of impressment of labour. Church building in the fifteenth century was more active in the provinces than in London. Moreover, the number of building contracts which have come to light show that new demands were replacing the old.[5] The main source of these was house-building, ranging from hovels for the poor to the splendid Tudor houses of which many fine examples are still in existence. While the largest buildings were constructed from stone, late medieval and early modern houses were built on a basic structure of a timber frame, and thus, in this branch, the carpenter and not the mason was the master craftsman. Together, these factors provided much greater opportunities for the more ambitious craftsman, who could now become a small contractor and not just the employee of another. To quote just two examples: the Grocers Company's accounts for 1429-31 record a payment of £100 to William Serle, one of the leading members of the Carpenters Company and an original trustee of the Hall, for building the roof of their Hall.[6] Secondly, in 1530, James Nedam, soon to become Surveyor of the King's Works and Master of the Company, contracted with Lord Henry, Marquess of Exeter, to make a wooden summer house and galleries to enclose three sides of a walled garden. Nedam received £100 for this work which had to be completed within four months.[7] In each case a considerable number of workmen were employed.

Much similar evidence could be quoted, but the general picture of the craft which emerges is that, by 1500, while the great majority of craftsmen, including 'forrens', worked as small masters or journeymen employees, there was a small but increasing number of men who were achieving more solid prosperity. This view is borne out by records of payments for building work.[8] The bulk of the payments were made by the day to individual craftsmen, but there were a few made to building employers who contracted for work 'by the piece', and not by the day; and over the fifteenth and sixteenth centuries the complaints that some master carpenters were employing 'forrens' and more apprentices than were allowed by the Company's ordinances grew steadily more numerous.[9] It is against this general background that the Carpenters' attempts to establish control over the craft in London have to be viewed.

The basis of the Company's authority was formed by those of the ordinances of 1455 which dealt with its control over its own membership: the regulations dealing with the binding of apprentices, admission to the freedom, and the practice of the craft. The ordinances laid down:[10]

'That every psone of the said Crafte the which hereafter shall take any app'ntice shall present and shewe the same app'ntice to the Maist and Wardeyns of the same crafte for the tyme beyng afore he be bounde to thentente that they may understand whether the same app'ntice be free born or not And also that he be not lame croked ne deformed . . . as than evy suche app'ntice as than he shall have and take by the aggremet of the said Maister and Wardeyns . . .'.

The fee for binding was originally 1s, but it was raised to 3s in 1508, and then, after a while, settled at 2s 2d for the remainder of the century. Apprenticeship was to be for a minimum period of seven years, but terms of eight and nine years were common, particularly among those who came from the provinces.[11] In 1569 it was ordered that no freeman could take an apprentice until he had been free of Company for three years,[12] and, by this time also, there were attempts to limit the number of apprentices which any master could take—although it was not until 1607 that new ordinances dealt with this problem.[13] No apprentice could be 'turned over' to another master without the permission of the Court and the payment of a small fine. 'Forren' carpenters could not be employed by freemen of the Company, except under licence. This licence, which gave the Company the power to limit 'forrens' wages, was not to be issued until the Master and Wardens were satisfied about the man's competence.[14] The Company also had the right to seize any materials used in the craft which were traded among 'forrens'.[15]

Before the mid-seventeenth century there were no separate apprenticeship registers, and details of apprenticeship were recorded in the Court Books.[16] Between 1533 and 1573 there is no record of the number of bindings, but there is a detailed list of those admitted to the freedom: 645 by servitude, 43 by patrimony and a further 30 by redemption. Between 1573 and 1594, 1,200 apprentices were bound at Carpenters' Hall, but of this number approximately only 40 per cent subsequently sought the freedom; in addition, a further 28 entered by patrimony, 18 by redemption and there were 4 translations from other companies. Apart from the possibility that some men technically remained as apprentices for periods longer than seven years, it has been suggested that their failure to seek the freedom resulted in part, at any rate, from the fact that as the majority came from the provinces, mainly from the northern and western counties, to learn their trade, they returned home when they had served their time;[17] indeed, only just under 15 per cent of those bound in 1574 came from London and the counties of Middlesex, Surrey, Kent and Essex, and by 1583 this proportion had fallen to some 13 per cent. So perhaps only 160 to 180 of those 1,200 bound apprentices were London-born. Lastly, it must not be forgotten that at least part of the discrepancy results from purely natural causes.

For some provincial-born men the migration to London was permanent. It was shown in chapter I that between 1546 and 1573 total membership fluctuated between 130 and 200, and from 1573 until the end of the century between 250 and 300. It is not possible to discover what proportion of the total in 1573 had died and had been replaced by 1600, but bearing in mind the low expectancy of life, it must have been considerable, and probably amounted to more than two-thirds. Even if all the 160 to 180 London-born apprentices had survived and had sought the freedom—which is unlikely—this number was not large enough to meet the replacement of members and to account for the expansion in total membership over the period, and consequently it follows that there was a considerable degree of recruitment from the provinces. This is borne out by the records, in which the careers of a number of provincial-born men can be traced from being bound apprentice to taking up the freedom.[18]

There is no straightforward method for determining the total number of carpenters in London, as little is known about occupational distribution before the nineteenth century, and those figures which do exist are mainly of interest as examples of the *lacunae* which dog any attempt to make such analyses. Nevertheless, with estimates of the population of London, it is possible to make some very broad but revealing comparisons between London employment and an extant occupational census relating to seventeenth-century Gloucestershire.[19] The census shows that in the three towns of Gloucester, Tewkesbury, and Cirencester, 2·3 per cent of the male labour force was employed as carpenters, either as masters, journeymen, or apprentices. The population of London is difficult to determine but it probably increased from 40,000 in 1300 to about 200,000 by 1600.[20] Now, if the conservative assumption is made that only one-third of the population of London could be classed as the male labour force, on the basis of the census this would give the number of carpenters in the City in 1600 as just over 1,500. Moreover, this calculation takes no account of the fact that, almost certainly, a proportionately larger number of carpenters was employed in London than in the provinces—this, after all, is why so many provincial carpenters went to London. Even on this minimum figure, the gap between the estimated number of carpenters in London and the number under the control of the Company is so large as to compensate for the very rough nature of the calculations and still to suggest the view that only a minority of those working at the craft were doing so legally. In fact, the combined number of freemen and apprentices represents, at the very most, 40 per cent of the estimated total. And, according to the Court Books, the number of licences issued authorizing the employment of 'forrens' amounted to no more than eleven between 1533 and 1573, and to three between 1573 and 1594, while the number of fines levied for failure to apply for such licences during the same periods were no more than twelve and seven respectively. Furthermore, there is no question of the law against 'forrens' being enforced through the City courts rather than through the Carpenters Company; their right to impose a penalty of 20s on those who employed 'forrens' illegally gave them every incentive, from a purely financial view, to enforce the law, and had they done so their annual income would have been far higher than it was in fact during this period. Nor do the records give any sign that the Denizens Act of 1524, or the Statute of Apprentices of 1563, strengthened the Company's hand; the one attempted to bring 'forrens' under craft control by forcing them to register with City companies, the other aimed to establish a standard period of apprenticeship of seven years. There is the usual problem, of course, of an unknown number of carpenters who were apprenticed to members of other City companies, but who at the same time would have recognized the ordinances of the Carpenters Company. But again, the procedure of translation from other companies would have kept this number very low.

Therefore, in addition to the constant migration into London of apprentices from the country who were bound at Carpenters Hall, there was a stream of unlicensed 'forrens' apparently completely outside the Company's control; though, no doubt, some of them would already have served their full term of apprenticeship in the provinces. Probably, these men were attracted to the capital by higher wage rates, for it can be shown by a comparison between an index of wage rates derived from the Carpenters' records and one based on evidence relating to the Southern Counties of England, that wages in London were from one-and-a-half to two times those ruling in the provinces,[21] although it is impossible to draw certain conclusions from this because little or nothing is known of comparative real wages. It can be suggested that at least part of this large body of non-affiliated carpenters was indirectly under the Company's authority, as a result of numbers of 'forrens' and 'long-serving' apprentices being employed by the small group of carpenter-contractors. But when due allowance is made for this, the foregoing analysis suggests that it is extremely unlikely that the Company represented, directly or indirectly, much more than a bare majority of City carpenters. To this extent the comprehensive authority vested in the Company through its ordinances was rendered weak and inoperative, and the reasons for this will be considered fully a little later. Altogether, this provides further evidence of the need to test carefully the degree to which the City companies were able to put craft and trade regulations into operation.

Fines imposed for breaking trade regulations were concerned mostly with the employment of apprentices and 'forrens', and the illegal purchase of building materials. Between 1573 and 1594 the details of only sixty-five such fines are recorded in the minutes of the Court, but it is clear that this is an incomplete record because a larger number of fines is recorded in the accounts as 'payments received'. How many of these related to domestic matters, and how many to infringements of trade regulations, it is not possible to discover. As well as craft ordinances, there were the ordinances dealing with the general behaviour of members. Usually, it was simply necessary for the Court to impose small fines on those who used 'approbrious' or 'unmannerly' language, but sometimes more serious offences occurred. One Anthony Bear, for instance, was fined thirty shillings because in the heat of a quarrel he 'drew out his dagger and would a done [sic] the said Christopher harm had not come neighbours and parted them'.[22] If the Court of Assistants proved unable to settle a dispute, it was empowered to issue a licence to the contestants to take their case before the City Courts.

Before the effectiveness of the Company's control over the craft can be fully assessed, it is necessary to consider two other aspects of its activities during this period. In each case this led to a close relationship with the City. From the fourteenth century onwards frequent attempts had been made to regulate carpenters' wages in London, but it is evident from such scraps of information about wage rates as we possess that these attempts ended in utter failure. The 'forrens', who, as we saw in the previous chapter, aroused the wrath of London carpenters in 1339, had attracted attention to themselves by working for less than 6d a day 'and an after-dinner drink', obviously the standard rate at that time.[23] In the summer the length of the working day was from sunrise to sunset; although these long hours were relieved by a liberal interspersion of Saints days and Feast days. In the winter, by reason of the weather the day was somewhat shorter, and on projects of Crown and Church building the officials in charge

would endeavour to so organize matters that much of the interior
and prefabricated work could be done during these months.

The Black Death, however, created a severe labour shortage
which drove up wages. In 1350, the Corporation,

> 'To amend and redress the damages and grievances which the
> good folks of the City, rich and poor, have suffered and
> received within the past year, by reason of masons, carpenters,
> plasterers, tilers, and all manner of labourers, who take im-
> measurably more than they have been wont to take...',

decreed that master carpenters' wages should not exceed 6d a day
in winter.[24] The persistent nature of the problem is shown, for
example, both by the need to issue further ordinances in a City
proclamation of 1372,[25] and by further general acts relating to the
country as a whole, passed in 1360, 1446 and 1495.[26] And the same
story is repeated in the sixteenth century. The Common Council
of the City, in 1521, issued a decree that a committee comprising
one each of the trades of mercer, grocer, draper, goldsmith,
fishmonger, merchant tailor, haberdasher, and skinner, together
with the two Bridge masters and the Wardens of the Carpenters
Company, should be appointed to 'Try the good workmen from
the Bad' amongst the four crafts of carpenters, tilers, plasterers
and paviours, and to assess their wages according to their
'deserts'.[27] And, in 1551, the Common Council instructed the
Company to ensure that carpenters would work for 'more reasonable and esyere wages than they nowe do', and that the best workmen would have a maximum wage of 10d per day.[28] The Company was ordered further to produce a report on the problem of
rising wage rates in the craft, together with its book of ordinances.
The Carpenters' accounts, however, contain many entries of wage
payments made for work done on their estates in London, and
these show that in 1443 craftsmen were then receiving 8d a day
and labourers 5d, while during the price rise of the sixteenth
century the rate for master craftsmen shot up from 12d in 1551

to 18d in 1579.[29] The pegging of wages proved to be an impossible task in such an inflationary situation;[30] and, in any case, it was not in the true interests of members of the Company to enforce wage regulations too conscientiously.

Nor was the City much better served by the Company in its attempts to enlist the assistance of Sworn Master Carpenters in an effort to enforce building regulations—most of which emanated directly from the Common Council, though on occasions the City became the agent for the enforcement of royal decrees. The first of these regulations was FitzAlwyn's Assize of Building of 1189, which dealt with building materials, the erection of party walls, and boundary rights. Further ordinances were issued in 1212 to prohibit any building which increased the already high risk of fire—the great menace in medieval towns—and on many subsequent occasions in the fourteenth century the City promulgated further decrees against this hazard. In order to supplement the various building regulations, the Company received specific powers under its ordinances of 1455 to seize sub-standard building materials.[31]

Indeed, the operation of this branch of the trade was a major cause in undermining attempts to enforce regulations. For instance, during the fifteenth and early sixteenth centuries those who cut and sawed timber outside London—timbermen and boardmen—brought their goods to the City and offered them directly to Companies, builders and carpenters;[32] and it was generally agreed that this ensured a regular supply of materials at 'fair' prices. By 1521, however, woodmongers and others, keeping wharves by the Thames, had supplanted the timbermen and boardmen in the business of distributing timber. Supplies were now brought in on barges from the surrounding countryside and wharf owners charged customers for storage and carriage. Moreover, it was alleged that woodmongers and wharfingers 'engross up all manner of timber, boards, lath, quarters, shipboard, shingles, hoops, etc.', by sending factors into the country to purchase all available supplies. The net result was high prices and the even greater use of inferior materials—mostly the use of unseasoned timber. The City responded to a petition from the Carpenters by decreeing that no wharf owner should henceforth buy any wood for resale, and should be entitled only to charge for wharfage and carriage. As soon as this order came into force it was openly flouted. Once again therefore, in 1529, the Company petitioned the City in this matter, drawing attention to the careless drafting of this decree, by pointing out that it contained no mention of how or by whom it should be put into effect.[33] To meet this criticism the Common Council declared that the penalty for engrossing should be forfeiture of the timber in question: 'half the value to go to the Mayor and Commonalty, the other half to the first finder thereof'.[34] Also, on pain of the same penalty, no carpenter or any other person buying wood for resale, which had been discharged from barges or lighters on to wharves, could do so until it had lain on the wharves 'three whole days'. To enforce this order the Council set up a committee drawn from the interested parties.

For all this paraphernalia of enforcement, however, the order proved to be, at most, a very qualified success. Eventually, in 1553, the issue was again discussed but with the same results.[35] The problem was made more difficult by the fact that the structure of most houses was based on a large wooden frame, often constructed in saw-yards in the suburbs, transported into the City by barge, piece by piece, and re-assembled on the required site.[36] It was, therefore, a relatively easy matter for 'forrens' and others not subject to the Company's control, to obtain supplies from the many wharfingers along the Thames. In 1554 it was reported that women were buying timber at the wharves for their husbands, who were 'forrens'.[37] And in 1572 it was ordained that:[38]

'... anie psone or psons of this companie or anie of their svauntes at anye tyme heareafter doe goe downe to the watersyd & buye of anye wharfenger or wharfekeeper ther or ther aboutes dwelling anie kinde of stuff belonginge to the occupacon of Carpentrie as tymber Rafters Joystes Lathes quarters or bordes or anye other thinge to the same belonginge or of anie other psone or psones not being free of this mysterye but onelie of the Tymber men whiche shall bring suche stuf to the water sid shall at everie tyme so offending forfeytt and paie to the use of this house six shillings & eight pence or more or lesse after the discrecion of the mr and wardens for the tyme beinge'.

Nevertheless, infringements of this ordinance continued unabated. In 1584 it was reported to the Carpenters' Court that a bill for reforming these abuses had been exhibited 'into the parlyemente house', but to no effect.[39]

Returning to the more specific building laws, the picture is much the same. The recurrent need to pass new regulations and to reaffirm old ones was due to the failure to devise effective means of enforcement. During the fifteenth century, the task of inspecting alleged infringements of the law for the whole of London was entrusted to a part-time staff of two master-carpenters and two master-masons; it is little wonder that City records provide a sad commentary on their success. In the following century the situation further deteriorated, particularly in periods of heavy building activity. Under booming conditions, those who were prosecuted for infringements of the regulations regarded a fine as no more than a small tax on operations, which could easily be passed on to the customer. An extract from the Court Book may be cited as just one example of this:[40]

'Adam Ramshaw ys contented and promyseth to paye unto the foresaid Gregorie Newland the yongest warden to the use of this Cominaltie the some of five shillings for making a compting house in Harte Streat contrarie to order wthoute licence before the fiveth daie of this instant moneth of October'.

It was very rare for more serious action to be taken. Though on a few occasions the Company was able to insist that shoddy workmanship should be replaced.

In the sixteenth century the Crown had been led to take a stronger hand in the regulation of building in London, and a very rapid spate of building in the 1570s led ultimately, in 1580, to a royal proclamation forbidding both new building within a radius of three miles from the heart of the City and alteration to existing buildings without a licence from the City Chamberlain; and the City appointed the Company to act as its agent in carrying out this decree.[41] Despite the proclamation, however, matters steadily deteriorated and in 1583 the Lords of the Council wrote to the Lord Mayor, 'complaining of the number of new buildings and the dividing of single tenements within the City and suburbs, contrary to Her Majesty's Proclamation'.[42] But the City aldermen preferred excuses to action. Moreover, the Company was trying desperately to repair some of the damage to its own authority. In 1583 it succeeded in obtaining a City decree against allowing 'forrens' to erect 'any frame, piece of buyldinge or worke whatsoever of tymber or woodd' within the City;[43] this was to be the sole privilege of the freemen of the Company—a vain hope. Site values in London were rising rapidly, and no doubt property speculators were easily able to defend their interests in the face of an over-burdened administration and a harassed Company.

In assessing the effectiveness of the Company's control over the carpenters' craft in London it is possible to distinguish two areas of operation. On the one hand there was its vicarious responsibility for enforcing City regulations dealing with wages and building construction. In this the Carpenters met with failure. And while this was of immediate concern to the City authorities alone, it did reflect the probability that the Company could achieve only limited success in its other sphere of operation, where it sought to regulate the supply and employment of London carpenters. The Company's ordinances applied to all London carpenters without exception, for this was the neces-

39

sary condition for successful craft regulation. Enough evidence has been cited, however, to show that this was far from being achieved. Before attempting to analyse the reasons for this it is relevant to pose the question of whether, from the outset, the Company was misled in its endeavours. In answer it can be said that, in the early fifteenth century, its founders had good reason to believe that with the changing nature of demand for building new opportunities were opening up for master carpenters, which could be best exploited by establishing a 'closed shop' in the carpenters' craft; and in the light of the success apparently being achieved by some other companies, no doubt there seemed little reason to question whether the same measure of success could be achieved by the Carpenters Company. Moreover, it was necessary for a small craft to mark its emancipation and independence by endeavouring to do this.

There were a number of factors which worked to falsify these hopes. Apart from anything else, it is obvious that even with the income from fines the task of enforcement of craft ordinances and City regulations was enormous when their detailed and comprehensive nature is considered in relation to the Company's administrative resources. This probably explains the irregular, as well as the restricted, activity of the Court of Assistants in trade matters. Even if the Company had been armed with more formidable powers of inspection, the jobbing nature of much of the carpenter's work would have made many infringements impossible to detect. Furthermore, once a carpenter had gained wide reputation he was little attracted to membership of the Company. Indeed, it is hardly meaningful to class such men as carpenters, being as they were the forerunners of professional architects and large building contractors; sometimes, they are to be compared to those who, like Sir Robert Rich in the mid-sixteenth century, made their fortune by speculation in land and building, regardless of City laws.[44] Certainly, the independent existence of this group inevitably weakened the Carpenters' position. Likewise, within the Company itself leadership was

1. Map of Moorfields district, 1559–60. Engraved on a copper plate in the *London Museum*

2. Page of the Carpenters Company Court Minute Book for August 21, 1604, showing the signatures and timber marks of Peter Cobb, *Master*, Robert Fisher, John Sharpe and Robert Bentley, *Wardens*

3. Engraving of Carpenters Hall in 1664, *drawn by Thomas H. Shepherd*

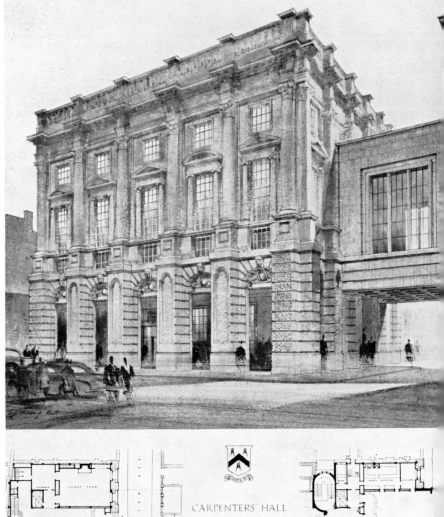

CARPENTERS' HALL
RECONSTRUCTION
SHOWING
NEW ARCADE
IN
LONDON WALL

WHINNEY, SON, & AUSTEN HALL ARCHITECTS

GROUND FLOOR PLAN

FIRST FLOOR PLAN

4. The Architect's sketch of the present Hall, including plans of Ground and First F

assumed by a few relatively prosperous master carpenters, some of whom gained the distinction of holders of Crown and City appointments. But in turn, it was not in the interests of this group that control over the craft should be made thoroughly effective. William Serle and James Nedam were cited earlier as examples of enterprising master carpenters; but these men, and others like them, operated on a scale which made it difficult for them to avoid contravening ordinances. Nedam's contract with the Marquess of Exeter, for instance, shows clearly that he engaged in the work of cognate crafts, thus directly breaking regulations:[45]

'And also the said Jamys couenauntith and grauntith by these presentes to fynde all manner of tymber bourde lathe nayle lyme sande bryk tile and plaster of parrys for all the outeside of the said galleres And all the inside of the said gallares to be seasid clenly with lyme and here and in likewise the roffes And also all glasse ironwerke and all other thinges belongynge to the makinge and fulfynesshinge of the said galleres in all thinges belonginge to the crafte of carpentry masonry smithes wark glasiers werke plastery bricklaiers tilars and plommers warke'.

And in 1510 a contract between a London prior and a carpenter for building a town house contained a clause which illustrates open defiance of the Company's ordinances:[46]

'And the same prior covenauntith and grauntith by these presentes to save and kepe harmles the same William [carpenter] agaynst the Wardens and occupacion of Carpenters of the Cite of London during all the tyme and space that the forsaid house shallbe in setting upp wtin the Cite of London as it is abouesaid'.

It will be shown in chapter IV that it was only by the lower ranks of the Company that demands for more effective regulations were

beginning to be made, because they were most affected by competition from 'forrens' in a period of falling real wages;[47] a 'closed
shop' being looked upon by them as the best means of safeguard-
ing their position.

The relative failure of the Company in craft matters could have
meant that its continued existence was uncertain. Apart from its
increasing activities as a landlord, however, it was still able to
serve special craft interests in an indirect but very real way.

There were a number of important offices either under the
patronage of the Company, or which went traditionally to its
leading members. In the first category were the appointments of
Sworn City Carpenters, Master of the Bridge-House, and Master
Carpenter at Guildhall, references to which have already been
made.[48] It may be added that Sworn City Carpenters were
exempted from 'all Taxes of Tenths, Fifteenths, and other
subsidies to our Sovereign Lord the King raised and levied in the
city . . .', because these officers were 'often ill paid for their
labour . . . '.[49] In the second category were the Crown offices of
King's Carpenter and Surveyor of the King's Works.[50] The post
of King's Carpenter had been created in 1256, and it carried the
responsibility of supervising the practical side of royal building
operations. After 1269, however, it had fallen into abeyance and
neither Edward I nor Edward II made any appointments to it,
although both employed a number of carpenters on royal works.
Among the earliest carpenters so employed, of whom there is a
record, was Robert Osekyn, already noted as the first Sworn City
Carpenter.[51] It is not possible to establish a direct link between
this office and the Company until 1426 when John Goldyng was
appointed to the post. He shortly afterwards became one of the
original lessees of Carpenters' Hall.[52] In 1451 Goldyng was
succeeded by Simon Clenchwarton,[53] a Warden of the Company
in 1455, who held this post until 1461 when he in turn was
succeeded by Edmund Graveley,[54] who became Master the
following year. Graveley was followed by Thomas Mauncey,[55]
three times Warden, to be followed by another Warden, Hum-

phrey Coke,[56] in 1519. Coke's successor in 1532 was James Nedam,[57] thrice Master of the Company. Shortly afterwards, Nedam was promoted to Surveyor of the King's Works, and his position of King's Carpenter was filled jointly by John Russell and William Clements[58]—Russell was four times Master, while Clements was an ordinary freeman. After 1565 the Company ceased to have any direct connection with this office.[59]

The post of Royal Surveyor involved the responsibility for repair and upkeep of all the King's properties. Nedam remained Royal Surveyor until his death in 1544, and in 1547 this vacancy was filled by Lawrence Bradshaw, who was eight times Master.[60] The last appointee from the Company was John Revell who died in 1564.[61] One remaining Crown office for which it is possible to trace a connection with the Carpenters, was that of Chief Carpenter in the Tower, which was held during the 1540s by Richard Ambrose, Master in 1546.[62] Finally, from time to time leading members were called upon to take charge of specific royal building projects—for example, William Crofton, John Bird and Richard Fowler advised the King on the defences of Guisnes and Calais,[63] and Edward Stone was in charge of building work in the Duchy of Lancaster from 1461–1478.[64]

The value of these offices is illustrated by the careers of Humphrey Coke and James Nedam; although it must be added that for most freemen these careers proved to be an inspiration rather than a guide. In 1509, Coke was made Master of the Bridge-House,[65] while in the same year he became Master Carpenter of Savoy Hospital; and by 1510–11 his reputation was such that he was commissioned to draw up plans of Eton College Cloister. In 1514 he was appointed Master of Carpentry at Corpus Christi, Oxford, for four years, and with William Vertue was responsible for providing the plans of the college. Bishop Fox, its founder, had a high opinion of Coke's ability and wrote of him: '. . . he is righte cunnynge and diligente in his werkes . . . if ye take his advice . . . he shall advantage you large monee in the building thereof, as well as in the devising as in the werkinge of yt'. By the time of his appointment as King's Carpenter in 1519 Coke was established as a successful general builder—for example, he was able to contract with James Yarford, Alderman of the City, to build the latter a town house for the sum of three hundred pounds. From 1525–9 Wolsey employed him in Cardinal College, Oxford (now Christ Church), and his roof for the Great Hall has been described as 'the last great work of medieval carpentry, uncontaminated by Renaissance influence', and judged to be second only to that of Hugh Herland at Westminster Hall. These achievements certainly place Coke among the great architects of the later Middle Ages.

James Nedam was obviously a man of different character from Coke.[66] It has been written that 'the events of Nedeham's life and his somewhat spectacular career leave an impression that he was a pushing and able administrator, well able to pick the brains of the most creative artists around him . . .'. To a large extent he owed his rise to Thomas Cromwell, who employed him on important work in the Tower, and on building Cromwell's house in Throgmorton Street, which later became Drapers' Hall. As Royal Surveyor Nedam was responsible for the repair of the King's houses and palaces at Greenwich, Eltham, Windsor, Dover, Ampthill, Moor Park, Woking and other places. An illustration of the manner in which these duties were discharged is provided by Nedam's accounts for work on the Placentia Palace at Greenwich, which have been carefully edited.[67] These show that his duties included the direction of a large labour force and the purchase of materials of all kinds, altogether involving considerable financial responsibility. Finally, it is interesting to note that John Russell, who became King's Carpenter in 1532 and who was probably responsible for designing the roof of Trinity College, Cambridge, owed his fortune to his marriage to Humphrey Coke's daughter, Christine.[68]

Apart from the direct benefits conferred by these posts in the City and under the Crown, they were clearly of indirect value both to their holders and to members of the Company generally.

As a City Carpenter, and therefore of proved ability, a man would command the most profitable work; moreover, a customer would be attracted by having the additional safeguard of being unlikely to fall foul of City regulations—which was always a risk on large buildings because infringements were easier to detect. And, of course, similar competitive advantages were open to those carpenters holding royal office. For members in general, it meant that some of the prosperity of the leading figures was bound to rub off on those less fortunate—and, for instance, when Nedam was working on St Thomas's Tower in the Tower of London he employed Richard Ambrose, Thomas Sheres, William Walker, John King and Thomas Hall, all of whom were men of standing in the Company.[69] For the Company itself these connections were an important element of its *raison d'être*. Membership could open the door to fame and fortune, or more probably to a solid level of prosperity. But those whose ambitions were helped towards realization in this way, seemed to forget the debt which they owed, as with John Nedam, who died a wealthy man, but who failed to remember the Carpenters in his will, and whose son became free of the Grocers.[70] If this and similar actions by others are anything to judge by, it is difficult to avoid the conclusion that while membership of the Company was often regarded as a means to success, it was not a mark of the notably successful carpenter.

In some ways it may seem strange that the Company should have bothered for so long to maintain what was, at times, little more than a semblance of control over the craft. But inasmuch as it was able to serve less immediate interests of its members, even a semblance of authority helped to ensure that it was not supplanted by a rival organization. By the sixteenth century, however, the Company's friendly society, civic, and social activities were assuming major importance as a result of its increasing prosperity and wealth; it is to these aspects of the Company's life that we must now turn.

CHAPTER III
INCOME AND PROPERTY
1438-1600

THE first account book was received as a gift in 1429 from a freeman named Crofton, and the accounts which it contains emphasize the Company's small beginnings.[1] Total annual revenue was never greater than £39 before 1516, it fell as low as 26s 8d in 1453, and on average was £28.[2] Unfortunately, these accounts do not give us a complete record of the Company's financial position. To use modern terminology, they must be regarded as the revenue or current accounts; the capital or deposit accounts were quite separate. Capital reserves were accumulated both from the surpluses of annual accounts and from lump sum payments received as fines for new leases, or as interest on loans. Some attempt to estimate the capital assets of the Company will be made at a later stage, but in the meantime this complication must be borne in mind. The reserves were kept in the 'black box' the first mention of which occurred in 1438.[3] It was kept in a 'Cheste wy a loke and key' but for greater security a 'Treser house' was made in 1469 in which the chest could be deposited.[4] At first this was simply a large cupboard in one corner of the Hall, but in 1478 it was turned into something more like a strong-room,[5] and in 1503 it was made even more secure with the aid of 'vj barrys of Iron'.[6] The treasure house, chest and black box were secured by a number of keys which were held by certain members of the Court.

The accounts show that current income fell into five main categories. First, quarterage payments, which have already been noted as providing a convenient way of estimating membership. Each freeman was required to pay 4d quarterly at the Hall, to which was added the subscriptions which the Livery made towards the cost of the dinners on the day when the Mayor went to Westminster, and of the annual feast day.

The next and largest source of income came from the operation of the apprenticeship system. On presenting a new apprentice at the Hall a master paid a fee of 2s 2d. Sometimes a master wished to turn over an apprentice to another employer and this was possible on payment of a fine of 12d. For failure to comply with these regulations, or for setting an apprentice to work before his seven-year servitude was completed, further fines could be levied. The number of apprentices which different ranks of the Company might have was controlled by ordinance, but at times for a fee the Court of Assistants was prepared to waive the rule. Quite clearly it was not averse to doing so as it proved a convenient way of supplementing income; and to have adopted a less flexible attitude would have been pointless during a period in which craft control was becoming less and less practicable. On the completion of their apprenticeship those who wished could receive the freedom of the Company on payment of a fee of 3s 4d; but for someone seeking the freedom by redemption it was a matter for bargaining between the individual and the Court. Finally, as well as small fines imposed for disciplinary purposes, larger indemnities were paid by those who were unwilling to accept the Livery or, more usually, the office of Warden. Overall this branch of income increased as a direct result of the growth in membership, and on average it accounted for between 50 per cent and 60 per cent of total income. But as the major source it had a dragging effect on the total increase over the period, because most apprenticeship fees and fines remained fixed despite the general rise in prices. The unwillingness to raise rates was, once again, partly a reflection of the increasing difficulties associated with the control of the craft—to have raised dues would have given added encouragement to many carpenters to elude Company control— and partly the natural reaction to regard such a measure as a last line of defence should the needs of solvency demand it.

Some part of income came from fines arising from the Company's attempts to enforce control over the craft in London. A number of its ordinances dealt with matters such as the purchase of timber, building licences, and the employment of 'forrens'. It has been noted that in a great many cases it is impossible to determine the nature of a fine as it was simply recorded in the accounts or minutes as an amount 'paid' or 'to be paid'. It is evident from the accounts, however, that attempts to enforce these controls—attempts made with increased vigour during the last twenty years of the century, largely as a result of pressure from City authorities[7]—were never successful enough to make this more than a small, erratic source of revenue.

Finally, income was drawn from property and what are best termed miscellaneous receipts; but it is doubtful whether the latter can be properly regarded as income as it was made up of a number of non-recurring items—gifts, bequests, subscriptions, and collections—which are best considered at a later stage. Revenue from property was made up of rents, which were quite straightforward, and fines for new leases, a consideration of which takes us beyond the purely current income position.

The first acquisition of property by London Wall in 1429 has already been noticed in chapter I. The site, on which the new Hall and four houses had been built, was held on a lease for ninety-eight years from the Prior and Convent of St Mary's Hospital, Bishopsgate, at an annual rental of 20s. In order to avoid the law of mortmain this lease was held by leading members of the Company who in fact acted as trustees, new members being appointed to replace those who died.

The first freehold owned by the Company, namely the Lime Street estate, was bequeathed to it by Thomas Warham in 1481, and it then consisted of a timber house and five gardens.[8] There is, however, evidence which not only provides very real doubt whether this was a straightforward bequest in the generally understood sense but also suggests an alternative explanation, which becomes even more appealing in the light of the Company's subsequent history. Confusion has arisen in connection with the complicated law of mortmain (1279) which forbade the bequest of real estate to the Church without royal licence. In 1391 this statute had been extended to cover guilds and fraternities,[9] but in this case there was a loophole, for, by the Charter of London of March 6, 1327, real estate bequeathed by a freeman of the City of London to a company within the City was free of mortmain.[10] It was, therefore, quite simple for land held on trust for a company —a cumbersome and even risky procedure—to be transferred to a senior freeman, who was not expected to live for many more years, and he in turn bequeathed it to the Company. In this way a clear title was established. This technique, known as testamentary devise, was widely used in the early fifteenth century. Indeed, in 1434 it was found necessary to pass an Act in Council,[11]

'to prevent unlawful grants in mortmain by wills of citizens, [and] it was ordained that from thenceforth no will of any citizen devising ... in mortmain shall be admitted for enrolment except after strict inquiry made on oath before the Mayor and Recorder for the time being ... whether the said legacy be without deceit or fraud, and be concerned with land and tenements justly belonging to the testator by inheritance or just acquisition, and not of lands or tenements belonging to others conveyed to him by feoffment *a latere* for bequeathing the same in mortmain without the King's licence, under the colour of his franchise ...'.

Despite this Act, however, the previous custom seems to have been continued and the City authorities reaffirmed this right in 1482 after its legal force had been questioned in the Court of the King's Bench.[12] After further attempts to challenge the privilege, it was eventually confirmed by the decision of Mr Justice Brian in 1488.[13]

Considered in this light there is good reason for doubting the traditional account of the acquisition of the Lime Street property. The first extant document linking the property to the Company is a deed dated June 12, 1454, which recorded the transfer of the land alone—no buildings are specified—from Edmund Wydewell and Reginald Harneys to William Wangford, Thomas Warham, William Thawaytes, William Clon, and William Warham.[14] (Both Thomas and William Warham were leading members of the Company.) On the same day Thomas Barnard and Thomas Sexteyn—the former an ordinary member of the Company and the latter its Master in 1460—were granted a letter of attorney from Edmund Wydewell and Reginald Harneys to convey their interest in the property to those mentioned in the deed of that date. This was almost certainly a transfer from one group of trustees to another either as lessees or owners; on whose behalf we do not know. Nothing more is heard directly about this property until the will of Thomas Warham, drawn up in 1477 and proved in 1481, by which it was bequeathed to the Company. Over the same period the accounts record a number of payments made for legal advice in connection with this will until in 1478 it was recorded:[15] 'Itm. paid for the makinge of Warhams Testemet xs'. According to this will the property, which now contained a timber house, was to be held by the executors for one year and then transferred to the Carpenters. It is perhaps significant, too, that in 1475 the Company made its first move to obtain a charter of incorporation which would enable it to hold estates in its own right. Moreover, when these facts are compared with parallel entries in the accounts (although it must be accepted that there are a number of gaps in the records) the result at least points to this as being a case of testamentary devise.

So far as can be ascertained, over the period of the first set of accounts three new houses were built.[16] Between 1457 and 1458 two houses were erected next to the Hall as almshouses.[17] But from the lists of tenants it is clear that they were not used as almshouses for very long and were soon let on ordinary terms.[18] More important in this context, at about the same time Thomas

Warham was responsible for supervising the building of a timber house, for which he received a final payment of £8 in 1457.[19] At this point there is nothing to suggest that the work was done at Lime Street. In 1479 and 1480, however, the Company paid for repairs to Warham's house in Lime Street, presumably because he was either leasing it from the Carpenters or holding it on their behalf.[20]

The evidence does not provide conclusive proof that the house mentioned in the will, the house in which Warham lived, and the house which was built in 1457, were one and the same; but at least it is consistent with the possibility of a testamentary devise. The deed of 1454 could have been for the original purchase by the Company of the land at Lime Street, or for its transfer from one group of trustees to another; however, the former alternative is more likely as neither Wydewell nor Harneys can be traced as members of the Company. The accounts are of no assistance as they do not record capital expenditure; and until the will had been proved, for fear of prosecution, it would have been unwise to enter any additional rents. In either case, with formal incorporation in 1477 it could well have been that the Company decided to establish its own clear title to the property by testamentary devise through the will of Thomas Warham. This does not preclude the possibility of some part of the estate, maybe in the form of improvements, to have been the bequest of Warham, and for this reason part of the income from it was to be used for an annual memorial service to him (technically known as an obit); in addition this would have provided ostensible evidence that the property was a bequest, and thus make the transaction less likely to be challenged by those who held that the right of testamentary devise was being abused. The bequest was to be held for one year by the executors just as an extra safeguard. Finally, from the scant remainder of Warham's will it appears that if this was a genuine bequest he put the claims of his Company before those of his wife and family.[21] For all this, it is emphasized that this is merely an alternative explanation, but it does provide adequate grounds for doubting, although not disproving, the traditional account. After 1481 the property was improved,[22] and by the time the accounts, interrupted in 1516, were resumed again in 1546, there were two tenements and stables at Lime Street.

The next acquisition of property provides much more positive evidence of testamentary devise. In 1517 Thomas Cony, five times a Warden of the Company, bequeathed to the Carpenters the property known as the Dog and Bear, London Wall, consisting of The Bear, three tenements and seven gardens.[23] On the west side it adjoined Carpenters' Hall and to the north formed a frontage with the Hall abutting on the highway, with the City wall opposite. The extent of this property is shown in the diagram on page 54. An indenture dated March 23, 1514, recorded the sale of it to Thomas Benkes and John Byrde, citizens and carpenters, for the sum of £72;[24] at this time Benkes was Master. This was followed by a deed poll dated August 31, 1517, by which Thomas Benkes (or Bynckes, who was Master six times), John Byrde, Thomas Smart, and John Wyneates (as trustees), transferred the property to William Cony—one day before he drew up his will. Although incomplete, the accounts for 1521 record the repayment of a loan of £40 to William Cony's executors.[25] This suggests that Cony was chosen as the benefactor for a testamentary devise and that he had lent the Company at least part of the purchase price of the estate in question. The fact that the transaction took three years to complete is probably explained by the intent of the Company to avoid any criticism that it was abusing the privilege of testamentary devise; while the situation of the property next to the Hall estate reveals the whole operation as a very shrewd piece of business.

A similar explanation undoubtedly applies to what was apparently the bequest of Thomas Smart in 1519.[26] Smart, a leading Carpenter, having been a Warden in 1494, 1495 and 1499, and Master in 1509 and 1513, purchased the Hall estate from the Priory of St Mary for £100 in January 1519.[27] Less than one month after this, and shortly before his death, Smart drew up his will by which he bequeathed the estate to the Company. Unfortunately, the account and minute books for these years are missing, but the sequence of events, and more importantly the sum of money involved which, judging from the rest of his will, was far beyond Smart's individual means, leave little doubt that this was a purchase by testamentary devise. Moreover, the Company was unlikely to have taken the risk of the freehold of the Hall passing into other hands without making a strong effort to purchase it. It is improbable, however, that the Carpenters made an earlier attempt to acquire the estate while there were still many years to run on the Hall lease; in the meantime the contents of the black chest could best be used for acquiring other properties.

The extent of the Hall estate in 1519 is illustrated by the diagram overleaf.

Until now it had been assumed that the next acquisition of property came by the bequest of Thomas Gittins in 1588,[28] consisting of tenements and lands at London Wall adjoining the Hall estate, the income from which being subject to an annual payment of 11s to three poor men. A will of Gittins dated November 3, 1587, and proved in January 1587/8[29] makes no direct mention of the property. However, the following rather unusual codicil was attached to this will:

'A CODICELL made by the testator at the time of making of this his will; MEMORANDUM That the Daye and yeare first above Written the saide Thomas Gittyns at suche time as he was Devising of this his will and testament uppon some communicacon had betwene him the saide Thomas Gittins and one John Blande Citizen and Carpenter of London concerning certain Landes whiche the saide Thomas had conveyed and assured by a former will to the company of Carpenters of London The saide Thomas Gittins then Declared that his meaning and intent was betwene god and his sowle that the saide company of Carpenters shoulde have the same And that for all the goodes in the worlde he woulde not otherwise, but that they shoulde inioye it; And that his meaning and intent was not by the will whiche he was then amaking (being this will above written) to preiudice the conveyaunce of the saide

LONDON WALL

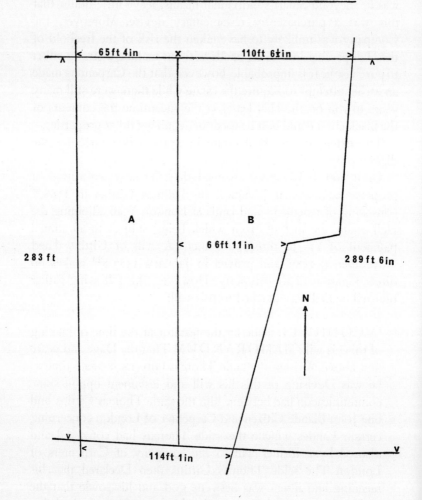

A : 'Smart' purchase 1519

B : 'Cony' purchase 1517

Landes before by him made in a former will bearing Date the thirteth Daye of July 1587 Last past Then being present and hearing the promisses John Dixon, and the saide John Blande and others'.

Furthermore, the Abstract of Deeds relating to the Company's estates contains a reference to the effect that the earlier will (alluded to in the codicil) was enrolled in the Court of Husting; and the Company undoubtedly paid to have this will drawn up and to be enrolled.[30] A thorough search of the Hustings rolls has not revealed this will and there is no known extant copy of it. However, the seemingly difficult problem of discovering the location of this property can be solved in a manner which has a surprising result. Apart from the Gittins 'bequest', there has only been one minor alteration in the size of the Hall estate since 1519, so that when the present-day dimensions of the property are compared with those shown in the diagram opposite the situation of Gittins' property should be clearly revealed. Allowing for the minor alteration, when the comparison is made, the measurements are found to tally exactly—in other words, Gittins did not make a bequest of property. Further positive proof of this is provided by the fact that the Warden's accounts show no change for a number of years after 1588 in the total number of tenants or in the amount received in rents. Moreover, although it will be shown later that the Hall was being extended at this time, these additions were built on adjoining gardens already owned by the Company. While the present authors are convinced on the matter, they can only offer a highly probable explanation of why the earlier will was drawn up and from what source the income for the charity was derived. For this it is necessary to look at the more general history of the period.

In 1547 the Chantries Act had been passed to deal with land which had been formerly used for religious purposes. It was held that after the dissolution of religious houses the income, and in effect the land itself, fell to the Crown; and in order to recover such property it was necessary for the owners to pay an indemnity. Thus, in 1550 the Carpenters had paid an indemnity of £8 on the Lime Street estate, because part of the income from it had been used for Thomas Warham's obit.[31] After these fines had been settled it was generally believed that there would be no more claims for chantry revenue; but this was not to be and, in the late 1570s, the whole question was revived under the guise of 'concealments'. The Queen, ever short of money, had been advised that some contribution to the easing of her difficulties could be made by searching for land which had been concealed from the investigations made under the Chantries Act. This was simply a device for casting the net wider and, among other things, catching land which had been sold by religious houses before their dissolution. Thus, Elizabeth granted patents to certain men to search for 'concealments', and if they were found the resulting indemnities or confiscations were to be apportioned between the Crown and the patentees.

As early as 1576 the Company was troubled 'Concerninge the sute for the Hall and the rest of the Landes at London Wall'.[32] It was necessary to prove that the lands in question had been investigated under the original Chantries Acts, which involved searching through the records at Guildhall, and in having the wills of Cony and Smart formally enrolled. In the following year the matter was again brought before the Courts but no decision was reached; but already, the cost to the Company of these proceedings amounted to over £50.

Nothing more is heard on this score for ten years, when, apart from the expenses incurred through the drawing up and enrolment of Gittins' will, there is one other entry in the official records which seems to have some connection with the matter, and this occurs in the accounts for 1588.[33]

'Paied unto Walter Moyll executor of Thomas Gittins for certaine money laied oute by the said Thomas in charges for matters aboute the companie } lxx^{li}

It will be shown later that, as a senior member of the Company, Gittins was closely concerned with, and seems to have been its spokesman on, property matters. Moreover, parallel to this the Abstract of Deeds shows a series of indentures and deeds to have been sealed on dates in May 1587, detailing the transfer of the 'Gittens' property at London Wall from Theophilus Adams and Thomas Butler to Thomas Pope and Thomas Gittins—and the last indenture records a 'ffyne levyed in Easter Term 29th Eliza.' This was followed by a deed poll, by which Pope conveyed his interest in the property to Gittins, and then by Gittins' will dated July 30, 1587. Lastly, included among these conveyances was a receipt of payment from the Exchequer of 'Lands lately belonging to the late dissolved Priory of the New Hospitall of Saint Mary without Bishopsgate London'.

It has proved impossible to trace any of these documents, but despite this a fairly clear pattern of events emerges. Adams and Butler were probably the two patentees claiming that part of the Hall estate, namely part of Smart's 'purchase', had been concealed from the Chantry Commissioners. After protracted legal argument the matter was finally settled—for £70?—and the land was re-devised through Gittins. In appreciation of Gittins' services, or to put the finishing touches to the matter, or both, provision was made for the poor of the Company and for the annual reading of the will. Certainly this provided the strongest tangible proof of the legality of the operation securing the Company's inalienable title to the property.

Before leaving this aspect of the Company's history, it is interesting to note briefly its more general implications. So far as other City Livery companies were concerned, it is unwise to assume that the details contained in wills are sufficient evidence of bequests of property. In each case it is necessary to make a thorough search of the deeds and indentures relating to apparent bequests.[34] It is also questionable to what extent other kinds of corporation, such as hospitals and educational foundations, resorted to the use of testamentary devise; and finally, to speculate whether the right of testamentary devise existed in other leading towns which were among the first to be incorporated by royal charter. Moreover, there seems reason to believe that this legal manoeuvre was used quite frequently at the end of the sixteenth century when 'concealments' became an issue—and this may account in part for the apparent rise in philanthropy during this period, as described by W. K. Jordan.[35]

In the very early years the Hall had been rented out for short periods, often just for a day, to fraternities or small companies which had no permanent headquarters of their own. Among the regular tenants during this period were the 'Dutchmen',[36] who were perhaps merchants living in London and on occasion wishing to celebrate together. But the house, stables and gardens adjoining the Hall provided the greater revenue. These were usually leased for twenty-one years, although a case of fifty years is on record.[37] A lease was granted on the basis of an initial fine and an annual rental, and tenants were usually responsible for repairs. Sometimes leases were drawn up on the basis of part of the annual rent being paid in kind. For example, one tenant gave a buck for the annual feast day,[38] a practice which had much to commend it during a period of rising food prices.

Rents formed between 25 per cent and 30 per cent of total recurrent income. After 1481 Lime Street had accounted for the larger proportion of the total, but by 1547, if not earlier, the Hall estate had become more valuable and by the end of the century produced nearly twice the income of Lime Street. Over the period there was a marked increase in the fines paid for leases, although unfortunately it is impossible to get a complete account of this increase, or to trace the rise for any particular house or garden, as many of the details are missing. But, as some rough indication, in 1477 John Shuckborough was fined only £2 6s 4d for the lease of a garden,[39] whereas in 1558 Master Mayes agreed to pay a fine of £35 for the lease of a house,[40] and in 1591 Thomas Daniell paid a fine of £40 for the lease of The Bear[41] (excluding the stable which had been rented earlier at £5 per annum).[42] Carpenters would have naturally possessed a very close knowledge of the rising value of property and there can be no doubt that by the mid-sixteenth century fines for leases formed the most rapidly increasing branch of income. Even so, the rapid inflation of this period must have meant that the returns on property would have been greater if shorter than customary leases had been granted, although bigger fines must have given some compensation. Indeed, the pressure on accommodation was so great that the Court minutes witness the growing practice of individuals suing for leases before the present occupant's term had finished.[43]

Tenants were drawn mainly from the minor crafts, with carpenters and curriers figuring very largely. The Master and Wardens exercised general supervision over the property and tenants by means of the annual view day, when they made a tour of inspection noting necessary repairs and any other matters. This was all done with the care and detail befitting master carpenters, and it paid ample dividends. Despite this vigilance, however, a stern line sometimes had to be taken with recalcitrant tenants. In 1566 John Burton, currier, refused to carry out repairs and his lease was duly foreclosed.[44] A more uncompliant tenant was Syslie Burden who seems to have been a somewhat redoubtable character. In 1567 it was noted that the Renter Warden was endeavouring to obtain possession of her house and that the Company was prepared to compensate her to the extent of 26s 8d, on the condition that she went 'quyetlye and peaccablye'.[45] After repeated efforts to dislodge her the Wardens were eventually successful. In 1570 John Pettie, currier, who was the tenant at the Bear, replaced the sign of the Bear with one representing a harrow and he was ordered 'to pluke it downe and sette up the signe of the beare', and to carry out overdue repairs.[46] More generally, in 1577 it was recorded with more than a hint of exasperation that 'the defaultes whereof whiche was viewed the laste year as by the view thereof made appereth are still remaininge unadmended in all respects'.[47] Nevertheless, unlike some of the larger companies these administrative difficulties never gave rise to serious deficiencies.[48]

Apart from Warham's and Gittins' 'bequests' to the poor, the Carpenters also benefited in 1570 under the will of Thomas Rowe,[49] citizen and alderman and a freeman of the Merchant Taylors, by which £4 was to be distributed annually among poor carpenters. Another bequest was made by John Holgate,[50] carpenter, in 1568. For overseeing his property in St Giles, Cripplegate, the Carpenters were to receive 40s per annum. But the Company became involved in an expensive legal battle with Holgate's widow, and in 1573 it was thought best to drop all claim to the property.

Because the accounts are very incomplete, it is difficult to obtain a reliable picture of the Company's income during the sixteenth century. In money terms it rose considerably, but when the general price rise is taken into account, there was apparently no increase in real terms.[51]

THE COMPANY'S INCOME DURING THE SIXTEENTH CENTURY
(10-year averages)

Period	Money Income			Real Income		
	£	s	d	£	s	d
1491-1500	27	15	0	27	16	1
1555-1564	80	6	3	29	5	10
1591-1600	126	6	4	27	5	0

It must be emphasized, however, that price indices for this period are by no means accurate, and it is a commonplace that inflationary factors do not have uniform effects. In this sense, while current income showed no real increase (in large part due to the fixed rates of trade fines and fees), it is probable that, both as a result of inflation and the heavy demand for accommodation, the value of the Company's property rose at a more rapid rate than the general level of prices, thus yielding capital gains—how large, it is impossible to say.

On the expenditure side the accounts fall into obvious categories. To start with there were the amounts disbursed to the poor each quarter according to the conditions laid down by the ordinances and subsequent bequests. Not that charitable activities were limited to formal obligations. Whenever there was a healthy balance a part was used to relieve members in straitened circumstances.[52] These benefits formed a very real advantage to be gained from membership of the Company. Even for highly paid carpenters, work was often irregular in an age when the economy was incapable of providing enough employment for the total available labour force. The level of activity in building construction has always been closely related to the general fortunes of the economy, and while, taken as a whole, this period was one of expansion of building in London, there can be little doubt that periods of national depression brought corresponding declines in the activity of the industry. Again, building has always been a somewhat seasonal industry, with the result that high wage rates are not altogether reflected in high average earnings over the year. Those carpenters who lived permanently in London were almost certainly completely dependent on their earnings from their craft and, therefore, a freedom admission fee followed by regular quarterage payments was a small insurance to pay for some measure of sickness, unemployment, and pension benefit. Incidentally, it is not improbable that a large proportion of 'forren' carpenters who flowed into London during periods of boom did so on a temporary basis; following a well-known pattern when trade declined of returning home where the rest of their family had remained engaged in some form of agriculture.

An increasing number of pages in the accounts were taken up by expenditure on festivities. The most important dinner was that held on Election Day, but there were others held on Court Days, Quarter Days, Reckoning Day, View Day, Lord Mayor's Day, and on 'Search' days (when the Master and Wardens inspected alleged infringements of building regulations). Inevitably, as these celebrations became more lavish they became more expensive, quite apart from the rising cost of food.[53] In 1500 the total cost of dinners had been £11, by 1550 it had risen to £23, and by 1600 to £72, and forming something like 50 per cent to 60 per cent of total regular expenditure at this date.[54] Quarterage receipts met the expenses for the dinners held on the days when these dues were collected, but it was acknowledged that increasing expenditure in this direction should not be met wholly from regular income, and from time to time special collections towards these costs were made from the Livery and Yeomanry.

Again, there were the everyday running expenses, which included the salary of the Clerk, and the wages of the Beadle and lesser servants such as the cook and scavenger. The Clerk's stipend had increased from 33s 4d in 1487 to £10 per annum by 1600, although it is interesting to note that this only represented an increase of 5s 5d in terms of 1487 prices. Nevertheless, this post like that of Beadle carried 'perqs'. For example, in 1561, when the Beadle's wage was under review, it was decided that he should have the house in which he lived for his lifetime free of rent.[55] Other items under this head ranged from the quite small, such as payments for pruning the vine or cleaning the stable, to much larger sums spent on repairs to the Hall. The Court paid careful attention to this latter and any defects were quickly attended to. More generally the decor of the Hall was being constantly enriched. The first mention of a 'green carpet' [i.e. tablecloth] occurs among an inventory of possessions drawn up in 1572,[56] and in the following year a further eight yards of 'carpet' was purchased for 10s 8d per yard;[57] and from time to time when there was a healthy cash balance the Wardens added to the Company's cutlery and plate.

Of great interest is the decision taken by the Court (probably in the 1560s although it is not possible to discover the exact year) to commission a series of paintings depicting scenes from the Bible which had a direct connection with the craft of carpentry, to which reference will be made in chapter VIII.[58] There were also various gifts of plate from members. Unfortunately, only the descriptions of these fine objects remain, the pieces themselves having been lost, sold or destroyed over the years. Sometimes a freeman would show his appreciation to the Company by paying for the repair of some part of the Hall; in 1586, for example, the whole of the Livery paid for the re-glazing of two clerestories on its north side, and their names and timber marks were engraved in the glass.[59]

The final branch of expenditure brings us once again to the blurred distinction between current and capital accounts. Together with the surpluses from the other branches of income, it was the uses to which rents and fines for leases were put that provides the greatest interest. In fact, this revenue was spent mostly on property. The additions made to the Lime Street estate over the period covered by the first book of accounts have already been noted, as well as minor alterations to the Hall. Moreover, it is clear from the rent accounts that one new house had been built at London Wall between the end of the first set of accounts in 1516 and the beginning of the next in 1546. It is even possible that a further house was added to these between 1546 and 1600 as the number of tenants at London Wall increased from seven to eight over this period; however, there is no record of such an addition and it might simply have been that one house was divided between two occupants. But between 1546 and 1600—at all times in fact—by far the principal investments were made in the Hall itself.

The first major alteration was the addition of a new parlour in 1501 at a cost of £23 2s 11½d.[60] It appears to have been partly wainscoted, lit by a bay window, and furnished with tables and forms. Although there is a gap in the accounts there do not seem to have been any further investments on this scale until 1561 when major repairs were carried out,[61] the main item being the replastering of the ceiling. This is of additional interest because it was the first recorded case, in what proved to be a series, of money being received from the 'black cheste' towards the cost of building operations.[62] In 1569 the layout of the garden was improved and a bowling alley was built.[63] This provides the first example of another new development, namely of the Company levying a subscription on its members to cover part of the cost. In 1573 extensive improvements were made costing over £80,[64] and part of this was met by a transfer of £30 from the chest and a subscription from the members amounting to just over £20. Both sides of the Hall were wainscoted in the same pattern as the upper end, a clerestory was constructed, and the existing gallery was refurbished and enhanced by a new carol window. Shortly afterwards, in 1580,[65] an unprecedented sum of £195 was spent on the addition of a new parlour and other sundry repairs. The new parlour was a major addition and might have almost doubled the size of the Hall. Of the sum involved, £80 was drawn from the 'black cheste', £64 was raised by subscription, £10 came by way of repayment of debts, and the remainder was met by the year's surplus. Even more surprising was the fact that this heavy expenditure was only the first of a series: in 1585[66] a new kitchen and new ovens were built at a cost of over £27; in the following year a new pantry was added which cost £13 and a new parlour costing £31;[67] in 1588[68] over £37 was paid for a new gallery on the south side, the money being subscribed by members; and finally between 1593 and 1595[69] another £121 was spent on enlarging the Hall on the east and on building a new counting house. With these added facilities, in addition to being the administrative centre of the Company, the Hall had become a place for relaxation and entertainment, perhaps making membership attractive for this reason alone.

These investments were marked evidence of prosperity, especially when account is taken of the heavy legal fees incurred at this time in connection with the Hall property and, more particularly, with the Lime Street estate. The purchase of Warham's obit has already been noted as well as the reopening in the 1570s of the question of 'concealments'. Thus it was that the Company was sued by Sir James Varmyn for certain concealed income alleged to be derived from Lime Street. The matter was first brought to law in the Michaelmas term of 1581.[70] No decision was reached and the affair dragged on until 1585 when, after protracted legal arguments, the Assistants were at a loss as to what course to take, and Richard Smithe and Thomas Gittins were deputed to look into the question,[71] 'And to answer compound and agree concerninge the same in all thinges at their descressions as other companies doe wch are in the like predygerments'. In the event it was agreed to settle with Sir James to have the subject closed. In total this dispute had cost nearly £50.[72] It is perhaps revealing that after this settlement and what was probably a similar argument over the Gittins property, the Court thought it necessary to pass the following ordinance,[73]

'that if the m^r or wardens or anie of the assistance that now ar or hearafter shalbe be so miseadvised to reveall or declare anie matters in question in this courte wch shalbe at anie time to be kept in silence and not to be declared upon proof thereof [or even to be recorded in the minutes?] had everie suche persone or persons so offending shall peremtelie be exiled oute of the assistaunce of this companie and not to be admitted againe untill suche tyme as everie suche person or persons hathe made reconsiliacon of his faulte and paid suche a some of money as shalbe assessed for him to paie by the Mr Wardens and Assistantes'.

There were many informers at large.

The tally of claims made on the Company's resources during what was a period of national economic difficulty, is still incomplete. After the economic stability of Henry Tudor's reign, that of Henry VIII was in marked contrast. The son had not inherited the financial caution and prudence of the father. After the rupture with Rome reckless expenditure and unprofitable wars led the Crown to the brink of bankruptcy. The financial schemes of Henry and his advisers exhibited ingenuity, but economically they were disastrous and helped to inaugurate the first great inflation in the modern world. For a variety of reasons Henry's successors did little to restore the balance. Mary, in her short reign, accumulated debts amounting to £250,000,[74] and Elizabeth began a series of wars on the unsound basis of credit. It has been estimated that between 1588 and 1603 war alone involved an expenditure of £4m.[75] It was not surprising that successive monarchs should have turned to the wealthier of their subjects to help them out of difficulties. And as the greatest concentration of wealth in the kingdom was represented by the City of London, it was the merchants and companies of the City that were regularly called upon to bear part of the growing burden.

In the fifteenth and early sixteenth centuries the Carpenters had contributed towards the cost of fitting out soldiers, and they had paid a small sum towards the forced loan of 1488.[76] But it was after 1550 that these demands became more oppressive. In 1557[77] the Company collected £10 4s 8d towards the cost of fitting out soldiers for the Queen. The following year brought a demand from the City to raise £40[78] towards a loan for Mary, the Carpenters being forced to borrow this amount and then to sell part of their plate to repay the debt. This was followed by a series of loans and levies totalling £408 between 1560 and 1600.[79] As if this were not enough, they also bore their share of the responsibility for avoiding some of the worst effects of famine. The Government operated a scheme of purchasing foreign corn when prices were low, storing it, and then selling it at reasonable rates during periods of dearth. The first assessment for 'corn money' was paid in 1574[80] when £52 10s od had to be raised from members, though there was no further contribution on this count until 1598.[81]

Outside demands on income were sometimes associated with more pleasurable occasions of royal and City pageantry. For example, in 1560[82] £4 7s od was laid out on coronation banners, and the Carpenters took their stand alongside other companies lining the royal route. Fortunately, for the Company the pleasure of these occasions was not marred by the heavy expenses which were often incurred by those companies playing more prominent roles.[83]

The following table adds totals of expenditure to those of income already given:

THE COMPANY'S EXPENDITURE DURING THE SIXTEENTH CENTURY

(10-year averages)

Period	Expenditure					
	Money			Real		
	£	s	d	£	s	d
1491–1500	24	8	5	24	14	2
1555–1564	71	11	0	26	0	5
1591–1600	118	8	9	23	13	5

The course of real current income has already been noted; a very small increase between the end of the fifteenth and the middle of the sixteenth centuries, followed by a decline of 7 per cent by 1600 —although this figure compares very favourably with the estimated decline of 20 per cent in real national income per head over this period. But, more important, it has been shown that the accounts give us a decreasingly accurate picture of the Company's fortunes. A more reliable indicator would be the number of years in which abnormal expenditure occurred, which drew on the Company's rising capital reserves—and there is no doubt that this number increased over the period. To put it another way it was the 'extraordinary receipts', a mixture of current and capital income, which became the major element in income generally; in addition to fines for leases the substantial amounts raised from members were a marked feature of the latter part of the sixteenth century, and there is no hint in the accounts or in the minutes that these contributions were made unwillingly. Indeed, they were added to by a constant flow of gifts. Thus, the impression left is that against a background of national economic instability the Company enjoyed a steady growth in prosperity. An important element in this success was that, while many craftsmen were experiencing hard times, master carpenters were enjoying relative affluence under conditions of boom in building.[84] It is not surprising, therefore, that they should have been willing and eager to display this by their generosity and by an obvious determination to raise their Company to a position of some prominence in the City; and no doubt this feeling of importance was fostered and strengthened by the appointment of leading members to City and Crown offices. Although the Company still remained one of the 'lesser' kind in all respects, and none of its members achieved aldermanic status, it had become a leading member of this 'lesser' group. In 1591 it was listed as twenty-eighth out of a total of fifty-five companies paying an assessment;[85] and although some of the 'Great Twelve' paid eighteen times as much as the Carpenters, there was by no means such a large difference between the Carpenters and those immediately following the 'Twelve'. More significant, the Company showed no signs of decline or decay, the most tangible proof of this being the size and appointment of its Hall, which could bear comparison with those of the great companies. And its growing concentration on developing its property was in line with future needs, as craft control generally became less and less effective.

CHAPTER IV

DEMARCATION DISPUTES AND WEAKER CRAFT CONTROL
1600-1670

A T a series of meetings of the Court of Assistants in February 1606/7, new ordinances were agreed upon.[1] In the following December the whole Company was summoned to hear a reading of the new ordinances which had been granted under the hands and seals of the Lord Chancellor, the Lord Treasurer, the Lord Chief Justice, and the celebrated Lord Coke of the Common Pleas. The minutes record that £33 was taken out of the chest to help meet the legal expenses which had been incurred.[2]

The ordinances of 1607 were much more comprehensive in craft matters than those of 1467.[3] In a number of cases, however, it was simply that formal recognition was given to customs and practices which had grown up in the intervening period to meet changing circumstances; yet there was more to this reform than mere codification of existing practices. There were the usual general requirements that all those practising the craft within the City and for a radius of two miles around it should be members of the Company, and that members should inform on anyone not complying with this. But most attention was given to the regulation of building operations and to the apprenticeship system. Hence, the custom by which the Company had nominated two of the City Viewers was now formally recognized—'and they [the Company] to name such persons as shall be hable as well in cunnynge as otherwise for the same office of viewers, the Kinges subiects, . . . shall be indifferently well & justly served as appertaineth'. There was, moreover, firm insistence on maintaining demarcation between the building crafts, and masons, bricklayers, tylers and plasterers were singled out as being the main offenders in this respect—an abuse which often arose as a result of master craftsmen having the resources to undertake large building operations but for which it was necessary to employ men from allied crafts. To give effect to this the Company was empowered to carry out searches, at not less than quarterly intervals, of all building work in progress. As regards building materials the Carpenters bound themselves to enforce, so far as possible, the long and detailed City regulations applying to the weights and sizes of timbers, as well as the regulations concerning trading in timber. Any materials seized by the Master and Wardens were to be shared equally between the City and the Company; and in every search made for such offences outside the City it was agreed to give notice to the King's Carpenter in order that he might accompany them if he so wished. No effort was to be spared, and at a Court in 1607 it was agreed that a Bill then before Parliament 'for the assising Stuff' should be 'prosequnted' at the charges of the Company.[4] Indeed, the amount of attention given to this matter in the ordinances is an indication that it was considered to be fundamental to effective craft control; and there can be little doubt that the consistent failure to regulate the supply of timber in the sixteenth century had seriously weakened the Carpenters' authority. Moreover, this was a period during which the King introduced much detailed legislation to limit the growth of London and under these circumstances any proposals for strengthening this control were bound to be received favourably.[5]

Strict limitations were imposed on the number of apprentices which a freeman could take—the Master and Wardens were allowed three, members of the Livery two, and ordinary freeman one. But an exceptional clause permitted the Master and Wardens to waive these requirements and to allow any freeman to have an additional apprentice on payment of a fine of 2s 6d. Under no circumstances, however, could a freeman who had not practised the craft for at least three years have more than one apprentice, while for more than three but less than seven years the limit was two apprentices. Following this were the usual regulations concerning binding, freedom, and the obedience of apprentices.

Immediately, a vigorous line was pursued with trade offenders. In the early months of 1608 the unusual step was taken of committing a number of men to prison for offences which were no more serious than usual, and for which a fine would normally have been judged as an adequate punishment.[6] There was, too, an increase in the number of fines levied on members for employing 'forrens' without a licence.[7] Not surprisingly, therefore, there is more than a hint that the Court of Assistants was somewhat over-zealous in the use of its powers, and on two occasions it was necessary for it to justify its actions in response to enquiries received from Mr Portington, the King's Carpenter.[8] There is every sign, however, that the Company's concern to enforce its regulations was often amply justified beyond its own self-interests—'Jeames Baylye free of the Commonaltye, Richard Gressam a forrener:— for building and working soe insufficientlye for one Broune in Chicklane that the house fell downe to the great Danger of his majestyes subjects—both committed to prison'.[9]

Similarly, close attention was being paid to membership matters. There were a number of translations of carpenters free of other companies, while there was a smaller number of transfers in the opposite direction; and for the first time there was a steady trickle of redemptioners.[10] This was part of a general movement among City companies to achieve more effective demarcation.[11] But the Carpenters went further than this and took the unusual step of admitting to the freedom a number of 'forrens' working in the City. For all this, the Company was sadly mistaken if it thought that it could stop, for once and for all, the unrestricted flow of carpenters into London.

Despite determined efforts to enforce regulations fresh difficulties soon began to appear. Towards the end of 1609 the Court decided to set up a standing committee to consider what steps should be taken to enforce the fines levied on carpenters using 'defectyve stuff', and to decide whether to begin proceedings on this matter before either the Lord Mayor, or the Court of Aldermen, or the justices.[12] Shortly afterwards an extraordinary case occurred of a 'forren' being fined for taking an apprentice without complying with the Company's ordinances.[13] From the record of this it would appear that 'forrens' were being allowed to take apprentices provided they were presented before the Master and Wardens and their indentures duly drawn up. If this was the case then it implied that a rapid and serious decline in the Company's control had occurred. Neither does this appear to have been an isolated incident, for in 1610 two justices of the peace visited the Hall for the purpose of hearing the answers of six 'forrens' who had been appointed as spokesmen for their fellows on matters of apprenticeship[14]—unfortunately, no further details were recorded. Nevertheless, the Company continued its efforts and during 1612 and 1613 there was a steep rise in the number of fines for 'insufficient work' and for transgressing building regulations.[15] But this burst of prosecutions was short-lived and was followed by a steady fall in the number of fines, and for 1620 only three were recorded.[16] Later discussion will show that this decrease did not represent a growing respect for the ordinances but the opposite. And to maintain a semblance of authority the Court granted a growing number of exceptions to its ordinances, which in effect simply gave its official approval to what it was powerless to prevent. In 1628, for example, a 'forren' was granted the freedom by servitude even though he had served his apprenticeship outside the City.[17]

If attention is focused on the growth in membership over this period considerable progress appears to have been made. From a total of just over 300 at the turn of the century, the number increased to approximately 500 by 1670.[18] Similarly, the number of bindings and admissions showed upward trends. Between 1654 and 1670, a period for which detailed records are available, the annual number of bindings averaged ninety-one as compared with thirty-eight for admissions to the freedom.[19] (At the beginning of the century the approximate corresponding figures were sixty and thirty per annum.) It is clear, too, that since the figures do not fluctuate significantly only something less than 50 per cent of those who were bound at the Hall subsequently took up the freedom. This has been explained already in terms of the training facilities offered by an apprenticeship in London, and of the number of apprentices who remained in London for some years after their servitude without seeking the freedom.[20] Furthermore, a closer examination of the figures reveals important underlying changes. For although the growth in membership was impressive, it was not so rapid as that of the population of the area under the Company's jurisdiction. Originally this area had been limited to a two-mile radius around the City, but under a new charter of 1640 this was extended to four miles.[21] If a similar calculation to that made in chapter II on the number of carpenters working in London is made for this period, it suggests that the Company accounted for no more than 30 per cent of the total number of carpenters working in the City, and for an even lower share of those working within a four-mile radius.[22] This was accompanied by a change in the pattern of recruitment.[23] At the end of the sixteenth century under 15 per cent of apprentices came from London, the suburbs, and the Home Counties, but by 1655 this figure had risen to 30 per cent and by 1660 to almost 60 per cent. In other words, the Company was drawing a growing proportion of apprentices from the area over which it sought craft control, but in turn this represented only a minor proportion of the number of young men taking up the craft in this region. Consequently, it was still necessary to contend with a large body of 'forrens' working in the City. Right down to the Civil War the Court of Assistants spent a great deal of time discussing the problem and expended much energy and money in attempting to bring offenders to book.[24] But the difficulties attendant upon enforcing these regulations remained the same; a large area had to be inspected, the ubiquitous nature of carpentry made detection impossible in many instances, and the regulations were so involved that their enforcement demanded financial and administrative resources which the Company could not hope to command. As a result success was very limited.

During the years of crisis between 1642 and 1644 activities in this field almost ceased, and for the remainder of the period the number of offences punished by the Court never returned to its former level. This could imply that more effective craft control had been achieved under the depressed conditions which affected the building trade during the late 'forties and early 'fifties. But whatever the case, these conditions were temporary, and by the mid-'fifties London's population was expanding rapidly once again, bringing with it a heavy demand for building.[25] It was as a result of this that the Company passed a new ordinance in 1655, expressed in language which certainly betrayed disappointment with the existing state of affairs.[26]

'Whereas divers persons of this Company have at present great imploym^t in building (worke being now very plentifull & still increasing) & yett by the strict rules of the ordinances of this Company are limitted in their apprentices whereby they are in want of workemen & so are not able many times to performe their worke undertaken in due time To the great prejudice of themselves & damage of their worke masters wch hath caused divers suit^{r}s to repaire unto the Court for apprentices extra-ordinary who upon deniall of their requests have gone pri-vately to other Companys & procured them to be there bound & afterwards assigned over to them & such apprentices doe afterwards come to be made free of other Companyes & have & doe daily multiply and increase To the great injury and destruction of this Company (if not timely remedied) where-upon this Court for prevencon of that evill for the future as much as in the Comp^{te} lyes & upon reading of the ordinances wch enables the M^r & wardens for reasonable cause to allow an apprentice extraordinary doth think fitt & so order That liberty be given by the M^r & wardens to any person desiring the same that hath worke sufficient to imploy an apprentice extraordinary in to have & take one apprentice over & above the number limitted by the ordinances And likewise that the same liberty be given to any person requesting the same (though not compleatly three yeares a freeman) to have & take an apprentice Soe as such persons be thought capable thereof by the M^r & Wardens.'

Once again, if this raised hopes that effective control would be restored by providing a means for undercutting the 'forrens', they were to be frustrated. This relaxation of regulations did little, if anything, to stem the influx of 'forrens', and a note of exasperation was struck monotonously in the Court minutes on this subject. Yet the Company remained determined to preserve its apprenticeship system so far as possible, and in 1664 it again sought the assistance of the law to enforce its ordinances.[27] Among the expenses so incurred was an unabashed entry for £21 4s od paid to the Lord Mayor 'for his own use'. And in the furtherance of their purpose the Company made a similar payment to the Clerk of the Common Council, as well as making gifts of 'wine, sugar, lemons and tobacco' to the jury—clear evidence of a determined will to succeed. An imminent catastrophe, however, defeated their scheming. Involved regulations for controlling the flow of labour into the craft were thrown to the winds, while in the midst of the turmoil that followed protests against this were heard as a feeble lament.

Troubles were not limited to the apprenticeship system. Even more serious complications arose between the companies in the building crafts. The first rumblings were heard in 1605 when the Court was informed that the Woodmongers Company 'drew out of the Carpenters' Company persons free of the Carpenters to the great prejudice of the Company'.[28] It was determined that this should be stopped forthwith and that if any 'sute or trouble growe

75

thereuppon the Chardge to be borne by this house'.[29] Nothing further is heard on this matter, but in 1612 the Court became involved in a dispute between the Woodmongers and one of its own prominent members, Richard Wyatt.[30] The Privy Council had directed that Wyatt should pay immediately all the arrears that he owed to the Woodmongers for the use of his three 'carres' [timber carts], according to the rates laid down by the Woodmongers, and further, if the Carpenters refused to endorse this decision, Wyatt should be committed to prison. To avoid arguments of this nature it was decided that these rates should rule in the trade. Although this particular matter was settled, it was indicative of the kind of dispute which was to recur in more severe form in the future. The Woodmongers were attempting to organize the carting of timber, which inevitably led to questions of demarcation between the transport of timber and trading in timber, the latter sphere regarded by the Carpenters as their exclusive preserve.

Peace with the Woodmongers was short-lived. In 1616 another dispute arose over the use of carts 'about which the . . . [Wood-mongers] . . . trouble Mr John Blinkhorne of this companye and will not suffer him to use Carres for his wharfe without he be translated unto them'.[31] It was decided that Blinkhorne should not be translated and the Carpenters compensated him with 20 angels [£6 13s 4d], and undertook to start legal proceedings on his behalf if it should prove necessary. These were the opening shots in what became a major battle between the two companies. Several legal actions were started by the Woodmongers in the Court of Aldermen, and elsewhere, both against the Carpenters and against some of its individual members.[32] By 1619 Blinkhorne's action seems to have developed into something of a test case. After referring to its decision of 1616 to take any legal steps necessary, the Court of Assistants thereupon expended money in order 'to preserve their rights as a corporation'. Blinkhorne also met similar expenses on his own account and it was therefore directed that £20 should be paid to him as recompense.[33]

The Company, however, was not willing to allow matters to deteriorate while the law took its course. In 1622 a committee of Assistants was set up to consider a proposal that the Carpenters should purchase a 'Wharfe on the bankside'.[34] The location of this wharf was at 'Sackvyle manner neare Whitefryars', adjoining Blinkhorne's wharf. In fact, the Company took a lease on it as it proved impossible to raise enough money to purchase it.[35] The details of this 'adventure' will be discussed more fully at a later stage, but for the moment it is interesting to question why it should have been decided to invest such a large sum of money in this way. The records contain no direct reference on this point. Nevertheless, the great lengths to which the Court was prepared to go in order to raise the money for the purchase,[36] the manner in which it appointed a treasurer and four overseers to supervise the enterprise, and the fact that John Blinkhorne took so much trouble over the whole business on the Company's behalf, suggests that this was not primarily, if at all, a business speculation. Against the background of the disputes with the Woodmongers it is seen as a direct attempt to compete with an 'upstart' company which was attempting to monopolize a branch of the timber trade.

Meanwhile a more fundamental dispute arose between the Carpenters and the Joiners. The Joiners Company had been independent since 1307,[37] but it remained a weak organization until the end of the sixteenth century. In 1591, however, the City assessed it for £4 8s od, which placed it close behind the Carpenters who were assessed at £5 10s od.[38] Moreover, it gradually became evident that the Joiners were strengthening their hold over those branches of woodworking not directly concerned with building construction. In doing this, they had fastened on that section of the craft which was to prove easiest to regulate in the seventeenth century. Besides, while the Carpenters had always claimed to represent all aspects of the craft they had never clearly defined this, although in practice most of their activities were concerned with building construction.

The discussions with the Joiners seem to have begun amicably enough. In 1621 Mr Allen, Mr Issack, Mr Petley and Mr Thornton were appointed to meet with representatives of the Joiners about differences between the Companies over the work to be properly under the control of each.[39] At this stage it would appear that meetings were taking place at fairly regular intervals to iron out disputes which from time to time appeared. During 1624 and 1625 the number of meetings increased, even so, they were still conducted in the convivial atmosphere of 'business lunches' in local taverns.[40] But from this time onwards matters deteriorated. In 1628 the Carpenters' Court reported, with stern disapproval, that joiners were building shop-windows and generally doing carpenters' work.[41] Matters came to a head in 1629 when the Court of Aldermen set up a committee to hear questions in dispute between the two Companies.[42] Eventually, in 1632, after calling before them the Masters, Wardens, and other chief members of both Companies at 'diverse tymes' the committee presented its decision. The basis of the dispute is best shown by quoting from the adjudication *in extenso*.[43]

That the following are the work of the Joiners:

1. All bedsteads 'except boarded Beadsteads and nayled togeather'
2. All chairs, & stools, made with mortise or tenon joints
3. All tables of wainscot, walnut or other wood, glued, with frames 'mortesses or tennants' [mortices and tenon joints]
4. All forms, framed, made of boards with the sides pinned or glued
5. Chests framed, 'dustalled [dovetailed], pinned or glued'
6. Cabinets or boxes dustalled, pinned, glued or joined
7. Cupboards framed, 'dustalled, pinned or glued'
8. Presses pannelled, dustalled, pinned or glued 'for wearing apparel Mercers Silkemen Millenors, or Napkinpressers'
9. All sorts of wainscoting, 'sealing' of houses, and 'setling' made by 'the use of two Jages'

10. Shopwindows 'made for ornament or beauty which Cannot be made without glue'
11. Doors framed, panelled or glued
12. Hatches 'Jaged', framed or glued
13. Pews, pulpits, and seats with desks, framed panelled or glued
14. All sorts of frames upon stalls, framed or glued
15. Picture frames, 'lattesses for Scrivenors, or the like'
16. All signboards of wainscot or carved
17. All work made by one or two 'Jages' with the use of any kind of nails
18. All carved works, using carving tools and not planes
19. All coffins of wainscot; but if of other wood, can be made by either company

And that the following are the work of the Carpenters:
1. All tables for drapers, taverns, victuallers, chandlers, countinghouses, all tables of deal, elm, oak, beech or other wood nailed together without glue, but not movable tables [i.e. trestles]
2. 'Cesternestooles, washing stooles, bucking stooles' and all other stools headed with oak, elm, beech or deal and footed with square or round feet, except framed stools which are glued or pinned
3. All sorts of frames made of elm, oak, beech or deal heads as long as the feet are not lathe-turned
4. Laying of floors of elm or oak (except 'groved' floors which are Joiners' work). Deal floors can be laid by either company
5. 'Deviding' warehouses and rooms, unwainscoted and unpanneled, with split or whole deals or other materials, except wainscot, and 'except all particions grooved glued battened or framed'
6. Shelving all rooms unwainscoted and unpannelled with seats and brackets, 'except worke in studies which wee conceive fitt to be left Indifferent to both Company'
7. All signboards not made of wainscot or carved

8. All pillars or ballasters for lights in a partition are to be made by whichever company made the partition itself
9. All galleries in churches and elsewhere unless wainscot or panelled or carved
10. Shelving in kitchen with racks
11. Floors for pews in churches, if of oak or elm; if of deal, then either company
12. All frames for screens not made of wainscot, glued carved or panelled.

Also, the 'jage' to be used by the Carpenters only for the work listed above. [A 'jage' was probably some kind of metal device for strengthening joints.]

In broad terms this amounted to the Joiners being granted fine work while the Carpenters were left with the rougher building and jobbing work. The Committee also heard a number of un-settled complaints of individual joiners against the Carpenters Company, resulting in the latter being directed to pay £4 to one litigant joiner, and 10s each to four others.

After such an exhaustive enquiry it might have been thought that matters between the two companies were finally settled, but this was not to be. Representatives of both companies met again in 1633 to discuss new disagreements that had arisen between them.[44] Following this yet another aldermanic committee was called in 1636 to hear a catalogue of differences which had accumulated since 1632,[45] and it was charged to call before it all concerned and to enforce the original decision as necessary. But in view of the fact that the adjudication of 1632 had in some ways given the Carpenters an inferior status to the Joiners, it was too much to ask that the senior and wealthier company should accept this without very strong resistance. In the 1640s, therefore, the Carpenters began to counter-attack by prosecuting joiners who were alleged to be doing carpenters' work.[46] Indeed, it could well have been that the Master and Wardens of the Carpenters, who enjoyed a tradition of shrewdness, were attempting to render the judgment unworkable, while the fact that much of the work assigned to either craft had to be carried out in conjunction with that assigned to the other didn't make this too difficult. But whether this was the policy or not, the impossibility of maintaining exactly those demarcations was recognized when, in 1642, the Joiners made further complaints that the Carpenters were violating the mutual settlement, and the Lord Mayor's Court lamely replied that both companies must observe the agreement[47] —no heavier or additional penalties were threatened.

The demands being made on the Court of Assistants by the mid-century were heavy. They were fighting a running battle with the Joiners, exercising constant surveillance over the Woodmongers, trying desperately to stem the flood of carpenters into London while attempting to control those already there, and endeavouring to enforce building regulations—all this, when yet another invasion was mounted. This time it was the sawyers.

Before the seventeenth century sawyers had had no effective organizations. Often they went under the general title of labourer and were employed by carpenters and others in the City or in large sawyards along the reaches of the Thames.[48] Whether it was the result of the weakening hold of the companies in the building crafts, or the steady rise in the demand for sawyers' services, or some other factor, a growing number began to move into London. Those already there soon sought to establish an independent organization and to raise their wage rates by restricting the entry of more sawyers into the City. As a result, in 1648 the Carpenters petitioned the Lord Mayor against the activities of the free sawyers,[49] and meanwhile proceedings which the free sawyers had instituted against their 'forren' brethren were stayed, pending the Lord Mayor's decision. This time the Carpenters were not alone but were supported by the Joiners and the Shipwrights.[50] It was argued that sawyers were essentially labourers because they worked under the direction of other master craftsmen, who also provided them with their material. Moreover, the Carpenters were concerned about the current shortage of free sawyers.[51] Eventually, in 1655, an order was obtained from the Lord Mayor regulating sawyers' wages and, for the time being at least, refusing recognition of their right to limit the influx of 'forren' sawyers.[52] However, the need to watch the activities of the sawyers added yet another burden to the already overworked Court.

There was further co-operation between the Carpenters and the Joiners, in company with the Bricklayers, Plasterers, Weavers, Feltmakers, and Hat-band Makers, in 1653, when a petition was presented to the Common Council 'for the bringing in of all persons into that respective Company whereof their trade is . . .'.[53] Only in this way, it was argued, could the public be assured of sound workmanship. Similarly, in the same year, the Carpenters independently petitioned a committee of trade which had been set up by the Common Council to look into the matter of demarcation between crafts.[54] The City seems to have been somewhat in sympathy with these demands for, in 1656, a committee under Sir James Vyner gave its decision on another petition which the Joiners had made in that year.[55]

'The petition is that all apprentices of working joiners, free of other Companies, and such of their sons as shall be bred up in the same craft, shall henceforth be presented and bound and made free by the Joiners Co. Precedents for granting such a petition have been found: similar grants were made in the Mayoralties of Sir James Pemberton and Sir John Jolles, to the Glaziers and to the Painter-stainers, and lately in the Mayoralty of Aldn. Andrewes to the Glovers Co. The state of the Company merits this grant, and a draft as that made for the foregoing companies has been prepared.'

The Carpenters, however, had to be content with the re-affirmation of their ordinances.

Petitions and litigation were the main theme of the Carpenter's craft activities for the following twenty years. The outcome was usually stalemate, sometimes failure. Even the lowly sawyers were more than a match for the combined forces of the Carpenters, Joiners, and Shipwrights. In spite of the settlement of 1655, sawyers steadily increased their wage rates, much to the annoyance of their 'masters'.[56] Amid all these troubles it must have been some consolation to the Carpenters when they had been able to conclude a successful pact with the Bricklayers in 1631.[57] Each agreed not to intermeddle with the other's trade and a standing committee was set up to deal with disputes as they arose. But this was a bright spot in a period of general gloom affecting all the companies in the building crafts, pointing to the fact that their several disagreements and contests were symptomatic of more fundamental changes affecting the building trade during this period.

Both James I and Charles I issued a number of proclamations on building in London with the aim of controlling the expansion of the capital; but the failure of these regulations, as well as of those emanating from the City itself, ensured that there was no break with tradition in this respect.[58] For example, in 1638 a list was drawn up showing that in previous years 1,316 buildings of divers kinds had been erected by 450 persons contrary to building laws, but in each case the matter was settled by a fine, and it is therefore assumed that the buildings were allowed to stand.[59] Much of this new building was promoted by big City landlords; the method adopted was for the landlord to offer contractors a reversionary lease of thirty-one to forty-one years. In this manner the Earls of Bedford, Holland, Salisbury and Clare, for example, added substantially to their income.[60] In the light of all this, it has been suggested that, for the greater part, the general regulations were not sincerely meant and were simply intended to provide yet another source of revenue for an extravagant King.[61] Moreover, by concentrating on the limitation of new buildings these regulations were self-defeating in that they encouraged people to make alterations and additions to existing buildings, thus increasing overcrowding; at the same time this provided a great deal of cheap jobbing work which was practically impossible to inspect.[62] The Carpenters, for their part, constantly urged the Corporation to take a stronger line in building matters. In 1621, for example, it petitioned that retailers of timber, deal, boards and other carpenters' stuff should be forbidden from selling 'under a load of anye of the severall sortes of the said stuff nor to alter the propertye thereof but to sell it as they bought it'.[63] The aim behind this would seem to have been to stop individual, probably 'forren', carpenters from obtaining small quantities of 'unsized' timber. Along with this the Company redoubled its efforts to sue those guilty of 'insufficient work'. In this connection the Wardens viewed some of the now famous London churches which were then under construction, and among others visited were St Clement Danes and 'a church in Covent Garden'.[64] They must have decided, however, that the costs of vigilance in terms of time, energy and money were not warranted by the results that were achieved, for in the 1650s there was a falling off in the number of fines and committals for trade offences, until in 1660, for the first time, no prosecutions were recorded. Moreover, the Master and Wardens found difficulty in enforcing their decisions in trade matters, and they successfully appealed to the City recorder for a general warrant which made it possible for them to commit recalcitrant offenders to the Lord Mayor or the Justices of the Peace. This did nothing to change matters, however, as the real problem was not the enforcement of penalties but the detection of offenders.[65]

What had been major trade issues in the early 1660s became matters of small importance after the Great Fire of 1666.[66] The impact of this disaster was relatively far greater than the similar shocking events of the 'Second Fire of London' of nearly three hundred years later. To recover from the devastation that was wrought demanded the highest degrees of ingenuity and resolution from those who directed the rebuilding of the capital. Their success proved to be one of the remarkable feats in English history. Moreover, the destruction could not be measured wholly in tangible form. The flames both hastened and symbolized the sweeping away of many old traditions and institutions. Nowhere was this more evident than among the ancient craft guilds, and in particular among those in the building trade.

The Act sanctioning the rebuilding took care to ensure that there would be an adequate supply of labour. All those working on the reconstruction who were not freemen of London were given the same rights as freemen. This privilege was for seven years in the first instance, but it could be extended if the rebuilding had not been completed within that period. Those 'forrens' who had exercised this privilege for seven years were given the right to claim freedom of the City for life. Under these critical conditions the Carpenters realized that concessions would be demanded from them, but, at the same time, they were determined to preserve some position of authority in building matters—indeed, it was possible for them to view events as a *deus ex machina* allowing the Company to claim itself as the most effective agency for regulating the supply of labour for building operations. Accordingly, in 1666 it petitioned that no carpenters should be allowed to work within the City unless they had duly served a seven-year apprenticeship, and to ensure this it offered to examine the indentures of incoming carpenters;[67] if this had been granted, it would have given the Company a formidable degree of control. Shortly afterwards another petition was presented that 'forrens' should only be allowed the status of journeymen or servants, not that of master.[68] In these demands the Company was not alone and in 1669 was joined by the Masons, Bricklayers, Joiners, and Plasterers in presenting a protest against 'forrens' 'intruding themselves upon the callings and businese of the Petitioners in the work of rebuilding the Citty'; and in the following year the Carpenters petitioned against the London sawyers' attempts to exclude 'all those ['forren' sawyers] who dayly resort to the Citty of London and parts adiacent to worke and labour att the whip sawe and frameing sawe and by that meanes keepe the wages & prizes of those sort of Laborers att an equal and indifferent rate . . .'.[69]

The problem was the same as in the 1650s; the increasing demand for sawyers' services had encouraged them to seek incorporation. Against this the Carpenters, Shipwrights, Joiners, Boxmakers and Wheelwrights put up strong resistance, arguing that sawyers' work was common to all their trades as an ancillary operation and that to submit to the sawyers' demands would result in an unwarranted increase in their wages, from which the general public would suffer; besides, it would form '...an evill president All other Laborers of Masons Bricklayers Plaisterers and all other trades having the same (if not greater) reasons to alleadge for their incorporacon'.[70] At least, the companies concerned could not be accused of sticking doggedly to the principles which they applied to themselves.

At one time these disputes might have been treated by the City authorities as matters of substance, but now they were regarded as petty and irrelevant squabbles. On a number of occasions the Carpenters urged the Court of Aldermen to be more vigorous in the enforcement of those clauses in the rebuilding Acts which dealt with the employment of 'forrens'; and they even took it upon themselves to bear the cost of legal proceedings against those 'forrens' working in London who had not served a seven-year apprenticeship.[71] The authorities, however, were guided by two cardinal principles: to remove any obstacle which impeded the rebuilding of the capital, and to ensure that the disaster would never be repeated. On the one hand this entailed a free and unrestricted flow of building labour into London, while on the other it led to the insistence that the basic materials in building should be of a non-combustible nature; brick and stone replaced timber.[72] This alone was enough to seal the fate of the Carpenters Company in craft affairs. Of course, the need to settle disputes between craftsmen remained, but City officials quickly assumed full authority in this sphere under their general responsibility for the rebuilding, and in order to effect quick decisions;[73] even in this field the Company was made redundant.

So far as the building crafts were concerned the Great Fire lent drama and brought suddenness to events which were the natural outcome of the preceding sixty years. It was inevitable that the Company would suffer a decline in craft matters. Somewhat paradoxically, the swift and radical fashion in which it was shorn of such authority in the craft as it did possess brought it short-term loss and long-term gain. It was given no opportunity for wasting its energy over many years in chasing the fantasies and irrelevancies of medieval craft regulations.

The decline in craft control was not the result of the Company's internal inefficiency. For the period as a whole there was a substantial rise in London's population which put heavy demands on the building crafts. At certain periods, therefore, it was impossible to stop large inflows of 'forrens' especially from the immediately surrounding area. Generally, prosperous conditions offered opportunities for some master carpenters to become building contractors who were prepared to undertake the complete range of building operations, thus cutting across established practices. As early as 1624 the Company had passed an order requiring any-one undertaking 'taskworke' exceeding £10 in value to record the agreement at the Hall, as a safeguard against under-pricing and supplanting.[74] Although large-scale contractors remained rare, the number of men who were competent to take on major operations in the rebuilding of London is evidence of their importance.

In 1666, for example, 'Mr Wildgoose[75] [and Mr Aldridge, bricklayer] ... gave their reports concerning the view made by them att the ground of the late Salters Hall and they declared that it is very necessary that the vault which is now standing [sic] be covered forthwith for the preservacion of it and have drawn a design for the building to be over the vault'.[76] Building of the new hall began in February 1666/7, but in the following June Aldridge was discharged and Wildgoose assumed full responsibility for the work, which was completed in 1668. The same year Wildgoose was employed by the Coopers 'to survey and measure the whole ground ... [for a new hall, and he] ... produced and explayned a draught or modell of the Hall to bee rebuilt'.[77] The Coopers were so delighted with this that their Court unanimously agreed to vote Wildgoose five gold pieces as a present.[78] Wildgoose's talents were employed also by his own Company, when between 1670 and 1671 he designed extensive alterations to Carpenters' Hall.[79] Thomas Fitch, carpenter, was another notable example. He undertook the task of turning the Fleet Ditch into a canal to be served by a number of wharves, and for a period he was receiving £1,000 a week on account of these operations.[80] Opportunities were not limited to building alone. Richard Wyatt, one of the Carpenters' leading benefactors, made his fortune during the early years of the century as a wharf-owner and dealer in building timber.[81]

The careers of Wildgoose, Fitch, Wyatt and others illustrate certain aspects of the general developments under discussion: new types of contractor were emerging, either as builders or as wholesale suppliers of building materials; the demand for major building operations was increased greatly as a result of the Fire—of the City companies alone, forty-four of them lost their halls;[82] and lastly, master carpenters of Wildgoose's calibre were coming to be distinguished as much for their talents as architects as for their abilities as general builders.

Changes of this nature underlay the growing rivalry and strife between companies in the building crafts. In the struggle that ensued what had been originally feeble craft organizations were able, for a brief period, to increase their influence by engrossing specialist sections within a general craft. One of the best examples of this is that provided by the disputes between the Carpenters and the Joiners. The latter drew its recruits from the largest skilled element among carpenters generally, and in relation to the growing demand for joiners' services—especially for making furniture —the supply of joiners was inelastic, and therefore more easily controlled than that of ordinary carpenters.

In trade matters the Carpenters Company gradually came to represent, with decreasing effectiveness, small independent master

carpenters who formed a transitional class between three unavoidable alternatives: the most able could aspire to become
building contractors or 'architects'; a larger, but still minor,
proportion could concentrate on specialist branches of the craft,
of which joinery was the most prominent; while the majority were
forced to suffer reduction to the status of journeymen employees
—a development which was re-enforced by the constant influx of
'forrens' into the City, who were prepared to work for wages
which were lower than those earned by London carpenters but
higher than those that could be obtained outside London.

Yet with all its failings in the field of craft regulation the
Company's membership continued to rise throughout the period.
Even in craft matters it still offered opportunities to some and
hope to many more. Those bent on success continued to be
attracted to it for reasons similar to those of a century earlier.[83] It
was still the avenue to the indirectly lucrative posts of City
Viewers; and its leading members were in regular contact with
City Officials, who could be very useful sources of business—on
a number of occasions gifts were made to the Chamberlain and
other officials to 'be kind to us'. And, although by the seventeenth
century the Company had ceased to have any formal connection
with the royal appointments of King's Carpenter and Surveyor of
the King's Works, it took very great care to foster friendly and
informal relations with successive holders of these positions;[84] for
example, in 1637 Mathew Banks, Master of the Company in that
year, marked the event by the gift of a portrait of William
Portington bearing the following inscription:[85] 'Wm. Portington,
Esqr. Mr. Carpenter in ye office of his Mate buildings, who served
in ye place 40 yeares, who was a well wisher in this Societe, this
being ye gift of Mathew Bankes who served him 14 yeares . . .'.
Through leading members a direct link was retained with the
subordinate office of Chief Carpenter in the Tower,[86] Mathew
Banks, Edmund Hedlond, William Wheatley and John Hort
being successive appointees to this post. Thus, for some, membership of the Company could bring pecuniary advantage and civic

honour, but this did not imply that they were always willing to accept office in the Company, or to follow the slow progression from Assistant to Master. The reason was simple; it could be an unprofitable use of time and energy, and consequently, from the 1640s onwards there was a steady increase in the number paying fines to avoid office.[87] As might be expected, this became more frequent after 1666.

But, for all this, over most of the period the strongest attraction exercised by the Company was of a more immediate kind. The energy behind the efforts to enforce its ordinances sprang from the bulk of the membership, who stood to lose most if those efforts should fail—namely, the small master craftsmen whom circumstances were reducing to the status of journeymen employees.[88] It was the small master who demanded the enforcement of the apprenticeship system, the translation of carpenters free of other companies,[89] and strict demarcation between the building crafts. In the 1650s, too, these small masters were strongly critical of the activities of the Company's Yeomanry— those who, as a result of choice or circumstance, were prepared to accept their lot as wage-earning employees—because they were felt to be undermining the very basis of craft regulation. Yet none of this must be taken to imply that the lot of the journeyman was becoming harder. In fact, taking the period as a whole, quite the reverse was happening; between 1600 and 1670 carpenters' real wages evidently rose by approaching 25 per cent.[90] This probably reflected a corresponding rise in earnings as it is unlikely that there were higher degrees of unemployment and underemployment in the seventeenth century as compared with the sixteenth. While the first half of the new century was marked by a number of severe depressions in trade, the impression is that the building industry was comparatively prosperous and that for ordinary employee carpenters work was relatively plentiful; this being the main reason why some apprentices married before their term was completed, caring little when they had to surrender their indentures at the Hall[91]—which, incidentally, was another factor accounting for the difference between the number bound and the number subsequently seeking the freedom. The strongest impression of full wage packets is gained from the 1650s and 1660s. In 1655, for example, the Lord Mayor and Court of Aldermen desired the Company's '. . . opinion for the reducing of the excessive wages of Laborers & workemen in these times of great plenty . . .'.[92]

More generally, the disputes which arose were not the counterparts of modern trade union disputes, but the reactions of small employers to the growing pressures of industrialization; and in this these men were able to attack only symptoms of their distress and not its causes, while any advantages which they gained were temporary. Yet naturally, while there was some hope of preserving their privileges, master carpenters determined to do all in their power to realize it. But finally the events of 1666 brought a sudden and decisive break with the past, which forced the Company to turn its attention more to the welfare of its members and to the development of its property. This was an aspect of its life which had continued to flourish throughout this difficult period and to provide a more lasting reason for its existence.

CHAPTER V

INCOME AND PROPERTY
1600-1666

⸺⸺⸺⸺⸺

W E have already noticed, in chapter III, that it is impossible to assess the Company's true economic position from the earlier accounts because these do not distinguish between current income and capital. Nevertheless, sufficient evidence has survived from the seventeenth century to outline the broad changes that occurred in its fortunes. By this time property was the basis of its prosperity, with rents accounting for over half of current income and fines for new leases amounting to nearly the whole of capital receipts. From £50 in 1600, rents rose to £325 by the 1660s, and by then it was quite common for a fine of £200 to be received for the renewal of a lease. It is, therefore, to the expansion of the Company's property that attention should first be directed.

In 1622 the Court of Assistants considered a proposal to rent a wharf at Whitefriars, as we noticed in connection with the dispute between the Carpenters and Woodmongers.[1] After negotiations the Carpenters obtained the lease of the wharf for a rent of £105 per annum, and the lease included the right of reversion on an adjoining wharf then held in her own right by Margaret, the wife of John Blinkhorne. Margaret Blinkhorne was the daughter of Richard Wyatt, and formerly the wife of John Bland, Wyatt's original partner; the wharf in question was one that Wyatt and Bland had operated for a number of years.[2] After further discussions the Court decided to purchase the two wharves outright for £3,000, but the contributions towards this 'Adventure'—£1,000 from the Master, Warden and Assistants, £1,000 from the Livery, and £1,000 from the Yeomanry—came in very slowly, and a small committee, consisting of a treasurer and three over-seers, was set up to hasten matters.[3] In the meantime, the Company instituted a writ against Richard Wyatt's widow, who was also his executrix, to surrender the lease of the wharf occupied by her daughter; but this seems to have been for legal form only and not to have involved any substantial disagreement.[4] So far as raising the £3,000 was concerned, matters were still not proceeding satisfactorily. Moreover, for the day-to-day running of the wharves until 1626 the Court relied on one of their number, Peter Petley, but in April of that year he announced that he was unable to continue because his own business was suffering through neglect.[5] At this juncture, John Blinkhorne assumed control while a course of action was decided upon. Eventually, in June, the Court gave up the plan to purchase the wharves and agreed to underlease them for £105 per annum. The lease was taken by Thomas and Michael King, and Richard Slade, for a period of six years on the condition that the Company made them a loan of £400 free of interest for a term of five years—to be made up to £300 in the form of stock at the wharf and £100 in cash.[6] To this the Company agreed, and repaid to its members the sums that they had subscribed. After the first few difficult years of occupa-tion, the venture became profitable and in 1629 the Company improved the facilities there by the construction of a crane costing over £119.[7]

It must have come as a pleasant surprise when, in 1629, a bequest was received under the will of Edward Fennor, who had been Master the previous year.[8] It consisted of a tenement in the parish of St Helen's within Bishopsgate. From the income of this property £20 first had to be paid to Fennor's heir, but when this was met the rents were to be divided equally between poor Carpenters and the poor of the parish. Within a few months of this gift another was received, this time from John Day who had been Master in 1621;[9] the rents from a house without Bishopsgate were to be used for the relief of ten Carpenters' widows.

Shortly after this, the Company, having evidently recovered

from its unhappy experiences with the Whitefriars wharf, again took steps to increase its independent income. In November 1630 a committee was appointed to consider a proposal to purchase property at Norton Folgate,[10] and a little while after this another three members of the Court were appointed to inquire into an offer for sale of land in Tower Street.[11] Nothing more is heard about the latter, but the Norton Folgate estate was duly purchased for £660.[12] This amounted to a large increase in the Company's property consisting, as it did, of eleven houses on a site measuring 100 yards in length and varying between 20 and 25 yards in breadth. The purchase was made through trustees drawn from the Assistants, who were charged 'to receive and dispose of the rents and profits thereof for the relief of the Poor of the Company, and for the aid and ease of their [the Company's] taxes . . .'.[13]

Just over three years later, in 1634, negotiations were begun to purchase a house in Crutched Friars, known originally as The Cork.[14] Having taken legal advice, a Committee of Assistants completed the purchase for the sum of £500 and an annual payment of £5 4s od to be made to the Parson and Churchwardens of the parish of St Helen's.[15] This was a surprisingly large investment so soon after the acquisition of the Norton Folgate estate. In terms of rent, its value was approximately half that of Norton Folgate; but somewhat later it was to yield an unexpected capital gain.[16]

The Civil War unavoidably postponed further private bequests or Company investment. In 1650, however, came a gift from John Read, who died in office as Master.[17] Under a complicated will the Company became trustees of property in Naked Boy Alley,* Bermondsey Street, Southwark. A number of legacies were to be paid annually from the rents, among them £10 to his brother, 10s to ten poor carpenters, £5 to the Master, Wardens, and Assistants for new gloves, 14s to the Clerk, 6s to the Beadle,

* A name probably derived from the common craft sign of coffin-makers or undertakers.

and £4 to a poor scholar at Cambridge. On the decease of Read's
brother the greater part of the income released was to be used
towards the upkeep of a school in the parishes of Penton and
Weyhill, Hampshire, and the remainder was to be distributed
among the poor of those parishes. If, however, the trustees
judged that the school was not being run satisfactorily then,
instead, the income was to be used to help five poor scholars at
Oxford or Cambridge.

This was followed, in 1653, by a gift from James Palmer, BD,
the son of a former freeman, who wished, no doubt, to show his
gratitude to the Company for their assistance to him some years
before when he was a poor scholar at Magdalen College, Cambridge.[18] He sealed a letter of attorney empowering the Company
to receive the rents from his three houses in Great Almonry,
Westminster, which then yielded £12 per annum.[19] He explained
that this was to replace his original plan to make a gift of £500 for
the foundation of almshouses. It was soon discovered, however,
that the houses in question were in a very dilapidated state and
the Carpenters had to spend the large amount of £545 repairing
them.[20] By way of recompense, Palmer, in 1656, granted the
Company the lease of the property for 2,000 years at a nominal
rent of 4d per annum.[21] Meanwhile, in 1654, the Court had
successfully bargained for another house in Crutched Friars. This
was completed in December of that year when £156 was paid for
the house, being the equivalent of thirteen years' purchase.[22]

Individually, the most valuable houses were the Bear Inn at
London Wall and 'Gyttens House' at Lime Street. As to their
size and appearance we can only guess, but no doubt they were
attractive examples of the smaller types of Tudor timber-frame
houses of which many still survive. The only houses constructed
of brick were the two at London Wall adjoining the Hall; and an
attractive feature of the Hall property was that of the house 'over
the gate' forming an archway into the Hall garden.[23] The occupations of the tenants were no longer recorded but the rents which
they paid suggest that most of them were prosperous craftsmen.

Moreover, a further indication of this, as well as of the rise in the capital value of the property over this period as compared with the sixteenth century, can be gained from the amounts charged as fines for the renewal of leases. In 1620, for example, Richard Middleton agreed to pay a fine of £100 and an annual rent of £5 for the lease of a house at London Wall;[24] or again, in 1636 Christopher Ball sealed a lease on a house in Crutched Friars by agreeing to pay a fine of £140 (by instalments) and an annual rent of £25;[25] and between 1661 and 1664 Richard Peckett paid a fine of £400 in four instalments for the lease of the 'Gyttens House'.[26] Even bearing in mind price changes over this period these figures can be taken as representative of considerable rises in property values.

So far as tenants were concerned, the Court had little cause to grumble. On one occasion those tenants in arrears with rents were threatened with legal action, and in 1655 an order of ejectment was served on Dr Engham—one of the tenants of Great Almonry —for non-payment of rent;[27] this soon brought the desired result and the Doctor remained in occupation. Control over the upkeep of property continued to be exercised by means of the annual 'view', when necessary repairs were recorded and the appropriate directions given to tenants. At the same time, every opportunity was taken to improve the property. In 1604 new stables were erected at the Hall, and the existing 'long stable' was extensively renovated, which included the building of a covered way between the houses and the stable.[28] It is possible that the new stables were built a little way from the Hall estate on a garden which had been purchased a year earlier (the Minutes contain a reference to a discussion to purchase a garden, but no further details are recorded).[29] The total cost of these operations was over £80. Furthermore, in the same year unspecified alterations were made to the houses adjoining the Hall;[30] and three years later the Clerk's House received extensive renovation including the addition of a study[31]—no doubt an indication of the growing burden of work carried by this official.

Apart from the construction of the crane at the Whitefriars wharf, for nearly twenty-five years remarkably little was spent on the existing tenanted property. In 1653, however, as has been noted, it was necessary to spend a considerable amount on the houses in Great Almonry.[32] And shortly afterwards, an urgent note was entered in the minutes recording that the tenants of the houses immediately adjoining the Hall had been ordered to put new, sound and substantial 'plate all along the passage or entry leading into the Hall of this Company upon which their respective houses are supported', because it had become rotten and dangerous;[33] and as part of this reconstruction the door to the Beadle's house, which appears to have been inside the Hall itself, was blocked up and an external door was made in order to afford the Beadle 'better accommodation'.

But, apart from the large amounts which the Carpenters laid out on new property and on altering what it already possessed, the Hall claimed most attention and money. For some years after the extensive work on it in the 1590s only minor repairs were necessary, such as underpinning the well in 1603.[34] In 1613, however, nearly £40 was laid out for the complete rebuilding of the 'upper end' of the Hall,[35] and in 1619 over £60 was spent on repairs to the parts immediately adjoining the two houses occupied by the Beadle and Clerk.[36] Meanwhile, in 1609, the estate had been considerably enhanced by improvements to the surrounding area carried out by the City authorities; 'what had been a most noysome and offensive place, a rotten morish ground, . . . was reduced from its former condition into most faire & royall walkes . . .'.[37] No further large alterations or repairs were made until 1630. Then it was noted that the roof was very defective and 4,000 tiles were used for its repair.[38] Indeed, the roof seems to have required fairly regular attention for, once again, in 1644, large parts of it had to be re-tiled.[39]

During the remainder of the 1640s and in the 1650s little was done, apart from the paving of the upper end with 'purbeck & Dunkirke' stone.[40] In the main, this lack of expenditure on the

Hall was due to the heavy outside demands being made on the Company during this period. But eventually, almost fatefully, two years before the Great Fire the Court ordered that:[41]

'... there shall be a new building erected on the west side of the Garden, of aboute twenty foote in breadth from the wall there, and in length, and from the Pastry [sic] to the Drapers Garden wall; the same to be for a Gallary or roome for the Mr. Wardens assistants and livery to meete on the Elleccon day of new Mr. and wardens, and other occacons when the Company pleases, the old dining roome over the parlo[r] being too little for the assembly of the whole livery ...'.

A committee was set up to decide between three alternative draft plans for the extensions, and to examine the cost of the operation as well as ways of raising the money necessary to meet it.[42] After due consideration Mr Wildgoose's drawings were adopted; although, for the new staircase into the 'new great roome' and a new passage leading to the garden, a quite separate plan was chosen. This had been drawn by William Taylor, who had been Master in 1658.[43]

Twenty-two carpenters were employed on this work, as well as bricklayers, plasterers, painters, paviours, joiners, and a glazier.[44] Much of their time was occupied on the 'Great Room', the building of which entailed the reconstruction of the kitchen and 'paistery' [sic]. A number of small rooms were built to lead off from the 'Great Room', and a new buttery was added 'towards the garden' with a passage joining it to the main Hall. The original staircase was much altered and refurbished with more elaborate carving, while delicate carving in the 'Great Room' was done by Ambrose Andrews, for which he received £25. William Taylor was paid £50 for building the new staircase and passage. John Smith and Edward Perwich, plasterers, received £80 'for worke done in seeling the great room' as well as other work about the Hall. Another £20 was paid to Herbert Higgins, joiner, for wainscoting half the 'greate roome & for the chimney piece &

halfe the cornishes there & for making of wainscott doors and other ioyners worke'; the remainder of this work was done by Christopher Webb, for which he received £28 5s od. Outside the Hall, excavations had provided an opportunity for re-designing the layout of the garden. In total, the cost of these operations amounted to £1,259 19s 8d, of which the greater part was accounted for by journeymen's wages. For this, the Company was by 1665 possessed of a fine and imposing Hall, but which was, as yet, a sign of prosperity rather than a mark of status among the London Livery Companies.

The growth in the Company's property was by far from being trouble free. With the record of the 1580s behind it the Court was probably not surprised when, in 1605, its title to the Lime Street estate was challenged:[45] the question of 'concealments' was still a live issue. To meet the legal expenses arising from this it was decided to cancel the Candlemas dinner.[46] Similar trouble was experienced by other companies, and with the costly disputes of the sixteenth century in mind, a joint endeavour was made to settle the matter once-for-all. In 1607, the Carpenters contributed £10 towards promoting a 'byll' dealing with so-called 'concealed' income.[47] This became an Act confirming to thirty-three companies, including the Carpenters, lands which had been under dispute.[48] In view of this, it is surprising to find that another, and much more expensive, suit arose over Lime Street between 1616 and 1619. The Court first enlisted the help of learned counsel about their title to Lime Street.[49] The gravity of the matter was shown by the decision to take £55 out of the chest to meet any contingencies.[50] Conveniently, details in the accounts present a fairly clear picture of the dispute.[51] There were two groups of payments. One was headed 'Charges Laid out about the land in Lyme Street of Mr Warham's giyft, and about the purchase there from Mr Chard, who had the patent thereof in trust for the Countess of Sussex, and for whom Mr W. Bennett in Aldersgate Street was a dealer'. The charges totalled £66 4s 4d of which £52 was for 'the purchase'. It would appear, therefore, that the Countess of Sussex had originally been granted the patent for the concealed income from Lime Street, and £52 was paid to her trustees to settle the matter out of Court. A second account was headed 'charges for the discharging of the arrears of the whole rent of the said Lands in Lyme Street after processe out of the exchequer to extend for the same of seventy two pounds one shilling and sixpence'. This sum was made up of a number of payments: £5 for Bennett's expenses, £25 'for his paynes', 44s to make his wife a ring, 52s for his clerk, 7s 'for his mayde', £5 to the auditor for enrolling the record of the discharge, 52s to the auditor's clerk, and £22 to 'Mʳ Attorney to confesse the plea'. The seemingly odd nature of some of these payments suggests that they were *douceurs* given to Bennett for expediting matters; while the Bennett family enjoyed their gifts the Carpenters went without their Election Day Dinner.[52] Finally in this connection, in 1619 a further £20 was drawn from the chest to pay for the confirmation by the King of the Company's title to the lands in Lime Street.[53] This was obviously part of a joint action by City companies, as the money was paid into a common fund, and a general precept was issued by the Lord Mayor—Lime Street was safe at last. From its beginning in 1581, the whole episode illustrates the exceptional risks which were attached to property ownership in Tudor and Stuart times, as well as the somewhat arbitrary nature of the law.

Against a general background of uncertainty, in 1641 the Company's title to its property in Norton Folgate was challenged.[54] This threat was met by obtaining a copy of a *scire facias* from the Exchequer Office; two years later this was repeated, and thereafter for the next ten years, at the beginning of every legal term. The only remaining problem in this respect occurred in connection with the house in Crutched Friars purchased in 1654, for, in the following year, a 'certaine lady or her steward' claimed an interest in the house.[55] The Assistants flatly rejected this challenge and that was the end of the matter.

Quite apart from its own estates, property matters in a wider sense caused the Company unwanted concern and expense. In common with other London companies it became involved in a royal scheme to establish a Protestant colony in Ireland.[56] The idea was first put forward in 1608 when it was proposed that a large portion of Tyrone, including the City of Derry and the town of Coleraine, should be 'planted' by the City of London. The Common Council of the City signed a contract with the Crown for this purpose, and at the same time called upon the City companies to become shareholders in a chartered company— the Irish Society—which would finance and direct the establishment of the colony. At this invitation the Carpenters set up a four-man committee to consider the project, and in 1610 J. Burch, Middle Warden, joined a delegation which the Livery Companies sent to Ireland to inspect the area concerned.[57] Shortly afterwards, the Common Council called upon fifty-five companies to provide £40,000 to finance the Irish Society; for their part the Carpenters opened a subscription list to its members. Recognizing that they could not avoid the obligation and hoping that the venture might be profitable, the City companies decided that it would be best to form themselves into twelve groups, each group headed by one of the 'Great Twelve'. The Carpenters were in the group led by the Ironmongers. £5,000 was to be provided in the following proportions: Ironmongers £2,300, Brewers £700, Scriveners £570, Coopers £420, Pewterers £360, Barbers £350, Carpenters £300. The Carpenters did not complete their collection until 1616, when they then began to pay sums to the Ironmongers towards the cost of erecting buildings in the colony in accordance with the conditions laid down in the governing contract between the City and the Crown.[58] No dividends were received, however, until 1621, but thereafter receipts continued until 1634.[59] On average these amounted to £8 per annum, but as the Company was paying interest of between 6 per cent and 8 per cent on the £300 it had raised in the first place, its net loss was about £16 per annum. This loss was soon increased, when, in

1634, trouble arose between the Crown and the City over the Irish plantation, and in 1637 the unpopular Star Chamber revoked the titles by which the City and, in turn, the companies held their Irish estates. Consequently, the Carpenters received no further rents until 1650, and it was not until 1656 that the lands were firmly restored by Cromwell. For the Carpenters, as for the other companies, the Irish Society had—in the short run at least—proved to be a costly fiasco.

Minor gifts of property to be used for charitable purposes have been noted already, but there remains one which, because of its exceptional generosity, deserves some special attention. It came in 1620 by the will of Richard Wyatt, who had been elected Master three times during the short space of twelve years—proof of the esteem in which he was held by his fellow Carpenters. Although few details of Wyatt's career survive, its path seems fairly clear.[60] He was born at Slinden in Sussex and as a youth came to London to be apprenticed as a carpenter to Roger Sheres. His servitude was completed in 1578[61] and a few years later he married his master's daughter Margaret. It seems probable that Wyatt received a valuable inheritance from Sheres, whose standing may be deduced from his being Master in 1587 and 1592.[62] Wyatt's obvious business ability enabled him to build up a substantial fortune as a wharf-owner in the City, and some of this money he invested in landed estates.

His first bequest was of some land at Henley-on-Thames, the rents from which were to be used to support thirteen poor women.[63] He then left £500 for building almshouses at Godalming for ten poor men—five to belong to the parish of Godalming, two to Puttenham, and one each to Hambledon, Compton, and Dunsfold. Wyatt directed that the first ten men should be chosen by his executors but thereafter by the Carpenters Company. The almshouses were endowed with the rents received from a farm at Shackleford, near Godalming, while the income from some land at Bramshot, in Hampshire, was to be used to defray the expenses of the annual visit by the Governors from the Carpenters Company. Three years after Wyatt's death the almshouses were completed; an attractive row of ten brick houses with a gabled chapel at the centre, with the following inscription being placed above the chapel window:

'THIS OYSPITALL WAS GIVEN BY Mr RICHARD WYATT OF LONDON ESQ FOR TENN POORE MEN WTH SUFFICIENT LANDS TO IT FOR YEIR MAYN-TENANCE FOR EVER 1622.'

A brass plaque was placed inside the chapel, containing a representation of the Wyatt family at their prayers beneath a shield bearing their arms.

At this time the annual visit by horseback took just over two days to complete.[64] Godalming was reached on the first day, and the party returned the following afternoon staying the second night at Kingston. In 1625 the custom was started of giving the Governors a nosegay before they attended the sermon at the chapel. And in 1626 it was decided[65]

'... that certaine orders already agreed uppon for the poore people of the erreccon of Mr Richard Wyatt deceased, at the hospitall neare Godalmyne, shalbe fairely writt in parchment and sett in a table for the use of the poore to reade them fower times every yeare quarterly by him that readeth the prayers'.

In its early years, however, the charity was a source of trouble for the Company. In 1626 they were compelled to apply to the Chancery Court for a decree confirming that the lands at Bramshot were to be used for the maintenance of the Godalming Hospital.[66] This came about because the Company's title was challenged by Richard Wyatt's son Henry. Two years later another disagreement arose over the property at Henley-on-Thames;[67] a portion of the rents was withheld by Henry Wyatt and false receipts had been signed by the former Renter Warden. After investigation the finances were straightened out and Henry

Wyatt was paid the one-third share of the rents legally due to him. But, to avoid future disputes of this nature, four months later the Assistants purchased Henry Wyatt's share in the Henley property for £60.[68] Part of the sum was reimbursed by Henry's mother, who seems to have disapproved of her son's attitude.[69] She also gave £40 'to provide ten new coats once in every three years for the Almsmen, with the letters R. W. on each coat'.[70] It must be added that while this charity was not for the benefit of poor Carpenters it was one which the Company willingly maintained. Indeed, the income to support the hospital increased hardly at all over the period—the rent of the Henley property remaining at £7 per annum and that at Bramshot increasing only from £7 to £9.[71] The result was that the cost of supporting the Wyatt charity rose more rapidly than its income, and a growing deficit had to met by the Renter Warden.

The remaining sources of income declined relatively to the revenue received from property and extraordinary receipts such as subscriptions and collections from members.[72] So far as fines for trade offences were concerned, this, in fact, declined absolutely and had almost disappeared by the end of the period. Income received in connection with the apprenticeship system continued to increase with the rise in membership, and occasionally was relatively high, usually as a result of redemption payments or fines from new Liverymen—in 1661, for example, twenty-four new Liverymen paid £7 each. Taking one year with another, however, income from the operation of the craft system as a whole fell from being approximately 25 per cent of total income at the beginning of the century to less than 5 per cent by 1660.

The most onerous branch of expenditure arose from the outside demands made on the Company—at first to help support extravagant monarchs, and then to help finance a civil war. Almost as soon as James I was proclaimed king, the City was called upon to make him a loan, of which the Carpenters share was £40.[73] Furthermore, the new king required companies to renew their

5. The Almshouses at Godalming

6. The Banqueting Hall, 1880

Inſtructions for the Apprentices of the Company of CARPENTERS, *London.*

YOU ſhall conſtantly and devoutly, on your Knees, every Day, ſerve God, Morning and Evening, and make Conſcience in the due Hearing the Word preached, and endeavour the right Practice thereof, in your Life and Converſation ; you ſhall do diligent and faithful Service to your Maſter for the Time of your Apprenticeſhip, and deal truly in what you ſhall be truſted. You ſhall often read over the Covenants of your Indenture, and ſee and endeavour yourſelf to perform the ſame to the utmoſt of your Power. You ſhall avoid all evil Company, and all Occaſions which may tend to draw you to the ſame, and make ſpeedy Return when you ſhall be ſent on your Maſter or Miſtreſſes Errands. You ſhall avoid Idleneſs, and be ever employed, either in God's Service, or about your Maſter's Buſineſs. You ſhall be of fair, gentle, and lowly Speech and Behaviour to all Men, and eſpecially to your Governors. And according to your Carriage expect Reward for Good or Ill, from God and your Friends.

Instructions for Apprentices (c. 1750)

8.
Octagonal Oak Table dated
1606 and the Master's Chair
(See Appendix 5)

charters. For the Carpenters this brought additional expense but, at least, it also brought some benefits. They were now allowed to hold property free of mortmain to a net annual value of £40, and their titles to existing estates were confirmed 'free of *quo warranto ad quod damnum*'.[74] In 1609, the Company was pressed to provide money for the colonization of Virginia, but they replied that 'their hability for the same [is] small by reason of Continuall payments and Chardges and ... theire Particular estates [are] Decaying for want of work ...'.[75] That it, and other companies, were not pressed harder in this respect, was due to their plea that they were contributing heavily to the Irish scheme.[76]

No more heavy demands were received until 1621 when the Company was called upon to subscribe towards the cost of the recovery of the Palatinate, to be followed by a series of subsidy payments for the same purpose. Then, in 1627, the City was required to make Charles I a loan of £120,000, and the Carpenters were forced to sell some of their plate in order to pay their share of £300—but this measure produced only £200.[77] In the following July, however, the Court decided that 'considering the estate of our poore bretheren' it would be better to pay the remaining £100 out of the chest rather than make another collection.[78] To recoup on these outlays, in the meantime, the Court had started an economy drive and, among other things, ordered that not more than 20s should be spent on any one dinner day.[79] Fortunately, during the next decade things became easier, and in addition to the acquisition of the Norton Folgate and Crutched Friars estates, by 1635 the Company had become a net creditor to the extent of £50 invested at 6 per cent per annum.[80]

But this decade, during which the Carpenters made additions to their estates, proved to be a calm before a storm. The first rumble was heard in 1640 when the King forced all companies to renew their charters. This brought an unwelcome charge on the Carpenters' income while giving them the doubtful advantage of an extension of their jurisdiction to an area of four miles radius around the City.[81] The storm broke a few months later when

Charles I demanded £50,000 from the City.[82] The next year brought a demand from Parliament for £100,000, and in 1643 £50,000 was needed for the defence of London against the King. In the event, less than a quarter of the total borrowed by Crown and Parliament from the City at this time was repaid. It is not surprising, therefore, that efforts to evade citizenship increased, that there was a drift to the suburbs, and that there was an unwillingness among senior Liverymen to accept office in their respective companies. The Carpenters lent £250 in 1640, nearly £550 in 1642, and a further £250 in 1643.[83] Moreover, loans soon proved inadequate and too irregular to satisfy Parliament's needs, and in 1643 what amounted to a property tax was introduced; thus, the Hall was assessed for £4 3s 4d per week for three months, while in addition tenants had to be reimbursed for similar payments—which, in the state of uncertainty that existed, were sometimes described by those making them as being for 'King *and* Parliament'. Further expenses were incurred from training soldiers and providing arms and gunpowder for the Parliamentary cause. But while the Carpenters dutifully obeyed Parliament's commands, they remained uncertain as to the outcome of events and thus maintained a dual allegiance; while sending men to join Waller's army and paying an assessment for 'My Lord Generall's army', the Assistants regularly attended the celebrations for the anniversary of the King's coronation day—no doubt, they were not untypical in that their attitude to the war was coloured by their immediate interests rather than by more general principles.

When the outcome became clear, demands for money became less frequent and less burdensome, but the army still had to be supported. Besides making payments for this purpose, in 1648 the Court received notice that troops were to be billeted at the Hall.[84] The Clerk was at once instructed to remove all possessions from the Hall and deposit them with a number of senior Liverymen. The Clerk's resourcefulness made this unnecessary, however, for in the following April both he and 'his friends' were rewarded for successfully avoiding this inconvenience.[85] More generally, the years between 1640 and the mid-1650s form a remarkable period in the Company's financial history.[86] The total amount of money paid out, in one form or another, for the Civil War, approached £1,500, more than two-thirds of it between 1640 and 1643. Obviously, over such a short period, this amount was beyond the Company's independent resources, and more than £500 had to be borrowed. But no one, it seems, was willing to lend for a period longer than a year, and usually for only six months. The minutes and the accounts, therefore, contain numerous entries recording complicated financial arrangements for maintaining solvency; in short, a process of borrowing from Peter to pay Paul. Most of the creditors were drawn from the Court of Assistants although, in 1645, the increasing 'tightness' of money drove the Carpenters to seek a loan from the Fishmongers.[87] The Fishmongers were prepared to grant this at the relatively low rate of 6 per cent on the condition that they were first allowed to see the Carpenters' charter. Apparently regarding this as a sinister request, the Court replied that the seal should be considered a sufficient security for a loan, and that it had decided to raise the money elsewhere.

The steady inflow of income resulted in a gradual reduction of liabilities, but so far as claims on debtors were concerned the outlook was bleak. In 1652 the Court calculated that, to date, it had made loans totalling £1,036 12s 8d, and that the interest owing on this amount was £783 17s 4d; against this it had received £152 10s 0d, leaving an amount outstanding of £1,668.[88] This involved considerable sacrifice, and as late as 1659 the Court was pushed to sell more plate—which had not been given by members living—to discharge immediate debts.[89] Of course, the City companies constantly pressed for the repayment of loans and interest; in 1653, for example, they drew up a joint claim for the repayment of a loan made in 1643 for the relief of Ireland,[90] which had been given on the security of bonds backed by calls on land in that country. In view of this claim it was decided to sell the land and divide the proceeds proportionately. The Carpenters' share was £73 5s 4d which was less than one-third of the amount they had originally subscribed.[91] Furthermore, by the end of the period, and in fact for ever, the Company was owed nearly £780 plus a larger (although unrecorded) sum due as interest.[92]

Despite this it was not deterred from borrowing a further £1,000 towards the cost of alterations made to the Hall in 1664;[93] of this amount John Wildgoose lent £600, his son-in-law, William Sell, an apothecary, lent £100, a further £200 was borrowed from Samuel Berry, and £100 from Thomas Dorebarr. At the same time, the Company was forced to borrow yet another £300 because it received a demand from the City to contribute this amount towards a loan of £100,000 being made to Charles II. Again it was the resourceful Mr Wildgoose who came to the rescue. In one year, therefore, indebtedness had been increased by £1,300. Finally, in 1666 it had to subscribe £75 as part of the cost of building a new royal frigate to be named *Loyall London*, which was to replace the ship *London* which had accidentally blown up.[94]

Against this background of vicissitude the domestic life of the Company continued to flourish. Dinner and celebration days provided the main social entertainment and a major claim on expenditure. The members were frequently amused by minstrels and plays, although during the 1620s and again during the 1640s more pressing needs made these festivities very sober affairs. For the more permanent enjoyment of members the facilities of the Hall were continually improved. The garden had long been an object of special care and attention; in 1603 more flower beds were added,[95] somewhat later four cherry trees were planted,[96] and in 1644 thirteen vines were introduced and an area of the garden was made into a lawn.[97] Occasionally, the garden was a source of trouble, sometimes because it provided a convenient meeting place for young men of the craft in boisterous mood, and sometimes because the Beadle, for small 'perqs', allowed local residents to hang their washing there resulting in squabbles when no more space was available. On more than one occasion the Court issued stern instructions on the general use of the garden, and to make these restrictions more effective in 1622 the existing Hall gate was replaced by a stouter one.[98] More modernization took place in 1623 when the New River water was brought by culvert into the Hall.[99]

The increase in purely domestic possessions was a sign of growing affluence. At some time a large chained Bible had been acquired, for in 1605 a lectern was purchased for it.[100] Among other items of interest are a large State chair—which is still in existence—in richly carved mahogany, and an octagonal table bearing the date 1606 and the initials RW, GI, IR and WW, representing Richard Wyatt, George Isack, John Reave and William Wilson, who were Master and Wardens in the previous year. The chair provides something of a mystery as there is no record of its acquisition, and the lower part of it is undoubtedly of an earlier date than the upper.[101]

Very little remains of the plate from this period, apart from the Master's and Wardens' cups used on Election Days. Nevertheless, what must have been a fairly comprehensive list of plate was drawn up in 1648 when the Hall was chosen for billeting soldiers.[102] Apart from the ceremonial plate, silver wine cups, 'beare' bowls, salt cellars, spoons and tankards were deposited with various members. Among other things to be given to individual charge, or to be placed in the treasure house, were chairs, streamers, pewter, the great Bible, diaper tablecloths, flaxen tablecloths, twenty-seven dozen diaper napkins, a 'large greene carpett' [i.e. tablecloth], a burial pall, a clock, a number of books including 'Euclides Ellaments', and four Election garlands or crowns which were placed on the heads of the newly elected Master and Wardens. On a number of occasions it had proved necessary either to pawn or sell some of the plate to meet pressing debts, but as soon as possible it was replaced. Sometimes a temporary buyer would be found among the Assistants, who was willing to re-sell the plate to the Company when more prosperous times returned.

The growth in the Company's activities entailed much heavier burdens of work and responsibility for the Clerk and, to a smaller extent, the Beadle. But they were fully rewarded for their pains. In 1652, for example, Roger Goodday was appointed Clerk at a salary of £50 per annum, provided with a house valued at £15 per annum and granted the right to certain gratuities received in connection with his duties.[103] The Beadle's wages were raised to £20 per annum in 1659 to compensate him for the loss of certain 'perqs', and he also enjoyed rent-free accommodation.[104] Relations between the Court and the Clerk were usually cordial, although it is surprising that there is no recorded complaint about Goodday's handwriting. As much cannot be said for some of the successive Beadles. In 1644, for example, the Beadle's wife ignored the Court's order to leave the Hall, even though it was alleged that she had been in contact with a plague victim.[105] Perhaps of a more serious nature was the warning issued to the same Beadle, his wife, and son, in 1653. It made plain that if there was one more occurrence of 'disorderly and uncivil behaviour' towards the Clerk they would be dismissed and evicted from their house.[106]

Finally, this account would be incomplete without further mention of charitable activities. The gifts of Warham, Gittens, Wyatt, Fennor, Day and Read have already been noted. There was also a benefaction for poor carpenters received under the will of John Vernon, Merchant Taylor, in 1615.[107] This was shared with five other companies, and, apart from money, provided for a new coat for each almsman every third year. Another gift was made by Richard Cambden, Carpenter, by his will in 1642,[108] providing a sum of £10 for making interest-free loans to 'honest freemen' for periods of three years. And in 1654 Ann Bowers gave £50 to provide an annual income to be used for the relief of the poor in parish of Allhallows.[109]

Charity was also extended to offer scholarships for poor students at Oxford and Cambridge even before Read's bequest. The grants were made from general income, usually to the sons of Carpenters. The scholarships varied from 20s per year to £4 per year—although in 1619 exceptional cases occurred of two scholars, Samuel Bameford of Emmanuel College, Cambridge, and William Sherborne of St John's College, Oxford, receiving £8 and £15 respectively to enable them to proceed to their MA degrees.[110] In the following year there was an unusual decision to make a collection for a poor scholar at Oxford.[111] These were the early beginnings of what has become an important part of the Company's work.

It is now possible to make an assessment of the main changes in income and wealth over the period as a whole. The following table, based on the Wardens' accounts, gives some indication of the magnitude of receipts and payments. But because of the failure to distinguish income and capital, the figures should not be taken as giving a precise index.[112]

INCOME AND EXPENDITURE
(5-year averages)

	Money							Real						
	£	s	d	£	s	d		£	s	d	£	s	d
1601–5	140	0	0	113	0	0		28	0	0	26	0	0
1621–5	300	0	0	244	0	0		68	0	0	46	0	0
1641–5	1,098	0	0	805	0	0		156	0	0	144	0	0
1661–5	958	0	0	970	0	0		147	0	0	149	0	0

Despite the charges made on its resources for national purposes during the 1620s, and again between 1640 and 1666, the Company managed to make major additions to its property and substantial improvements to that it already possessed. A very rough estimate of the total current capital value of its property based on rental income—which unavoidably excludes the most valuable item, the Hall itself—is that it rose from £1,000 at the turn of the century to £7,500 by the 1660s. When it is remembered that debts of over £1,000 were never repaid to the Company, and that the money it borrowed to pay for the extension of the Hall in 1664 was paid off in three years, the achievement was remarkable.

A great deal of this success was owed to those directing affairs. While only one member, namely John Wildgoose, who became a Common Councilman at the end of the period, achieved civic office, the Assistants generally were prosperous master carpenters. Wyatt and Wildgoose were the outstanding examples and the only two for whom the merest shreds of biographical evidence survive; but there were others who were no less important as is shown by the ease with which the Company was able to raise large loans from its members during periods of financial difficulty, to say nothing of the regular flow of gifts which it received. Moreover, the skill with which the problems of borrowing and lending were solved shows these men to have been well acquainted with business matters. On only one occasion does it appear that the Company was ill served. In 1605 Robert Fisher was discharged from the office of Master, and a whole page of the minute book was devoted to the wry comment: 'Lamentally, knowe all men'.[113]

During the dark days of the 1640s the control exercised by the Court had to be strengthened, with the result that a division appeared between the Assistants and Livery on the one hand, and the Commonalty on the other. Matters first came seriously to a head in 1644, when a lawyer had to be consulted in order to define the power of the Court.[114] The issue arose in connection with the right to appoint the Clerk and Beadle. In the event, the Court retained its power to order affairs, but not without a warning from counsel that the peace of the Company was at stake. There was trouble again in 1650 when the Yeomanry voiced criticism of the Court's dictatorial attitude.[115] For the moment, the dispute was limited, but it marked an important change in the nature of the organization. In other words, it was becoming more representative of the wealthier elements within it, of those who came to attach more importance to its social functions than to its effectiveness as an agency for craft control. A Court order of as early as 1632 indicated that there was already a substantial number of middle-class members, most of whom must have entered by patrimony as they had no direct connection with carpentry:[116]

'... It is this day ordered by this Court that the Master Wardens and Assistants and liverye of this Companye shall paye twelve pence everye one apeece, and that all others of this Companye being Wharfingers Shoppkeeps and Alehouse Keepers shall pay every one eightpence apeece and all the rest to paye sixpence a peece'.

And in turn, greater stress was laid on increasing the prosperity of the Company as the means to increasing its status within the City.

But with all the will and ability in the world these aims would have been unsuccessful if it had not been for the favourable nature of more general conditions. The Carpenters had inherited a firm basis of prosperity from the previous century, and the rapid rise in property values during the seventeenth century swelled their income and produced an overall surplus which could be used for further investment. Moreover, rising property values implied a buoyant demand for the services of carpenters, who were thus enabled to make their contribution to the Company's financial strength. Lastly, although the Carpenters, in common with other companies, attracted the unwelcome attention of the Crown, it was one of the smaller fish and could more easily slip through the net. True, the calls made upon it were proportionately as heavy as those made on its larger associates, but unlike many of them its administrative body was not already under such strain that new burdens brought about its collapse.[117] So far as can be judged, therefore, the Carpenters' financial standing at the end of the period was strong. And, by an odd quirk of fate, the Great Fire of 1666, which was a disaster for many, in one respect was to be for the Carpenters a source of considerable advantage.

CHAPTER VI

A PERIOD OF STAGNATION
1666-1700

THE rebuilding of the City after the Fire brought prosperity to all sections of the building crafts. Once this had been completed, however, employment was less plentiful. The large number of new buildings required much less repair and maintenance than those they replaced, and as a result during the last quarter of the century for both small-master and journeymen carpenters times were not easy.[1] Moreover, the Carpenters Company was unable to offer much help to its members, for the Acts regulating the rebuilding had removed any remaining authority which it possessed in the craft. Now, its sole responsibility was to provide, along with the Bricklayers, Plasterers, Masons, Smiths, Plumbers and Paviours, two master workmen, four journeymen, eight apprentices and sixteen labourers to be ready at all times for fire duty.[2]

While the rebuilding was in full spate free carpenters voiced great concern about the heavy inflow of 'forrens', which acted as a brake on rising wage rates.[3] The Company realized, however, that in the face of insistent demands by the City authorities for an adequate supply of building labour, this influx could not be checked. As an alternative, therefore, it urged the need for some supervision of this labour, and naturally offered its services for this; but the City rejected the proposal.[4] For a while, the heavy demand for building ensured that free carpenters were not put out of work by 'forrens'; indeed, the Company itself gained from an increase in the number of redemptioners, who were, in most cases, provincial-born carpenters who were doing well in London and only too willing to pay £10 to become freemen.[5] By the early 1670s, however, unemployment among free carpenters began to appear; and although the Company now had practically no control over the craft, it was still the most effective agency through which ordinary journeymen could express their demands collectively. For a time the Court adopted the mistaken policy of seeking co-operation from the Joiners, Bricklayers, Masons, and Plasterers, to expel all 'forrens' from the City.[6]

A small committee of Assistants was voted money to enable it to search for and to prosecute 'forrens' who had not conformed to City regulations requiring them to give proof of seven years' apprenticeship.[7] Repeatedly, between 1671 and 1674, the committee was pressed to intensify its activites. Eventually, however, unemployment among free carpenters reached such a level that on their behalf the Company petitioned the Court of Common Council that they should be given permission to meet in Cornhill, before the Royal Exchange, every morning between the hours of 5 a.m. and 7 a.m., so that any available work could be given to them in preference to 'forrens';[8] apparently, a number of master carpenters frequently employed 'forrens' 'under pretence of wanting freemen'. The Court of Common Council agreed to the request, and to give it effect ordered that journeymen carpenters should 'have Liberty to stand in a peaceable manner during the pleasure of this Court on the Backside of the Royall Exchange in Threadneedle Streete every working morning from 5 of the clocke till seaven, in order to be hired provided at 7 of the Clocke they doe without faile quitt the said place'.[9] No doubt this did something to improve circumstances, but the plight of carpenters in the City was by no means solved. In the country at large builders' real wages were falling, and it is almost certain that in London the fall was greater than average.[10] Matters could have been improved had the Company been able to regulate the number of carpenters in London. But from the early 'seventies onwards, for the first time in many years, although London's population continued to grow, the population of the City itself ceased to expand,[11] and because of this the Common Council would not allow the enforcement of laws which in any way discouraged immigrants.

Against this background the Carpenters did not alter their uncompromising and somewhat ambivalent attitude towards the sawyers. For many years free sawyers in London had endeavoured to establish some control over 'forren' sawyers, though on each occasion when they had sought the backing of the Common Council, their efforts had been balked by the vigorous opposition of those companies which needed to employ 'forrens'.[12] In the 1680s free sawyers renewed their attempts,[13] causing the Carpenters to enter a *caveat* with the Lord Mayor's Court.[14] It was argued that sawyers were only labourers to carpenters, joiners, and similar trades, that there were insufficient of them to meet current needs, that even if there were enough the exclusion of 'forren' competition would advance the 'demands, power and prices' of the free sawyers, and that many 'forren' sawyers had proved themselves excellent workmen. The Lord Mayor's Court accepted this tortuous argument and instructed that while 'forren' sawyers could be employed within the City by carpenters, joiners, and like trades, wherever possible priority should be given to freemen.[15] Some time later, however, free sawyers complained that carpenters were employing 'forren' sawyers in preference to competent freemen. The Mayor's Court accordingly directed that unless carpenters complied with the earlier decision their freedom to employ 'forrens' would be withdrawn altogether.[16]

Only in the field of apprenticeship did the Company retain something of its former role. During this period over 2,000 apprentices were bound at the Hall,[17] although the annual average number of bindings—ninety-one between 1654 and 1674 as compared with fifty-four between 1685 and 1694—showed a marked fall. The proportion of apprentices from London and the Home Counties in relation to the country as a whole, which reached nearly 60 per cent in 1665, was not maintained after the Fire;[18] by the end of the century this figure had fallen to near

40 per cent. An analysis has shown that, as in the sixteenth century and almost certainly for the same reasons, only a small number of these apprentices eventually sought the freedom. Boys continued to be bound, no doubt, because their fathers thought that the best training in carpentry was provided by those London carpenters who were members of the Carpenters Company—in other words, the Hall became an efficient employment bureau. In any case, the small number seeking the freedom by servitude in relation to the number being bound becomes even less significant when account is taken of the increasing proportion of the total gaining freedom by patrimony and, to a much smaller extent, by redemption. Furthermore, among those admitted to the freedom during these years were twenty females, engaged in trades such as sempster, milliner, and child's-coat-seller.

After the Great Fire the Court of Assistants made no serious effort to enforce its apprenticeship rules, the most important of which limited the number of apprentices a master might take. In 1693 it gave up even the pretence by formally enacting that a free carpenter could take as many apprentices as he wished, provided they were bound at the Hall and the necessary fee paid.[19] To facilitate this, apprentices were bound in groups to the Beadle, who then turned them over to masters as occasion arose—often to master carpenters who were free of other companies.[20] This was coupled with an effort to have all apprenticed carpenters bound at the Hall, irrespective of their masters' trade; a claim which, in 1693, was upheld by the Common Council.[21] But this is seen simply as a device for increasing revenue, in no way as an attempt to retain, or indeed to restore, some measure of craft control.

Before the Fire had burnt itself out it had left a trail of destruction and 100,000 homeless citizens. It had ravaged an area bounded to the south by the Thames, to the west by Tyburn, and to the north by the City wall; to the north-east its advance had halted along a line running from just west of Moorgate to just west of Seething Lane.[22] The luck of the Carpenters was extraordinary; of all its property, only the Lime Street estate came within the area destroyed by the Fire,[23] and here only one tenement was burnt. The advance of the fire was, in fact, stopped two-thirds of the way along Lime Street, and it is possible that the fire was put out just as the flames started to lick the edge of the Company's property.

The Court of Assistants was quick to offer accommodation at its Hall to all companies which had lost their own halls 'by the late and dredfull fire'.[24] The first request came from the Drapers, and the rent agreed upon was £30 per annum for the use of certain rooms in the Hall on a specified number of days during the year.[25] Other lessees were the Goldsmiths, the Masons, the Feltmakers, the Weavers, and the Haberdashers.[26] The most august occupants, however, were four successive Mayors, who rented most of the Hall and the garden for £100 per annum.[27] In 1670 the rent was raised to £150,[28] but a few months later the Lord Mayor returned to the Mansion House.[29]

Samuel Pepys estimated that a house which before the Fire could be rented for £40 per annum afterwards fetched £150.[30] Unfortunately, the Carpenters gained little from the undoubted rise in rents, for all their property was let on a leasehold basis, involving an initial fine and a fixed annual rent for a period of years, and not one lease fell in during the period 1666–70. Some measure of the 'loss' suffered as a result can be gained from the fact that before the Fire, in 1665, John Godschall, merchant, paid a fine of £1,100 for the lease of two tenements at Lime Street.[31] Even the additional rents from the Hall were not pure gain, for in 1670 it was recorded that parts of the Hall had been left by the Lord Mayor in very bad repair, and that renovation would cost a great deal.[32]

After extensive repairs had been carried out in 1671—retiling the roof, rebuilding kitchen chimneys, repainting the exterior—a committee was set up to suggest means of 'beautifying' the Hall.[33] It was decided to add new wainscot in various rooms, to replaster the ceiling, to hang 'painted cloth' in the parlour, to have all the loose accounts bound in leather, to rebuild the hearths in the

Great Room, the Dining Room, and the Music Room with coloured stones, and to have the gardens 'handsomely trimmed upp'. The nineteenth-century historians of the Company, who knew this Hall well in its later days, remarked particularly upon the 'rich and beautiful ceiling' but thought that much of the remaining improvements which had been made at this time— particularly some additional windows on the north side of the building which had been decided upon a little later—was of considerably less merit.[34] Much of the new work had been designed by John Wildgoose, but it seems that his earlier successes at the Hall were not repeated. Moreover, the total cost of these operations was, no doubt, the main reason for the period of economy that followed.[35]

As usual, the first economies were achieved by reducing expenditure on entertainments; a number of minor dinners were suspended, and strict limits were placed on the number of guests invited to monthly dinners.[36] Despite these measures costs were not reduced, and the Company had to resort to a loan; £300 was borrowed from Mrs Purefoy, a tenant, in return for an annuity for life of £36.[37] As an additional measure the Court decided to dispense with the services of their standing lawyer, Thomas Knight, hiring instead a counsel when required.[38] Still this did not produce the required surplus. On Audit Day 1672, a long time was spent on examining the accounts and it was found that during the previous year there had been 'exorbitant expences on dinner and reparacions with divers frivolous and extravagant expences ... overlarge private expences ...'.[39] Stringent economy was to be the watchword henceforth; no extra money was to be given to the poor, and strict budgets were set for dinner-day expenditures. Moreover, a decision not to re-let the Hall, reached after an acrimonious debate in 1671,[40] was reluctantly reversed; and no doubt it came as a bitter disappointment when the Hall was let to the Sheriff-elect at a lower rent than formerly[41]—all the more so when it was found that even this did not restore a credit balance. Once again resort was made to short-term borrowing; in December 1672, £300 was raised from Thomas Charman, Upper Warden.[42]

The causes of these difficulties are not far to seek. The Company had incurred heavy expenditure when prices were high and then had to pay for it in a period of falling prices. It had been unlucky in not being able to raise its rents in the years immediately following the Fire, and now it was too late. Indeed, a number of its tenants successfully petitioned for reductions in rent and in one instance the Court had to order the arrest of a tenant for failure to pay his arrears.[43] It is probable that this phenomenon was quite widespread in the City of London where, as has been noted, population was practically stationary.

Luck had not altogether deserted the Company, however. In 1673 a fire broke out in Seething Lane, and before it was extinguished it had caused some damage to the Crutched Friars estate and to His Majesty's Navy Office which adjoined.[44] After some delay the Commissioners of the Navy Office decided, in 1676, to make the Carpenters an offer for part of their Crutched Friars property, in order to secure a larger site for a proposed new Navy Office;[45] the land involved amounted to about half the estate. The protracted negotiations form a vignette of seventeeth-century administration. The offer was, in effect, a compulsory purchase, and the price agreed upon was £464. After the transfer had been signed and sealed the Court of Assistants applied to the Lord Treasurer's Office for payment of the money due to it. Four months later a committee of Assistants reported that it had been unable to secure an interview with the Lord Treasurer about the matter 'that highly concerns the good and right of the Company'[46] and had met with nothing but prevarication and delay. The committee undertook to pursue the matter assiduously and requested an advance of money for gratuities 'to persons of that quality to espouse and effect the matter in their petition'.[47] Meanwhile, as a consequence, the Company was forced into even more stringent measures of economy. After another month had gone by, the committee discovered that Sir Anthony Deane was one of the Navy Office Commissioners,[48] the very man who, nine months before, had petitioned the Company for the lease of the land at Crutched Friars not sold to the Navy Office.[49] Furthermore, Sir Anthony had given the committee to understand that he could secure some satisfaction for them in the matter of the money owing, but in so doing 'large allowance' would have to be made to persons—anonymous—who would have to be 'treated with'.[50] Thus, it was arranged with Sir Anthony that £390 cash would be accepted in settlement of the debt, and £74 would be allowed to him to dispose of as he thought necessary.[51] Sir Anthony presented himself at a meeting of the Court a few days later when it was agreed to give him a receipt for £464 although, in fact, only £390 was to be received—'which this court promised to take particular care in'.[52] The business was completed with remarkable expedition after the meeting, while in addition to the £74 for gratuities Sir Anthony was granted the lease of the remaining property at Crutched Friars.[53] The money was a very welcome addition to the year's income, and the actual amount received, £390, represented a real capital gain of over 50 per cent on the original price paid for this part of the estate.[54]

Apart from the negotiations over the Crutched Friars property, a torpor settled over the Company in the 1670s. In 1673 it was decided to re-lease the Hall; this time to Gabriel Roberts, a Turkey merchant.[55] The Carpenters had little use for it, and simply reserved the right to use it on certain dates during the year. Meetings of the Court became irregular with intervening periods of three to six months. On occasions so few Assistants attended Courts that it was almost impossible to complete business. It did bestir itself in 1673, when, due to ambiguities which had arisen during and after the Commonwealth, it was necessary for companies to renew their charters. The new charter recited the provisions of the old,[56] with a little more stress on the ordinance which required all those exercising the craft to be free of the Company. But in the following year torpor developed almost into atrophy, when disagreements arose in the Court over the appointment of a new Clerk.[57] No attempt was made to resolve the dispute until 1676, while in the meantime nobody bothered to keep any minutes. The Clerk's appointment was eventually confirmed, probably for no other reason than to deal with the administration arising from the negotiations with the Navy Office. And, characteristically, one of the minutes entered by the new Clerk revealed that it was difficult to recruit new Assistants, because so many of the senior Livery had 'distant habitation'[58]—presumably in the suburbs. For the previous two years the barest essentials of administration had been attended to—the election of Masters and Wardens, the administration of property, and the annual audit. Financially, a policy of economy was steadily maintained, but it still proved necessary to borrow some of the money to pay off previous loans.

The 'eighties were destined to be more eventful, and even the Company approached them with some zest. In 1680 itself, a bequest of property came by the will of William Pope, Master in 1675.[59] The rent from a tenement in Coleman Street was to be distributed to seven poor members or their widows. In the same year it was decided to purchase an estate in Fenchurch Street, consisting of three messuages and three gardens.[60] The price paid was £516. To secure a firm title on this property the Company obtained a new licence from the King allowing it to purchase additional lands to the value of £40 per annum, free of mortmain.[61] While the reasons put foward to support the petition for this licence undoubtedly contained an element of exaggeration, they pointed out that after the sale of part of Crutched Friars the consequent reduction in revenue made it difficult to meet charitable or other commitments; and it had taken some time to accumulate enough capital to remedy matters.

Financially, with an annual surplus on current income averaging £60, things were easier, but far from satisfactory.[62] There were still large debts outstanding, and therefore, taken overall, expenditure was still more than total income could support. The only solution was to renew short-term loans, to maintain a favourable annual balance, and to replenish capital reserves by fines on new leases. But this was a solution compounded with a large measure of optimism. Indeed, just a few weeks after the Fenchurch Street purchase the tenant at Naked Boy Alley, Bermondsey, petitioned for a reduction in his rent; and the Court promptly 'conceived it a hard lease'.[63] This was the third such case in four years.[64] More were to follow. In March 1681 a letter was received from John Cheeseman,[65] tenant of the Shakleford Farm, the rents from which helped to support the Wyatt charity. Cheeseman gave notice that he would not take a new lease unless his rent was abated or, alternatively, a new barn was built. The Court replied that it could not meet these demands. It had provided for repairs to the farm over the past out of its own funds, as Wyatt's bequest had made no provision for the upkeep of the properties. Instead, the vestries of the parishes benefiting from the charity were offered the choice of either meeting the cost of the charities while the Company paid for the repairs to the farm, or vice versa. If the vestries refused to consider this then it was determined to seek legal advice about the possibility of being discharged from responsibility for the upkeep of the hospital and its lands. The churchwardens saw the force of this argument and quickly agreed to the former alternative.[66] Troubles did not end here, however, for in April 1682 the inmates at Godalming petitioned the Commissioners for Charitable Uses for an increase in their alms-money.[67] A quick inspection of the almshouses was made by a committee of Assistants, before it met with the Commissioners at Guildford.[68] After a full discussion of the affairs of the charity, the Carpenters agreed to increase the almsmen's pensions by 4d per week; and for the future, the Clerk was instructed to keep separate accounts for Godalming.

During the remainder of the period there was not one case of a new lease being granted without an unusual amount of haggling. The tenants' complaints were not always as convincing as that made by Edmund Buckley a little earlier, in respect of his two tenements at London Wall on the Bridge House Estate.[69] He pointed out that when he had taken the houses over they were 'extremely in decay' and he had spent £70 and upwards in making them habitable. But before he had been able to let the renovated tenements 'the building of New Bethlehem was carried up against the said tenements', resulting in a considerable drop in their value—and, therefore, he had not been able to let them economically. After much bargaining he was allowed a rebate of £3 per annum. Gone were the days when prospective tenants sued for leases months, even years, before the existing occupant's term was complete.

Things were not made easier by members' obvious lack of interest in the Company. It was hard to persuade Liverymen and Assistants to accept office, and, to provide stronger encouragement, the fine for refusal of an office was raised from £5 to £10.[70] Moreover, very few gifts were received from members, even the tradition of the youngest Warden presenting a piece of plate being discontinued by the end of the century. This lethargy was rudely interrupted, however, when Charles II began his *quo warranto* proceedings against the City in 1684. The King forced the City to surrender its charter and all its privileges, in an effort to gain control over the Capital which was unsympathetic to his views. He then proceeded to 'pack' the City government with loyal supporters. It followed that all corporations under the City automatically lost their independent rights and were forced to sue for confirmation of their charters and ordinances. So far as the companies were concerned, the royal authorities were mainly interested in the 'Great Twelve', although all had to toe the line. On June 19, 1684, the Carpenters surrendered their charter, and it was ordered *nemine contradicente* that their governing powers should be delivered up to the King.[71] By this act the King was empowered to elect, nominate or appoint the Master, Wardens, Assistants, and Clerk. But the Company was not supine in its obedience. Legal advice was taken lest anything in the surrender might affect its property 'or strike at the very being of the said

Company so as they should seas to be'.[72] The elections followed in August, 'At which Court was then Read the said warrant [from the King] wherein was inserted the names of the persons who were intended to serve as officers . . . And the said Stone unknown to the Company named Clerk'.[73] The name of the existing Clerk, John Smalley, was accordingly erased from this list and replaced by 'one Stone'.[74] Smalley, however, refused to hand over the account and minute books to the new Clerk, until he was arrested a few months later.[75]

Charles II died early in 1685, but this did not alter the situation for his brother pursued the same reckless policy even more vigorously. The new charter was granted by James II in June 1686,[76] and the several persons nominated were duly elected. James Stone was appointed Clerk. Entries in the minutes now became neat, concise, and formal, with little record of anything but routine matters. For a short while James II kept up the pressure, but it was a while too long; when he decided to restore the rights and privileges of the City and the companies, it was too late—William III had already landed at Torbay.[77]

Throughout this unpleasant episode the senior members of the Company were opposed to the King's policies. They seem to have agreed among themselves, however, to exchange offices as required so as at least to give the impression of conformity to the King's wishes. Probably, the office of Clerk was of most importance, as the royal appointee to this post was easily able to inform his superiors of any non-conformity. Yet in this respect events proved rather unusual.[78] Although Stone was originally forced upon the Company and the existing Clerk, Smalley, was dismissed, Stone appears to have served it well. When, in 1689, Smalley applied for reinstatement, the Court resolved to have nothing to do with him, and Stone was confirmed in office.

The Carpenters benefited from the greater political freedom following the Glorious Revolution of 1688, but this was not matched by any relief from their financial burdens. The King almost immediately entered upon a costly war with the Dutch.

The land tax was raised to 4s in the pound, but this and other revenues still left a deficit which could only be met by loans,[79] the most famous of which led to the foundation of the Bank of England in 1694. Out of an annual gross rental of under £500 in 1699–1700 the Carpenters paid over £110 in land tax.[80] More directly, in 1690 and 1691 it contributed a total of £350 in loans to William and Mary.[81] When £200 of this was repaid in 1695 it was immediately re-lent.[82] In March of that year, however, it was decided to deposit a reserve of £200 with the Bank of England.[83] This was something of an event because this new account replaced the 'black chest' which had served as the deposit account for over 250 years; and the Court commemorated the event by having the first two Bank receipts, each for £100, pasted in the minute book.

Lending to the Crown was not unprofitable, but the demands often occurred when the Company was short of ready cash. Thus, in 1694, the Court resorted to calling sixty persons to the Livery, when the fines for non-acceptance were included, this way raised £231.[84] For a time finances improved with the result that some of the old conviviality returned with more lavish dinners and entertainment. But the improvement was temporary. By 1697, in one form or another, £650 was on loan to the Crown, and reserves had shrunk to a mere £100 bank-note.[85] And when, soon after, the Crown repaid a loan of £400 with £9 16s od interest, it was accompanied by a request for another loan at below par; the Company lent the King £380 which he accepted as £400 at 8 per cent.[86]

After a slump in the 'eighties current income in both gross and real terms was beginning to recover again by the end of the century.[87] The share accounted for by rents rose from just under 50 per cent to just over 60 per cent. This was partly due to a slight increase in individual rents, and partly to the net increase in property when the Fenchurch Street estate was purchased to replace the part of the Crutched Friars estate sold to the Navy

Office. Despite misgivings the Hall was still included in the rent roll, having been re-let in 1689 to the Turkey merchant, now *Sir* Gabriel Roberts, for ten years for an unspecified fine and an annual rental of £100[88]—and, incidentally, it was insured for £1,000. If, moreover, account is taken of fines for new leases, on average income from property amounted to three-quarters of total income by the end of the period. On the other hand, this was a period of relatively stable, even falling, prices which, combined with the apparent slackness in the property market in the City, put a strong brake on attempts to increase rents. Luckily, only on the Irish estate was the point reached where the tenant was allowed an abatement of arrears, equivalent to two years' rent.[89]

Against this there were heavy and unexpected demands in the form of taxes and obligatory loans. Economy was unavoidable, and in turn this led to continued cheerlessness in the social life of the Company. The only extravagance, if it can be called that, was the improvement of the Hall in the 1670s; but even this was at the expense of the customary conviviality of dinner days. Despite economy, charitable responsibilities were never forgotten. These accounted, however, for no more than 15 per cent of total expenditure; and it is true that in comparison with, say, the Drapers,[90] the scale of the Carpenters' charitable commitments in relation to their income was not such as to be acutely burdensome. On the other hand, there were limits to cuts which could be made in expenditure on entertainments without seriously weakening *esprit de corps*. Supplementary charity to those in some special need and assistance given to poor scholars at the universities, therefore, had to be discontinued.

So the period was one of stagnation in the Company's life. In craft matters alone, there was an inevitable decline. And the loss in this respect was by no means compensated for by greater activity in charitable, social and business affairs. Total membership showed no increase above the 1670 level of 500.[91] As a Company wishing to increase its social appeal it did not contain, as yet, enough men of prominence in the City. Mathew Banckes was the only member to achieve wide distinction.[92] He paid fines for all three Wardenships in 1698, the year he became Master. From 1683 to 1706 he was Master Carpenter in the King's Office of Works, and as such was responsible for much work on royal palaces. 'In addition . . . he carried out the carpenter's work at six of the City Churches, and was employed as a surveyor in connection with several buildings designed by Wren, notably the Library of Trinity College, Cambridge . . . and the Upper School at Eton College. . . .' And among others, he worked for the Duke of Beaufort and the Earl of Rochester, while his reputation was high enough for him to maintain an official business residence in the Stable Yard of Chelsea Hospital. It was Banckes's father, of course, who had presented the portrait of William Portington in 1637, and he himself presented the Company with a portrait of John Scott, his former master and 'Carriage Maker to the Office of Ordinance', in 1698. Significantly, there is no record of Banckes's sons playing prominent parts in the Company.

The Company's main achievement during this period was to have survived at all. Without its unusually large property interests, it would probably have totally collapsed. Even by the end of the century it still had a long way to go before it had made the successful and complete transformation from a craft organization to a modern Livery Company; but, at least, it had started on its way.

CHAPTER VII

A CENTURY OF
UNSPECTACULAR PROGRESS

D
URING the eighteenth century the Company's
fortunes were slowly built up from the proceeds of
rents, fines and fees. In most years the Renter
Warden was able to hand over to his successor a
modest surplus of £100 or so. This annual profit was deposited
with the Bank of England from the mid-1690s onwards (as we
noticed in the previous chapter) or in the stock of the South Sea
or East India Companies.[1] Bank deposits and company stock
provided a welcome alternative to the Company's unproductive
chest, for they usually yielded a fairly high rate of interest; and in
1720, during the South Sea Bubble, the Carpenters successfully
timed the sale of their South Sea shares, worth a nominal £700
and bought before the boom started, so that they fetched a handsome £2,408.[2] When sufficient funds had been accumulated, the
stocks were sold and the proceeds laid out in the rebuilding of
property, improvements at the Hall, or purchase of land. So the
Company's capital grew. Annual income from all sources, of
which rents were by far the most important, rose from about £750
a year at the beginning of the century to about £1,300 in the
later 1780s, before the inflation of the Revolutionary War makes
direct comparison misleading. An income of just over £2,000 at
the beginning of the nineteenth century reflects wartime price in-
creases rather than a more rapid increase in real terms.[3]

The Company was still not yet in a position, however,
to afford those splendid social occasions in its own Hall with
which it was later to regale its members and their friends. An
inventory of plate, taken in 1756, makes rather sorry reading:

	oz.	*wt.*
The Head of the Beadles Staff	81	2
Largest Guilt [*sic*] Cup and Cover [1611]	41	3
A Guilt Cup and Cover, Mr Jarman's gift [1628]	30	18
A Guilt Cup and Cover, Mr Ansell's gift [1611]	31	4
A Guilt Cup and Cover, Mr Edmond's gift [1612]	28	11
A Tankard, Mr Hawkin's gift [1653]	21	
A Wrought Cup, Mrs Purifoy's gift [1664]	12	3
Two Cups, the Gifts of Mr Charman and Mr Jegens together [1665 and 1655]	26	6
Ounces	272	7[4]

The only addition between 1665 and 1756 had been a new silver head for the Beadle's staff, acquired in 1725.[5] None of this plate, however, graced an eighteenth century dinner in Carpenters' Hall, for the Company was obliged to lease the building to a succession of tenants, reserving only one or two of the smaller rooms for meetings of the Court or other business purposes. In the later eighteenth century it was rented by the firm of Luck & Kent and was used by them as a carpet warehouse.[6]

Not that the Carpenters were deprived of their convivial gatherings, but these were rather ordinary functions, held at places like The George in Ironmonger Lane, or the London Tavern. Nevertheless, throughout the eighteenth century, much more was consistently spent on food and drink than on charity. In 1699–1700, for instance—by no means an untypical year— £216 was spent on 'dinners etc.' (including £43 on Lord Mayor's Day and £40 on Election Day) and £127 on charities; in 1739–40, the totals were £417 and £357 respectively, and in 1799–1800, £333 and £252. Occasional economy drives were sometimes attempted, usually, as had happened in the previous century, after a bout of building which could not be entirely paid for out of reserves.

The worst crisis of this sort arose out of the building programme at the end of the 1730s, the details of which will be given later in this chapter. On January 6, 1740/1, the Court minutes record:

'A debate arose ... that the Company has been at great expenses occasion'd by having breakfasts before they proceeded to their business of the day.[7] And also the monthly Court Day dinners. And whereas the Company have greatly increased the number of their poor and inlarged their charitys to them, therefore to do some good and laudable act for the good of the poor of this Company rather than decrease them in number and their pay are desirous to take some method to reduce their expenses. Thereupon the question was put and seconded that the breakfasts on a Court Day and the monthly Court Day dinners be laid aside. And that every member of the Court of Assistants, the Clerk and the Beadle should in lieu of such breakfasts and dinners be paid the sum of 5s apiece by the Renter Warden for the time being for their trouble in attending and doing the business of the day provided such a member should appear in the Court Room before the hour of eleven o'clock in the morning, which this Court are well assured will greatly reduce their expenses and be of singular service for supporting their numerous poor ...'.

This attempt to cut costs, however, was not sufficient to balance the Company's accounts. The War of Austrian Succession pushed up Land Tax and ferocious winters in 1739–40 and 1740–1 affected the succeeding harvests and so brought distress to the economy as a whole.[8] The Company soon felt the pinch in reduced income from its property. The Court discussed the financial position again at a meeting on June 7, 1743, noting that:

'... Land Tax is now and has been for several years last past four shillings in the pound, many of their houses empty ...

several of their old tenants being poor and not able to pay their rents have applied to this Court to be forgiven their rent in arrears upon quitting the premises, which the Company have granted in order to get better tenants . . .'.

With reduced income, the Company was still not making ends meet, despite the abolition of breakfasts and monthly Court dinners. It was therefore driven to adopt the course which it had hoped to avoid two years before. It was obliged to cut its charity payments.

The Company was in 1743 paying £280 a year to its poor. Every quarter, 10s was given to 100 people, at Christmas a further 10s was given, and every other year 12s (known as the St James's gift).[9] The Company was also paying 8s every Christmas to sixteen poor freemen 'who stand next in turn to come on the pension list',[10] which was financed out of £100 given by Samuel Burgin during his year as Master in 1736, and £60 given by Colonel Williams, then Middle Warden.[11] In their efforts to economize, the Court decided to abolish the Christmas and St James's payments and to run down the pension list from 100 to 60 as the pensioners died. In this way the total charity payment would be reduced from £280 to £120, plus the 8s consolation at Christmas for those sixteen poor Carpenters who were waiting to be put on the pension list. No doubt it was a fairly long wait during the running-down period, though high mortality rates hastened the process: already by the end of 1744, for instance, there were only eighty-eight on the list.[12]

These were all Company pensions, as distinct from those paid from particular benefactions administered by the Company. The axe fell upon the latter in 1752 when the Carpenters embarked upon another, though less severe, economy campaign, following another bout of heavy spending. A committee of enquiry reported that the bequests of 10s per year, which had been given during the seventeenth century by Richard Wyatt to thirteen widows, by John Day to ten widows, and by John Read to ten and William Pope to seven poor members or their widows, were all, in fact, being paid at the rate of 10s per *quarter*, that is to say at the same rate as the Company's own pensions. Moreover, payments of

'ten shillings quarterly [were being made] to such poor members of the Company as the Court from time to time have directed to be set down in a list each Quarter Day, the particular gifts not being mentioned in one of the quarterly lists, which they should have been'.[13]

In view of the need to economize, the Court decided to abolish the incidental quarterly payments altogether and to return to annual 10s payments, as laid down by the benefactors. They thereby cut the regular payments from £80 to £20 per year. In future these were to be paid only on the Quarter Day before Midsummer Day, 'the Clerk to read part of the Will and the Beadle to say grace and bring in their allowances'. All the recipients were to be given a dinner, as the benefactors had laid down —all, that is to say, apart from those receiving the Pope bequest, for William Pope had made no such provision. They were to be served on Midsummer's Eve (provided the day was not a Sunday) with:

'2 legs of mutton and 1 sirloin of beef to be roasted with herbage proper and 3 plum puddings and a sufficient quantity of beer not exceeding a quart of beer each'.

Benefactors were soon forthcoming, however, to enable the poor to have a good dinner more than once a year. In 1764 William Robinson gave £150 4 per cent Bank Annuities, the proceeds from which were to be spent on a second dinner before Lady Day (March 25th) and for two dinners for those pensioners on the Company's own 'sixty' list (as it came to be called), none of whom had previously had any Company dinners at all. Robinson declared that he was 'desirous they should all be upon a footing and none sent empty away'.[14] A committee of the Court managed to find an innkeeper who was prepared to feed the pensioners for about 1s per head. The meal was to consist of

'boiled legs of mutton and roast ribs of sirloins of beef, with sufficient cabbage and carrots; and each poor person to be allowed one quart of porter. All of which Mr Rimington (who was present) undertook and agreed to do for £10, that is to say, £5 for each dinner'.[15]

When, in 1766, Robinson gave another £150 so that pensioners could have two more dinners a year, the Court decided that the time had come to add his name to the list of benefactors 'now fixed up in the Hall'.[16] (This 'handsome table' of benefactors, all inscribed in golden lettering, had been put up in 1737.)[17] The only other eighteenth-century addition to it was William Reynolds who left to the Company £300 South Sea annuities, the proceeds from which were to allow nine more poor freemen to receive 20s each per year.[18]

The economy drives and niggardly giving of the eighteenth century contrast sharply with the generosity of the earlier seventeenth; the eighteenth century, in fact, was quick to put up a table of benefactors but slow to add names to it. The Company even turned down an opportunity to possess its own almshouses, the gift of Sir John Cass.

In 1734 the Court of Chancery upheld an unfinished codicil to Cass's will directing that twenty houses be built in Portsoken Ward for the benefit of the Company's pensioners. At first the Company reacted favourably to the gift,[19] but the Chancery verdict was challenged and proceedings dragged on until the early 1740s when, as we have seen, the Company was doing all it could to curtail expenditure. The minutes of a Court meeting on December 7, 1742, record the conclusion of this sad episode:

'This Court taking into consideration the state of both wills made by Sir John Cass and the uncertainty of anything arising for the benefit of this Company from either of them, and having no trust under said wills but only the nomination of putting said poor men into intended almshouses do, notwithstanding they have put in an answer under the Common Seal wherein they have declared the acceptance of said Sir John Cass's charity, now put the question whether the Company would accept of said Sir John Cass's charity or not; and it was carried by a great majority that the Company would not act under the said will and do order the Clerk to give such instructions to the Counsel upon hearing the cause accordingly. And it is further ordered that the Master and Wardens be a committee on the occasion and are desired by this Court to be as frugal in the expense that may attend this suit as may be.'

Although the Company continued to be responsible for the upkeep and management of the Wyatt almshouses at Godalming,[20] it had to wait another hundred years before it came to possess almshouses of its own.

Such parsimony in matters of charity and occasional, more restrained attempts to spend a little less on its own social functions enabled the Company to go on increasing its worldly wealth. It was only by depriving the pensioners and occasionally tightening its own rather capacious belt that it could build up its reserves for periodical investment in land and property. Of these ventures the most important were the erection of Carpenters Buildings and the purchase of land near Stratford.

The Carpenters, having saved over £5,000, were already building on part of the Hall estate by the end of 1736.[21] On the following July 5th it was decided that a stone should be laid calling these new premises Carpenters Buildings. They started to produce revenue in 1737–8 and by 1739–40 were bringing in over £110 a year (to be compared with £67 which the tenant then paid for his lease of the Hall itself).[22] By the end of the century Carpenters Buildings produced £191 in rent, £51 more than the Hall and all the other Company property in London Wall.[23]

As early as 1721, the Company had instructed its Clerk to look for 'an estate of one hundred pounds p. annum or upwards', and, having heard of one about ten miles from London, 'being an inn, houses, lands, etc.' offered twenty-three years' purchase for it.[24] The bid was unsuccessful, however, and nearly fifty years elapsed before there was another opportunity to acquire land. At a special Court held on October 20, 1767, it was decided to buy for 3,000 guineas 'a freehold farm consisting of 63 acres of marsh land tithe free lying in the parish of West Ham', near Stratford, then bringing in £126 per annum.[25] The purchase owed much to private information supplied by Richard Mount, a member of the Court. He was subsequently presented with a suitably engraved piece of plate, the gift of the Master and Wardens, as a token of the Company's gratitude.[26]

Most of the Company's other investment was made on two occasions at the Hall itself. In 1722 it was decided to add an extra storey

'at least nine feet clear in height over the said Hall and the end room, divide the storey into the same number of rooms as are now five garrets, and likewise make a strong wainscot partition worked on both sides and make a clear passage of nine or ten feet wide from one end of the building to the other with doors out of the same into each room and a large sash window at each end of the said passage, the rooms in the storey all new floored and laid even from end to end, and the passage laid with old boards and a proper number of sash lights in each room and two chimneys in the new building and a door to each end room to the next room, the long passage one side lined with deal'.[27]

The second major alteration came in the later 1770s. Some of the Company's old houses at London Wall had then to be pulled down and the land was let on building leases.[28] This led to the construction of a new gateway into the Hall and the opportunity was taken to build a new entrance hall and main staircase within the Hall itself. In 1779 William Jupp, a leading member of the Company, was put in charge.[29] He designed and superintended the new additions, the entrance hall being decorated in stucco work both with figures and implements emblematic of carpentry and with heads of Vitruvious, Palladio, Inigo Jones and Wren. He also designed the archway forming the entrance to the street which contained a bust of Inigo Jones by Bacon on the keystone. £1,000 in investments were sold to pay for the beginnings of these improvements in 1779, and a further £2,200 had to be raised by the issue of annuities in 1781. In the following year the Court was embarking upon yet another economy campaign.[30]

These periods of investment and crisis punctuated what was otherwise a serene and unruffled existence. Most of the Court's time was taken up with purely routine matters. It visited the Wyatt almshouses at Godalming every year and there were fairly regular inspections of property elsewhere. The university exhibition, administered under the terms of John Read's will, occupied its occasional attention. Even the age-old problem of attempting to regulate the craft was raised once or twice during the earlier part of the century. The Common Council's decision of 1693 was invoked when, in January 1721, the Court heard yet again the familiar complaint

'that divers persons do use the Trade of Carpentry within the City of London and the Liberties thereof who are not free of the City, and also that others who use the said Trade but are free of the said City bind their apprentices at other Companies and not at this Company in manifest contempt and breach of an Act of Common Council dated the twenty-fifth day of April one thousand six hundred and ninety-three. Therefore that no person may plead ignorance of the said Act of Common Council, it is ordered by the Court that the Clerk to this

Company do cause the Order, together with the said Act to be printed and distributed to such as have been or are known to offend against the same, that for the future they may not be guilty of the same offences; and that the said Clerk do put the said Act in execution against any offenders as he shall receive direction from this Court'.[31]

The Court minutes, however, contain no evidence of any proceedings having been taken against defaulters. In July 1733 further complaints were heard and again the Clerk was instructed to 'sue such persons or their masters';[32] but again there is no indication of any action having been taken. Three years later, in 1736, the Court ordered that another 500 copies of the regulations be printed.[33] In 1739, however, the Company at last came near to accepting the reality of the situation. It decided that 'the Chamberlain was the proper person to regulate such complaints' and therefore ordered that

'when such complaints be made for the future Mr Poole the Clerk do go with such persons to Mr Bembridge one of the Mayor's Court Attorneys and if he shall think their information right, then to prosecute such offenders as the City's laws direct'.[34]

This seems to have marked the end of the Company's long and fruitless attempts to control the trade of carpentry in London. Paradoxically, however, while it was finally renouncing these unenforceable powers, it was enjoying much more success in enrolling practising carpenters as freemen. The Freedom Admissions Books at the end of the seventeenth century and beginning of the eighteenth show that most enrolments were of men practising other crafts. From about 1715 onwards, however, those who were actually carpenters by trade formed the overwhelming majority of those who were enrolled.[35] On January 3, 1726/7, the Court even went so far as to order that even those admitted by redemption had to be carpenters,[36] and although this order could not be too strictly enforced, it is clear from the enrolments in the mid- and later eighteenth century that the majority of redemptioners did, in fact, belong to the craft.[37]

The Court minutes occasionally shed incidental light on some of the Company's customs at this time. It was the habit, for instance, for anyone who became Father of the Company to provide the Court—twenty-four people in all[38]—with 'a treate'. Some new Fathers, however, preferred to put £5 in the poor box instead.[39] Another well-established tradition was the ceremony on Election Day. This consisted first of the Master and Wardens walking round the Hall 'with Musick and Cupbearers' (the latter being the four junior Liverymen), then the crowning of the new Master and Wardens by the old accompanied by mutual toastings, and finally the procession round the Hall again, but this time of the new Master and Wardens 'with Musick and Cupbearers as before'.[40] Other entries in the minutes which may perhaps reflect earlier customs rather than attempts to establish new ones include references to the reading of the Charter at 10 a.m. on Midsummer Day[41] and the presentation of medals to new members of the Livery, each medal bearing the arms of the Company on the one side and the Liveryman's name on the other.[42]

The duties of the Clerk, who lived at the Hall, were carefully spelt out. Apart from the taking of Court and committee minutes, he was to attend the Master and/or Wardens when they collected rents, to keep the Warden's accounts, to go on the yearly visit to Godalming, to make out bonds and rentals for the Renter Warden and to pay an assistant on Court days to fill up indentures. He was also to 'write yearly the Master and Wardens' names fairly on vellum paper to be put up in the Hall where the Court shall direct'. And, in case anything had been omitted from the list, the Court took the precaution of adding that he should also 'be obliged to do any other business for the Company that the Court shall find needful to be done'.[43] For these many services, in 1700 he received a basic salary of £8 a year. But, in addition, he was given a Christmas gift of £10 and binding and freedom fees, all of which brought his total income to about £50 a year. It would appear that he also received his lodgings at the Hall rent-free. In 1751 the Court decided to increase his salary to £40 a year plus fees, the fee for freedom being increased from 12s to 14s per person admitted.[44] Nine years later, in 1760, the Clerk pointed out that

'He being the Company's resident servant at the Hall was put to some extraordinary expense on that account, particularly in having a greater number of servants and those at extraordinary wages on account of the largeness of the rooms, also for the coal, soap, sand, mops, brooms etc. used in cleaning the Court Room and the rooms adjacent with the stairs and passage leading thereto and in keeping the said apartments and the furniture clean and dry'.

The Court was evidently impressed by these arguments, for it agreed to an additional allowance of £30 a year.[45]

The Company was well served by its eighteenth-century clerks, although one of them, Joseph Knapp, got into private troubles and had to resign. He wrote to the Court of 'unhappy misfortunes' which he 'would not enlarge upon' and added: 'My intention to seek my fortunes abroad and with what Your Worships please to allow me, I design to buy up necessaries proper for my intended voyage'. Christmas was approaching, so the Court allowed him the usual Christmas present of £10, plus a further £10 with which to pay off some of his debts.[46]

None of the Company's Beadles suffered such misfortunes, though one of them, Thomas Barnard, was reprimanded for 'following his business of carpentry' in the Hall Yard.[47] Barnard's successor, Benjamin Barlow, a member of the Court at the time of his appointment, was promptly dismissed from it, having (according to the minutes) 'degraded himself by his acceptance of the office'.[48] It carried a salary of about £20 a year for most of the century, though this was suddenly increased in 1782 to 45 guineas in view of 'the great rise of the common necessaries of life'.[49]

By 1800 the Carpenters Company was not yet in a position to attract into its ranks such wealthy men of business as other City Livery Companies were then doing, although the increasing Livery fines may indicate some slight growth in the prosperity of its Liverymen.[50] (In 1700, the 'first clothing' had cost £1; by the early 1770s the fine stood at 10 gns., and between 1772 and 1782 it was doubled.)[51] Nevertheless the Company drew its strength mainly from men of comparatively modest means who were connected with carpentry or with allied trades such as that of timber merchant. Perhaps Lord [Montagu] Norman's family was typical. Richard Norman, who left an Oxfordshire farming community in 1661 to become apprenticed to a London carpenter, eventually built up a carpentry business which employed others. He became Master of the Company in 1706. His son enlarged the business and was Master in 1733. His grandson, however, who went on to amass a fortune in the Anglo-Norwegian timber trade and bought himself a fine house in 37 acres of ground on Bromley Common, was altogether too great a man for the Carpenters Company. His name does not appear in its list of Masters and Wardens.[52]

The few outsiders who came on to the Livery were also people in modest walks of life. There was, for instance, a watchmaker, a seedsman, a glass seller, a couple of plumbers, a boxmaker, a tea dealer, a 'coffee man' and an obvious eccentric who described himself as 'a martial musical instrument maker'.[53] The only really wealthy businessman who became Master during the entire eighteenth century was rather an aberration so far as the Company was concerned. This was Sir John Cass (1666–1718) who has been referred to earlier in this chapter. Having made his fortune as a merchant, he was elected MP for the City in 1710 and became Sheriff in the following year. His father had been a carpenter and when he himself entered City politics he seized upon the Company as a means of attaining his immediate ends. He bought his way to the Mastership in 1711 by paying eleven years' quarterages and fines for the three subordinate offices which he had not filled. That a powerful merchant could prevail upon the Company in such a way, suggests the Company's weakness and vulnerability rather than its attractiveness, an impression that is confirmed by Cass's utter disregard for it once his Mastership was over. He never again appeared at Court meetings, and in 1713 he moved to the more influential and powerful Skinners Company.[54] It is true, as we have seen, that he remembered the Company in a codicil to his will, but, as we have also noticed, this gift was eventually refused. In some ways this was a not unfitting sequel to a rather revealing episode.

Yet, although the Company did not as yet attract eminent outsiders, it did produce some distinguished men from within its own ranks. The eighteenth century saw great building activity and considerable change in the structure of the building trade. Master carpenters, who, as Colvin has remarked, 'were quite capable of designing and building a church without the supervision of a member of the Royal Society' gave place to professional architects. 'The pressure of this new architectural discipline was to increase until, by the end of the eighteenth century, the craftsman had sunk to the level of a mere executant, dependent for every detail upon the working drawings supplied by the architect.'[55]

The 'mere executant', however, could do very well for himself in the later eighteenth century if he had a flair for organization and a head for figures, for larger building concerns were needed at a time when growing population and expanding business all called for more accommodation. Such a man was Sir William Staines (d. 1807), who started life as a labouring stonemason, made a fortune in building and eventually became Lord Mayor, the first member of the Company to achieve that office.[56] Unlike Cass, Staines was an active member of the Company, serving twice as Master, in 1793 and 1799. Little has been written about him, however, and his name rather surprisingly does not appear in the *Dictionary of National Biography*.

Of the Company's other distinguished members, two belonged to the age of master carpenters in the first half of the eighteenth century and two to the age of architects in the latter half. Sir William Ogborne (d. 1734), who was Master in 1724 and 1726, was Master Carpenter to the Office of Ordnance and became Sheriff of London in 1726.[57] John James (d. 1746), who was Master in 1734, as a young man became storekeeper at Greenwich Hospital and assistant to Nicholas Hawksmoor, the Clerk of Works there. He later became joint Clerk of Works with Hawksmoor whom he succeeded on the latter's death in 1736. He also succeeded Hawksmoor in 1736 as Surveyor to the Fabric of Westminster Abbey as he had Wren as Surveyor to the Fabric of St Paul's Cathedral thirteen years before in 1723.[58] He *has* been given an entry in the *Dictionary of National Biography*. So have the Company's two other notable members of the later eighteenth century, William and Richard Jupp. The sons of Richard Jupp, who had been Master in 1768, they—and particularly the younger son, Richard—represent the first generation of architects. William Jupp (d. 1788), as we have seen, was responsible for the alterations at the Hall in 1779–80. Richard Jupp (d. 1799) was for more than thirty years Surveyor to the East India Company and he is also said to have designed the west wing of Guy's Hospital. It is significant that he was an original member of the Architects' Club, described by Colvin as 'the first step towards a professional association', which was formed in 1791. Among the other founder members were James Wyatt, George Dance, Henry Holland, S. P. Cockerell, Robert Adam, Robert Mylne, John Soane and Thomas Hardwick.[59]

With the ascendancy of the Jupp family, the Company enters a new phase of its history. One of Richard Jupp's sons, Richard Webb Jupp (1767–1852), a trained solicitor, served as the Company's Clerk for over half a century, from 1798 until his death, and his son, Edward Basil Jupp (1812–1877), the Company's first historian, succeeded him as Clerk, a position which he also held until his death. William Jupp's eldest son, also called

William (d. 1839), became architect and surveyor to the Skinners, Merchant Taylors, Ironmongers and Apothecaries Companies, and District Surveyor for Limehouse, Blackwall, Wapping, Mile End Old Town, Poplar and Radcliff.[60] When he became Master, in 1831, the Company had not only gained a close connection with the new architectural profession: it was also soon to reap the reward of further commercial development and, in particular, railway building, which started to enhance further the value of its land. The Company's prosperity of the later nineteenth century owed much to its slow, unspectacular growth in the eighteenth.

CHAPTER VIII

GROWING PROSPERITY
1800-1880

ALTHOUGH the Company has inherited traditions and responsibilities dating from medieval times, its modern foundations were not really laid until the nineteenth century. Only then did income from rents and dividends reach proportions which would allow the Livery to dine in style in its own Hall. Only then could the Company develop from a cautious dispenser of doles to just over a hundred deserving poor into an owner of almshouses and a patron of technical education.

These important changes occurred in the middle, rather than in the earlier part, of the nineteenth century. For the first three decades, property values grew at little more than their eighteenth century pace. The Company's urban rents at the end of the 1820s were about one-third greater in money terms than at the beginning of the century[1] though somewhat higher than this in real terms when the fall in the cost of living since the end of the Napoleonic Wars is taken into account. The return to peace and unsettled agricultural prices, however, had reduced the value of the Stratford estate which was still pasture land; but the Company turned this fall to advantage by acquiring a little more property there while prices were low.[2] The loss of income from Stratford was, however, more than offset by higher rents in London itself. The Company's total income, which, as we have seen, had stood at about £2,000 a year in 1800, reached about £2,700 by the early 1830s.[3]

Although the Livery consisted of a hard core of practising carpenters and was well representative of the building industry as a whole, after 1800 it came to include more people from other walks of life. Indeed, there is a revealing Court minute on New Year's Day, 1805, which reads:

'It appeared by the Annual list of this Company that the Title of Esquire has been added to the name of William Payne of Temple Bar, one of the Livery, and the Court being convinced that he had no right to it and that many Gentlemen of the Company who did not claim the Title had a greater right to it, ordered that the same be omitted in the next list'.[4]

Of the eight Masters who held office between 1812 and 1824 and whose occupations can be traced either from the Company records or London directories, two were smiths and two were builders and surveyors; there was also a barge builder, an orange merchant, a timber merchant and a mason. A list drawn up at the end of 1823 gives the occupations of sixty-three people out of a total Livery of 125:[5]

carpenters 13; carpenter and builder; carpenter and undertaker; architects 5; cabinet maker; undertaker; timber merchants 5; timber and coal merchant; coal merchant; mason and brick-layer; mason; paviour; stone merchant; plasterers 3; bricklayer; glass dealer; fanlight makers 2; rope manufacturer; chemists 2; druggist; grocer; hop merchant; tobacconists 2; slopseller; hatter; potters 2; corn factor; linen draper; hosier and manu-facturer; seedsman; cheesemonger; surgeon's instrument maker; surgeon; brokers 2; banker; jeweller.

The Company was obviously attracting men from a wide range of occupations, a few of whom appeared to be quite well-to-do. But it still lacked sufficient appeal to prevent some of its more promising members from transferring their allegiance to a wealthier company, as may be seen by the transfer to the Fish-mongers Company of (Sir) William and Lewis Cubitt.[6]

No particular concern seems to have been shown for the Company's poor when prices rose during the war. Pensions remained at their previous levels, and, apart from the grant of £5 a year (the dividend from £100 worth of 5 per cent Navy annuities) which William Higgins gave in 1803,[7] the plight of pensioners seems to have attracted little attention until after the war was over. In 1819, a year of acute post-war distress and discontent, Robert Ashton, a member of the Court, presented a memorial on their behalf.[8] A committee was formed and this recommended that the Company's own quarterly pensions be raised from 12s (10s 6d plus 1s 6d for dinner) to 16s (14s plus 2s). Having noted that those who benefited from the annual payments made under the private gifts of Wyatt, Day, Read, Pope, Burgin, Williams and Reynolds were 'uninformed of their benefactors' and 'strangers to their kind regard for them', the committee seized the opportunity to recommend that the benefactors be named when payment was made; but it did not decide to increase these pensions to bring them into line with the new Company pension rates.[9]

There matters rested for a time. But at least one member of the Court, John Simmons, an architect who had served as Junior Warden in 1823–4, felt that the Company was behaving with less than justice towards its poor. In 1825 he pressed the matter in the Court, but he received a hostile reception. Indeed, at one meeting a dispute arose which led to fisticuffs and provoked Simmons into publishing an outspoken pamphlet attacking the Company. In it he noted that he had received

'from different persons . . . various intimations of wrongs, and [he had] collected from documents what appeared to be strong facts . . . [His] principal object was to improve the Company in its respectability and usefulness and to endeavour to extend its benevolence towards its distressed members'.[10]

The Court was, not surprisingly, furious. It claimed that the pamphlet contained 'a gross libel on the present Master, very offensive reflections and observations on the late Master, the late Renter Warden, the Court of Assistants and also on one gentleman of the Livery'. It deplored the fact that Simmons,

> 'by indulgence of private pique, by an assumption of superiority of abilities and disinterestedness and by behaviour contrary to the usages of civilized society, should assiduously endeavour to create dissensions in a fellowship that had for so long a period acted together with uniform harmony and cordiality'.

He was promptly expelled.[11]

The matter of the Company's poor was then dropped for a time. When financial matters were next discussed, in 1830, it was to launch yet another economy drive in order to raise money to repair the dilapidated old Hall and to shore up the front of it where there had been some subsidence.[12] The existing tenant was granted another lease, for seven years, at £300 per year on condition that the Hall was not to be used for any purpose other than as a carpet warehouse and that 'no feather, carpets or other things' were to be beaten on the premises.[13]

The coming of railways, in the 1830s, presented the Company with a capital windfall from which it was at last able to build its own almshouses. The London & Greenwich Railway paid £1,135 for property in Bermondsey, £210 in 1834 for seven cottages in Cross Keys Alley and £925 two years later for other premises in the vicinity of the Cross Keys Public House.[14] In 1837, the Eastern Counties Railway bought for £1,055 a ribbon of land at Stratford for its main line, which ran right through the Company's estate.[15] This was the first of a long succession of railway purchases there. And later in the same year Miss Hannah Acton, the widow of Samuel Acton who was the nephew of Nathaniel Wright (Master 1800), gave the Company £500 for the support of its poor.[16]

The Company was, therefore, in a financial position to consider the building of almshouses when, in November 1839, six acres of freehold land at Twickenham were offered to it for this purpose.[17] W. F. Pocock, Middle Warden in 1839 and an architect by profession, not only handled the buying of the land but also volunteered to design the almshouses without fee.[18] On June 24, 1841, Pocock's drawings having been approved, the Clerk was instructed to invite tenders from the twelve Liverymen who were in the building trade. Robert Hicks, who put in the lowest, for £2,250, was awarded the contract.[19] The first stone was ceremonially laid by the Master on Friday, July 30, 1841,[20] and the almshouses were completed during the following winter. On March 1, 1842, the Court was in a position to advertise for inmates, all of whom had to be either Liverymen or Freemen or their widows. Soon after this, the cloth for the poor men's clothing was chosen and a Twickenham doctor engaged at a fee of 10 guineas a year.[21] The Company launched an appeal for money to maintain their Twickenham pensioners and by the end of 1843 this had reached nearly £1,060. A gift in 1845 of £500 by Mrs Buhl, the widow of John Frederick Buhl who had been Master in 1817, came at a most opportune time.[22]

By the mid-1840s, R. W. Jupp, who had served as Clerk for nearly fifty years, was finding the task too heavy for him. He did not retire, however, but sought the assistance of his son, whom the Court elected as Joint Clerk at the beginning of 1843.[23] Edward Basil Jupp, who had been on the Livery since February 5, 1833, at once showed some concern about the preservation of the Company's old records. He sorted them out and, in January 1844, the Court voted him 30 gns. for his services. It thanked the Master and Wardens

'for the very able manner in which they have arranged the numerous deed books and other important documents belonging to the Company . . . and acknowledged the zeal and ability of Edward Jupp in performing the above work . . .'.[24]

Two years later, he was encouraged, by a chance happening at the Hall, to study these records. On December 19, 1845 (to quote the Court minutes),

> 'one of the workmen engaged in repairing the Great Hall, having driven a nail through some old canvas into the western wall and finding that he could not obtain a firm hold, proceeded to remove a portion of the canvas, when it appeared that the nail had merely penetrated the plaster on the face of which he discovered an old painting about 3 feet in height . . . He then removed the remainder of the canvas and found that the painting extended the entire length of the western side'.[25]

The committee of the Archaeological Society was called in, and on Christmas Eve it carried out a careful inspection of the painting which was found to represent 'four scripture subjects all in some way connected with the art of carpentry'.[26] The four subjects were, in fact, Noah's ark, King Josiah ordering the repair of the Temple, Joseph as a carpenter, and Jesus in his youth teaching in the synogogue.[27] (For further details, see Appendix 5.) This discovery caused Jupp to go hunting through the old records in an effort to establish the date of these paintings. He failed to find any clues there, although he was able to establish, from the Cottonian Manuscripts, that they had probably been in existence at the end of the sixteenth century. He came to the conclusion that they probably dated from the extensive repair and redecoration of the Hall in 1561.[28]

Jupp's search through the Company's records led him to go on to write its history. He spent nearly two years over this task, claiming when he had finished 'the credit of being the first to attempt anything like a detailed history of any particular Company'.[29] A committee of the Court met in three, separate four-hour sessions during December 1847 to hear him read his manuscript out aloud to them. At the end of these readings, they unanimously voted in favour of publication. Two hundred and

fifty copies were ordered to be printed and bound at a total cost of
£80. These were sold to the Livery at 10s each and to the general
public at 16s.[30]

E. B. Jupp eventually became sole Clerk—at a salary of £300
per year[31]—after his father's death on August 26, 1852. His father
had the distinction of being one of the select few whose portrait
had been commissioned to be painted by a distinguished artist—
John Prescott Knight, RA—at the Company's expense.[32] At the
time of his death he was in his eighty-fifth year, and his fifty-
fourth as Clerk. This long period of service the Court described as

'without precedent in the annals of the civic Companies . . . he
was alike distinguished in his integrity, assiduity and punctua-
lity, in the discharge of his various and onerous duties—by the
warmness of his friendship, the urbanity of his manners and
his comprehensive and untiring philanthropy'.[33]

It was in the middle of the nineteenth century that the Company embarked upon the development of its estate at Stratford.
The growth of this place, at the end of the French wars no more
than a village extending itself outwards along the main road,[34]
quickened when to the mills and factories of the Lea valley was
added, in 1848, the locomotive works of the Eastern Counties
Railway.[35] Unfortunately, the Carpenters' estate, by this time
bisected by the railway as well as by the meridian of Greenwich,
lay mostly in the marshy Lea valley and had no access to the main
road. Nothing could be done about its marshy situation; but
greater proximity to the road was gained as the result of some
deft negotiation with the Railway Company.

When, late in 1846, the Eastern Counties Railway approached
the Carpenters for more land, the Carpenters arranged to exchange this for railway company land, principally market
gardens, situated on the Stratford side of the Carpenters' estate.[36]
In the event, the Carpenters parted with land worth £324 and

bought further land worth £2,582.[37] Fortunately they were in funds, the South Eastern Railway having recently bought more property in Bermondsey—this time the Cross Keys public house itself—for £1,800.[38] They had also sold three houses in the Great Almonry, Westminster, a few years before[39] and Chancery permission was given for the proceeds of both these sales to be devoted to the purchase at Stratford.[40]

In 1850, when the existing tenancy of their estate was about to expire, the Carpenters sought the advice of a land agent about how they could best develop this property. He pointed out that the estate had deteriorated in value as pasture because 'the old system by which London was supplied with milk has been superseded by the supply through the instrumentality of railways'. He went on to suggest, however, that if the Company could improve the access to its estate, portions of it might be let for factory and house building.[41] This advice was followed a few years later. Having spent a further £2,120 on land which gave direct access to the main road[42]—out of additional money received from the Eastern Counties Railway for yet more of its land[43]—the Carpenters, in 1856, consulted a surveyor about 'the best mode of proceeding with a view to letting the land for building or manufacturing purposes . . .'.[44] It was decided to advertise weekly in The Builder and occasionally in The Times, and instructions were given for large 'For Sale' notice boards to be put up on both sides of the Railway.[45]

More years were to elapse, however, before any builder or manufacturer asked for a lease. It was not until the end of 1861 that a Romford brickmaker named Cosh took a fourteen-year lease of land for a brickfield; he was soon making over two million bricks a year there.[46] In September 1862, two acres of land to the north of Cosh's brickfield was let for building,[47] and at the end of 1863 Messrs Ritchie of Fenchurch Street, merchants and linen factors, leased a factory site.[48] In 1864 there is the first mention of Carpenters Road and Warton Road, the latter named after the Master in 1863–4.[49] Cosh was allowed frontages on the

east side of Carpenters Road for the building of forty houses at
the rate of ten per year and it was again decided to advertise the
land in the press.[50] One hundred plans of the site were litho-
graphed and some were pasted up on Stratford and Shoreditch
railway stations.[51] More roads were laid out: in 1868 and 1869
there is mention of Blyth and Rosher Roads[52] and presumably
they had both been named during the previous years when John
Blyth and Edward Rosher had served as Master. More factories
were put up, including one for the manufacture of lucifer matches.
The owner was excused from insuring his works.[53]

Meanwhile, railway extensions within the City itself were
bringing even more money into the Company's coffers. In 1862
the North London Railway bought property in Worship Street
and Bell & Dragon Yard for its Broad Street line, for which an
arbitration jury awarded the Carpenters £4,023 at the beginning
of 1863.[54] Two years later, in 1865, the Great Eastern (as the
Eastern Counties had then become) took two houses and the
back premises of three others in Norton Folgate for its proposed
extension to Liverpool Street; but that unfortunate railway got
into financial difficulties and it was not until early in 1869 that the
purchase price, £8,000, was received.[55] Soon after that, more of
the Company's Norton Folgate land was sold to the Great
Eastern, the North London and the London & North Western
for £5,400, £4,000 and £1,850 respectively.[56]

By the 1870s the Carpenters were in a position to join other
companies in two development schemes in the city. The first of
these concerned their Lime Street property and involved the
opening up of Lime Street Square by means of an avenue running
from Lime Street to Billiter Street and another running south
from the Square to Fenchurch Street (the future Fenchurch
Avenue). This development was undertaken jointly with the
Fishmongers Company and Bridewell and Bethlehem Hospitals.[57]
The second scheme was undertaken on the initiative of the
Drapers Company, who, having decided to build upon Drapers
Garden, situated immediately to the south and west of the old

Carpenters Hall, approached the Carpenters early in 1873 with the proposal to cut a road from London Wall to the southern end of Drapers Garden 'with room for carriages to turn at some point in the Garden'. This proposal was accepted and the work put in hand. The Court learnt at the beginning of 1876 that the new road was to be named Throgmorton Avenue.[58]

The laying out of Throgmorton Avenue meant that the Carpenters had to pull down their old Hall, which lay a little to the south of London Wall and was entered from a courtyard facing that thoroughfare. This old Hall, 'of no great architectural merit' as *The Builder* tactfully described it,[59] continued to be leased for business purposes until the 1870s. Indeed, the detailed ordnance survey map of 1875 labels it 'Warehouses'. For a time, during and immediately after the Railway Mania of the mid-1840s, it had been sublet to an enterprising Somerset man by the name of Emery who needed

> 'the Great Hall . . . for the meetings of directors and proprietors of railway companies and the remainder of the premises . . . for offices for conducting the business of the companies'.[60]

(It was during the repairs and alterations needed to adapt a carpet warehouse into a directors' board room that the biblical paintings were discovered.) The Mania over, Emery surrendered his sublease.[61] In 1850 Waterlows, the printers, became tenants[62] and as their business flourished, they were constantly pressing the Company for more space. In 1853, after the death of R. W. Jupp, they took over rooms at the Hall which he had previously occupied.[63] In 1859 their application to build in the forecourt was turned down, but they were allowed 'to carry a shaft under the pavement between the Great Hall and the new building in the courtyard'.[64] In the following year, 1860, they declared themselves anxious to treat with the Company for the whole of Carpenters Buildings, the Beadle's house and two houses in London Wall;

but they had to be content with a lease of a part of Carpenters Buildings only.[65]

The Company's total income, which, as we have seen, had stood at about £2,700 per year in the early 1830s, was by 1870 nearly twice that amount and it grew at an even more rapid rate during the 1870s.[66] It is rather difficult to interpret the income returns so grudgingly provided by all the Livery companies for the Royal Commission which reported on their affairs in 1884. But this evidence, for what it is worth, would suggest that the Carpenters, with an income of about £8,000 at the end of the 1870s, came only a short distance behind two of the twelve great companies, the Ironmongers (£13,200) and the Vintners (£10,000). Outside the Twelve, the Leathersellers (£17,700), the Brewers (£12,700) and the Saddlers (£10,200) had larger incomes, the Armourers and Brasiers (£8,100), and the Bakers (£7,600) similar incomes and all the other companies smaller ones.[67]

During these years of growing economic strength, between the 1830s and the 1870s, the Carpenters were able to boast among its members two Sheriffs and two Lords Mayor. R. W. Kennard, an iron merchant, served as Sheriff in 1846 and became Master in the following year. William Lawrence was Sheriff in 1849, the year after he had served as Master. He was a Cornishman who, early in the century, had come up to London as quite a young man and founded a building concern which, as William Lawrence and Sons, was to develop into a very thriving business with yards both in the City and at Lambeth.[68] Two of his sons, (Sir) William Lawrence[69] (Master in 1856) and (Sir) James Clarke Lawrence[70] (Master for part of 1860), both held the office of Lord Mayor, the former in 1863 and the latter in 1868. Although their allegiance was to shift to the Fishmongers Company (in which they were both eventually to serve as Prime Warden), their loyalty to the Carpenters during their lord mayoralty undoubtedly increased the Company's prestige in the City. It is also noteworthy that during the 1870s no fewer than fifty-two people became members of the Company by redemption to be compared with twenty-nine by patrimony and only one by servitude.[71] Clearly, when the Drapers' proposal to build Throgmorton Avenue brought the issue to a head, a new and splendid Hall had become not only economically possible but also socially imperative.

In August 1874 the Court ordered a ground plan to be taken of its London Wall estate and in the following summer it was discussing the kind of new Hall it needed. A special committee decided that it should cost less than £30,000 and be built in the Italian style, to the north of the site of the existing Hall and at the corner of London Wall and Throgmorton Avenue.[72] A leading member of the Company, William Willmer Pocock,[73] was instructed to prepare drawings. Tenders were invited in the summer of 1876 and William Brass's for £28,992 was accepted.[74] The foundation stone was laid on August 1st.[75] Meanwhile the development of the whole site went forward; in November 1876, for instance, it was proposed that it should be let in eighteen plots.[76]

E. B. Jupp, the Company's first historian and for many years its Clerk, died in 1877 while this major development scheme was getting under way. The Court solemnly noted that he had

'conducted the business of the Company at all times with such sound judgment, urbanity of manner and perspicuity of language as are seldom met in the same individual'.[77]

Jupp's place was taken by Stanton W. Preston, who had served as Master in 1875–6. The Company also appointed a solicitor, George Hensman, who had been Master in 1869–70. Preston, like Jupp before him, gave his early attention to the archives. Like Jupp, he found all in chaos, some of the documents 'being in boxes with lists enclosed that did not correspond with the deeds therein and others placed about the strong room in a very loose way without any system, more especially the charters which were very carelessly found, placed in a broken box'.[78]

By the spring of 1879 the building of the new Hall had reached the point at which speaking tubes were being fitted from the

Court room to the waiting room, and from the Livery Hall to the kitchens.[79] By the end of the year the kitchens themselves were being fitted up.[80] A dinner service was ordered from the Worcester Porcelain Company, and on January 27, 1880, the Court dined at the new Hall for the first time.[81] The purchase of candelabra, cutlery, wine glasses and wine occupied much of the Court's time during the spring and summer of 1880 and so did the furnishing of the drawing room. The first Livery dinner at which a future Prime Minister, (Sir) Henry Campbell-Bannerman, responded to one of the toasts, was held on November 25th.[82] In all, the new Hall and its furnishing had cost nearly £44,000.

It was a two-storey building with an exterior of Portland stone. On the ground floor and to the left of the entrance (in Throgmorton Avenue) were the Court room, the Court dining room and dressing rooms; and to the right were a waiting room, the Clerk's offices and a private office. Upstairs were a drawing room and the Livery Hall, one of the largest in London, the ceiling of which reproduced as nearly as possible that in the old banqueting hall.[83] Some of the fine wood carving from the old Hall was also used in the decoration of the new one and three of the four wall paintings were also included.[84] As befitted Carpenters Hall, timber joists and wooden floorboards were used throughout in preference to iron and concrete, a tribute to the craft which was remarked upon by *The Builder* at the time.[85] Its correspondent, who was allowed to scrutinize the plans while the Hall was being put up, also noted that, although there was to be a service lift between the Livery Hall and the kitchen, this would only be used for returning the empty dishes. Dinners would be passed up 'from hand to hand by a numerous retinue of servants stationed on the staircase from the kitchen upwards, it being found that this method is much more expeditious than the use of a lift'.[86]

The opening of the new Hall ushered in a new era in the Company's history, an era that was to be marked by a considerable extension of its philanthropic effort, particularly in the field of education.

CHAPTER IX

THE COMING OF THE WELFARE STATE

T HE Carpenters' increased interest in education, and particularly in technical education, reflected Britain's greater concern about her economic position then confronted by growing foreign competition. It was said that foreign manufacturers, and the Germans especially, were gaining economic advantages because of their superior facilities in technical education. Captain Donnelly of the Science and Art Department urged that the wealthy City companies should take the lead in developing technical education in London and he obtained very warm support from T. H. Huxley who, at a meeting in December 1879, told the London companies in no uncertain terms that it was their responsibility, as the wealthy inheritors of the property and traditions of the old guilds, to give generously to the recently formed City & Guilds of London Institute. The money was forthcoming and in 1881 the foundation stones were laid of both a City technical college in Finsbury and a national institution—the future Imperial College—at South Kensington.[1] The Carpenters Company began making an annual contribution of £250 to the City & Guilds in 1883, which was raised to £500 in 1887. It also gave a further £1,000 to the building fund between 1883 and 1886.[2]

By this time the Company's income had reached very considerable proportions. Perhaps not uninfluenced by the report of the Royal Commission on the City Companies, which was discussed at two meetings of the Court,[3] the Company formed a committee to consider the distribution of its income left over after the payment of charities and the mortgage repayments on the new

Hall. The committee reported at the beginning of 1886 that this surplus totalled £6,000 per year. It recommended that not more than £2,000 should be spent on causes connected with the craft, including technical education, lectures and exhibitions; not more than £500 each on (i) general education in the form of scholarships to universities, gifts to free libraries, prizes or contributions to schools in London, Stratford, Godalming and elsewhere, (ii) hospitals, convalescent homes, baths and recreation grounds, (iii) relief of infirmity, and (iv) objects not covered under the previous heads, such as local improvements whose claims might arise from proximity to the Company's estates; and the remaining £2,000 to be spent for a few years on completing the development of the Company's estates.[4] Having heard these recommendations, the Court decided to concentrate particularly on the Stratford estate, where 3,000 of the 5,000 inhabitants were under 20 years of age, most of those between 14 and 20 being employed in the sixteen factories there.[5] A sub-committee was formed to confer with the Rev George Towner on the matter.[6]

George Towner was a Baptist minister who had, in 1879, built a chapel at Stratford upon land which he had rented from the Company at £10 a year.[7] In 1881 he and others were also granted a lease of 11 Park Place at £5 a year for a schoolroom;[8] and in 1884 he had been given £50, and in January 1885 an additional £30, towards the building of a new schoolroom.[9] When he met the sub-committee in February 1886, however, his ideas for further educational developments were considered far too grandiose. The sub-committee recommended instead that a modest building be put up on a piece of ground in Jupp Road to house a reading room or lecture hall, two classrooms for cookery classes and a workshop for carpentry. The land between this building and Pickford's premises, which lay behind it, should be used as a gymnasium and recreation ground.[10] The building seems to have cost less than £750 to erect[11] and it was agreed that not more than £250 per year should be spent in running it, £100 for lecturers and teachers, £100 for caretaker, coals and general upkeep, and £50 for materials and tools.[12] The official opening took place in October 1886[13] and at the beginning of November it was decided that evening classes for carpentry and joinery should be held on Tuesdays, for plumbing and geometry on Wednesdays, for cooking on Thursdays and for mechanical drawing on Fridays.[14] The recreation ground and gymnasium were opened in June 1887.[15] Baths were added in 1889 and extended in 1890 and 1891.[16]

When, in 1891, this evening institute was changed into a day technical school—the only one of its kind in Essex at that time[17]—George Towner became its first headmaster.[18] The school was enlarged in 1894, at a cost of £2,770, and in 1897 £1,570 were spent on a new workshop.[19] By then, William Ping, 'a "round" man with a red face, red nose and gold spectacles' had become its much-respected headmaster. Hundreds of boys passed through the school before it closed in 1905. West Ham Corporation was by then providing alternative technical education at public expense and, in these circumstances, the Company did not feel that the school's continued existence, with costs rising, was justified. Despite its brief life, however, it left its mark, for many of the boys, who came from quite humble homes, went on to make distinguished careers for themselves in business (one became a director of B.T.H. and another a director of Kearle and Tonge), in the civil service, in journalism (P. W. Izzard), and on the stage (Stanley Holloway).

The closing of the technical school allowed the Company to spend more on the Trades Training School in Great Titchfield Street. The Tylers and Bricklayers were also associated with this modest venture, which was first launched in 1893. The Company granted £1,028 to it in the following year.[20] In all, up to £4,300 was voted for technical education in 1894, the other beneficiaries being the City & Guilds, King's College and University College, London.[21]

Exhibitions and lectures at the new Hall and examinations in carpentry were other prominent features of this period. The first carpentry exhibition was held, in conjunction with the Joiners, between May 26 and June 14, 1884. It was visited by 11,456 people, and twenty-five prizes (worth altogether £84) were awarded.[22] The second exhibition, held between May 14 and June 2, 1888, attracted only 7,000 but on that occasion the judges felt that the standard of exhibits was higher and they awarded forty-five prizes.[23] The first examination in carpentry and joinery was also held in 1888. It was an exacting one, for written papers took the whole of one day (from 10 until 4.45 and from 5.30 until 8.30), practical work the whole of the next day and *vivas* the afternoon of the third day.[24] The Company was fortunate to have as organizer of its examinations Bannister Fletcher (Master in 1889), who became Professor of Architecture at King's College, London, in 1890. Soon after his appointment he formed a joint King's-Carpenters Company wood-carving school.[25] (Sir) Henry Harben (Master 1893) gave the interest on £2,500 government stock to support these classes and £750 for the building of a suitable classroom at King's.[26]

The Company also maintained its long-established scholarships at Oxford and Cambridge under the terms of the Read Trust. One of the scholarship holders at Cambridge in the 1880s was (Sir) Walter Raleigh, soon to become a very well-known professor of English.[27] In 1890 the Company made its first Read award to a woman, Josephine Partridge, who also went up to Cambridge.[28]

Sir Henry Harben, Bt, who had been both secretary and president of the Prudential Assurance Company (which had advanced the Company a mortgage on its new Hall), was a prominent benefactor of the Company at this time. The Harbens were related to the Chamberlains—Joseph Chamberlain's mother was a Harben —and, more relevant for our present purposes, one of Sir Henry's sisters had married Stanton William Preston, who, as we have seen, had become Clerk of the Company in 1877, just a year before Sir Henry himself had come on to the Livery. In addition to his gifts to the wood-carving school, he gave £200 in 1894 for the purchase of books connected with architecture and a carved oak bookstand to house them. In 1894–5 he contributed £1,700 towards the extension of the Stratford technical school. To these gifts he added, in 1879, eighty-eight £5 Prudential shares for lectures on matters concerned with public health and for the provision of a gold medal to be awarded yearly by the Institute of Public Health. In the same year he established a convalescent home for working men in 17 acres of ground at Rustington in Sussex, for the management of which the Company was to be responsible. He also left 300 £5 Prudential shares for its maintenance. His daughter, Mrs Mary Woodgate Wharrie, subsequently added a further 300 £5 Prudential shares in 1915, an outright gift of £4,000 in 1922, and fifty £1 Prudential 'A' shares in 1933.[29]

While Harben deserves mention as the Company's benefactor of later Victorian times, other members also made their mark upon its life. When, for instance, William Willmer Pocock completed his term of office as Master, in 1884, the Court remarked upon the interest he had shown in the development of the Company's estates over the years, and went on to comment upon the care he had shown in the building of the new Hall which had 'made it a lasting memorial to his talent'.[30] He was to place the Company yet further in his debt when, very soon afterwards, he became responsible for a new edition of Jupp's *History*. When it appeared early in 1887, the Court decided that it should be distributed free to all the Company and supplied to Pickering & Co. for general sale at 10s 6d.[31]

Alfred Preston (Master 1881–2) seems to have been the leading figure in, if not the prime mover behind, the important educational developments of this period. If there was ever a committee appointed to consider educational matters, he was sure to sit upon it.[32] When one of the technical school boys won a County Council scholarship, it was he who conveyed the good news to the Court.[33]

As Clerk, the elderly Stanton W. Preston was not prevented by age from keeping a firm grip on the Company's affairs. He remained Clerk until 1902. He had then served in that office for twenty-four years.

The Carpenters were able to claim one Lord Mayor at this time, G. S. Nottage, who died in office in March 1885.[34] He was also Master of the Company in that year. He had been in the iron trade with his uncle, R. W. Kennard (see page 155), before setting up his own photographic business in Cheapside and Oxford Street in 1856.

The Livery remained 150-strong, though in 1890 it was decided to admit six new members in place of the six who then lived permanently abroad.[35] Some of the members lived some distance from London but managed to attend meetings regularly. H. C. Smith, for instance, who was Master in 1887–8, lived at Rugby.[36] There are two pieces of evidence which suggest that the Company was becoming more select or, at least, more exclusive. The presentation of gifts of plate became fashionable once again and Frederick Arthur Crisp (Master in 1904) issued a catalogue of the Company's plate which he had printed on his private press in 1906 (see Appendix 4). In 1890 the Freedom fine for redemptioners was put up from £15 15s od to £65; and in 1895 the regular visit to Twickenham was postponed so that members of the Court should not miss Ascot.[37]

By the early years of the twentieth century, the later Victorian burst of activity, a reflection of the Company's suddenly improved financial position, had spent itself. The Company settled down to half a century of much less impressive growth. Then, in the 1950s, the prospect of a further large jump in its income induced yet another period of rapid change. It, too, was associated with the building of a new Hall.[38]

So far as its charities were concerned, the Company was, between 1900 and the 1950s, mainly interested in reallocating its resources, for central and local government were now taking over and extending many of the services which the Company and other philanthropic bodies had pioneered. The closing of the Carpenters' technical institute at Stratford in 1905 and its replacement by West Ham's technical college was the first sign of the changing times. An even more striking example was the Twickenham Borough Council's acquisition, in 1947, of the Company's almshouses. It built flats on the site and became responsible for the rehousing of the displaced pensioners. When the Master laid the foundation stone of the flats, on May 15, 1950, he was, in fact, acknowledging a new order in which more ample public resources were replacing the Company's more tenuous private funds. Some of these funds now needed to be switched to other charitable purposes in which it was still possible to supplement public expenditure effectively.

In the field of education, for instance, the scope of the Read bequest, which had enabled two students to go up to Oxford or Cambridge in the later nineteenth century, was extended to finance a third such scholarship. Financial support continued to be given to the City & Guilds and to the Trades (later renamed the Building Crafts) Training School in Great Titchfield Street. During the Second World War the latter became a centre for the training of both soldiers and munition workers, and before it reopened for the training of apprentices, in 1947, it provided refresher courses for ex-servicemen who were returning to the building industry. The Company also provided a three-year scholarship tenable at the Bartlett School of Architecture, a three-year bursary at the Brixton School of Building, and a one-year travelling scholarship to a student at the Polytechnic, Regent Street. H. Westbury Preston (Master in 1926) gave money for travel grants, administered by the English-speaking Union, to assist British students travelling to universities in Canada, and these were supplemented by part of the income from a large bequest by Albert Evan Bernays (Master in 1941–2 and 1942–3) inherited by the Company after his death in October 1960. Other income from the Bernays Bequest was devoted to grants of an educational nature. The Company also continued to make, in deserving cases, individual grants for the schooling of deceased Liverymen's children.

Several members of the Company and others financed prizes to encourage those who were studying the craft of carpentry and building. In 1927 H. Westbury Preston gave £200 worth of 7 per cent Greek Refugee Bonds for this purpose. In the following year, George Charles Barnes gave £100, the proceeds from which were to provide an annual prize for students at the Trades Training School, and in 1938 Miss Marianne Paxton Willson presented the Company with £1,000 to be spent upon furthering its technical education work by grants to students. In 1949 and 1953 respectively H. Westbury Preston and Sir Bannister Flight Fletcher gave £1,000 and £1,500, in the former case for prizes and in the latter for medals, at Great Titchfield Street.

The general spread of competing courses elsewhere eventually brought the Carpenters Hall lectures on carpentry, joinery, architecture and building to an end. They ran successfully enough up to the Second World War and were restarted when the war was over; but the number of students fell and when, in 1955, only twenty candidates presented themselves for examination—of whom thirteen failed—it was decided that the time had arrived to recognize that the purpose for which the courses had been devised was being adequately met by other bodies, notably the City & Guilds and the Incorporated British Institute of Certified Carpenters, in the creation of which, in 1890, the Company had played a notable part,[39] and which had branches throughout the country and in Australia. The examinations were subsequently handled by the IBICC, but, despite encouraging reports of Australian entries, the examiners were very soon pessimistic about future prospects. Between the wars the Company also held courses and examinations on sanitary building construction; these lapsed, however, with the Second World War and were not re-started. Some lectures of a more popular nature were given between the wars by well-known speakers such as the Dean of St Paul's.

The Company also continued to help the poor and the sick by

individual gifts and by donations to institutions; and the Rustington Convalescent Home, which it managed, continued to receive patients, except during the years 1940–8 when it (but not the farm attached to it) was occupied by the Services. At Godalming, the ten Wyatt almshouses, which lacked bathrooms and indoor sanitation, were modernized between 1956 and 1958 and turned into eight flats. These were designed by Geoffrey Ridley (Master in 1955–6). At Stratford, a number of Liverymen continued the social work on the Company's estate which had been started by H. Westbury Preston.

Carpenters Hall, then little more than sixty years old, was destroyed by fire during the last big raid on London, on the night of May 10/11, 1941. A parachute mine fell in London Wall and set a gas main on fire, and there was insufficient water pressure for the firemen to quell the blaze. Nobody inside the warden's post situated in a passage between the kitchen and wine cellar was seriously hurt, however, although the blast from the exploding mine blew in a heavy wooden door and sucked another off its hinges.

By wise planning and good fortune, most of the Company's most treasured possessions and important working records were saved. The Master's cup, which was on exhibition at the New York Fair when war broke out, remained safely in America. The Company's silver, old records and microfilm copies of more recent ones were safely stored at the National Provincial Bank, Warminster. So, too, were the garlands, which were fetched by the Porter and Beadle for each war-time election-day ceremony so that custom should not be broken. The pictures, charter and Master's chair were crated and placed in a space outside the wine cellars below the Hall and escaped harm. The frescoes, on loan to the London Museum, also survived, although one of them was damaged. The only serious losses of historical interest were the window containing the glass from the previous Hall, two seventeenth-century chimney pieces, a Kneller picture of the first Duke of Marlborough, some oak panelling and two corbels. The Clerk's office was completely destroyed, but the safes containing ledgers and account books survived. In the Beadle's office, however, the safe was completely burnt out—though the Bank of England was able to calculate, from an examination of the ashes, how many banknotes it had contained and obligingly gave new ones in return. Fortunately, the only up-to-date list of tenants' names and addresses was contained not in the safe but in a steel filing cabinet and this survived the blaze as did the Company's stationery. But all the books in the library were lost and so were the examination records. The Company's wines and spirits, however, survived safely (much to everyone's surprise and joy) and the only losses sustained occurred subsequently on two occasions when intruders managed to get into the cellar beneath the gutted Hall—still used for storing the Company's bottles—and took a liking to, among other things, some 1878 brandy and claret.

Immediately after the fire, the Drapers offered the Carpenters hospitality at Drapers Hall, thereby returning the compliment which the Carpenters had paid them after the Great Fire of 1666. A committee meeting, arranged for May 13th, two days after the raid, was held in the Wardens Room there and this served as the Company's temporary office and headquarters for a time. Then three rooms were rented at the Bank of Ireland premises, 3 Throgmorton Street, for Court and committee meetings. The office was moved in 1941 to 28 Austin Friars, Drapers Company property. Accommodation there was very limited and all committee meetings and Court functions continued to be held at Drapers Hall.

Other losses suffered by the Company during the air raids were about a third of the cottage property at Stratford and the building opposite the Hall in Throgmorton Avenue. 171/3 Aldersgate Street was also badly damaged by fire but was rebuilt. The rest of the buildings in the City which stood on the Company's land, however, including the new property put up before the war at 38, 39 and 40 Lime Street and 4 Fenchurch Avenue, escaped unharmed.

For the first decade after the war, the building of business premises was held back in order to help the housing drive, and it was only after the mid-1950s that the Company was able to turn to the rebuilding of its Hall. At the same time, building elsewhere drove up site values and enabled the Company to increase its rents when a number of its leases fell in. It was at this juncture, in anticipation of increased rents, that the spirit of adventure reasserted itself. Despite some opposition, it was decided to build a modern and enlarged Hall. Designed by Austen Hall and built by Dove Brothers (W. W. Dove was Master in 1954), it spanned Throgmorton Avenue. The banqueting Hall was, in fact, built on a wide bridge across the Avenue and the new building also included a considerable amount of office space for letting. The foundation stone was laid on July 23, 1956. The Clerk and his staff were able to move into their new quarters on March 14, 1959, but the whole building was not formally opened until May 4, 1960. It cost more than twice what the Company had received in war damage insurance, but, on the other hand, the rents from office tenants made it a more valuable property than the old Hall had been. Members were urged to contribute to a furnishing fund and they did so most liberally.

In meeting the greatly increased expenditure incurred in the day-to-day running of the Hall, the Company was helped not only by income from its new office tenants but also from higher rents elsewhere in Throgmorton Avenue. The leases held by the City of London Real Property Company expired at the beginning of the 1960s and they were renewed very greatly to the advantage of the Company which then became directly responsible for their management. Soon afterwards the compulsory purchase of some of the land at Stratford, needed by the West (now New) Ham Corporation for its development scheme also proved of considerable financial benefit to the Company. It continued, however, to own the factory sites.

The Company continued to number in its ranks men of ability

9.
The Master's and
Wardens' Crowns
(See Appendix 5)

10. Silver-Gilt Seventeenth Century Steeple Cups
Left to Right: Ansell Cup, Reeves Cup, Edmones Cup
(See Appendix 4)

Wyatt Tankards and Jarman Steeple Cup
(See Appendix 4)

12.
Hawkins Tankard and Possit
Cup and two Baluster Stem
Cups
(See Appendix 4)

and distinction. It is worthy to note that the foundation of the Hall was laid by one Lord Mayor (Sir Cuthbert Ackroyd, who had been Master in 1952) and opened by another (Sir Edmund Stockdale, then Middle Warden). Sir Leslie Boyce, Lord Mayor in 1951, was also a member of the Company who served as Junior and Middle Warden. A full list of Masters and Wardens will be found in Appendix 2.

The Company's officers maintained the tradition of long and loyal service. Joseph Hutton Freeman was Clerk from 1902 to 1935 (when he became Master), and his successor, Henry Carl Osborne, who served the Company through the difficult years of the Second World War, held office until 1960 when he had to retire on account of ill health. Frank Carter, who was Beadle from 1895 to 1928, served the Company for thirty-three years, as Freeman had done. His successor, Frederick William Powell, who served for thirty-five years as Beadle, retired in 1964.

The size of the Livery, over which the Company exercises its own jurisdiction, remained at 150 until the mid-1950s when it was agreed that up to five additional members might be admitted provided they were sons or grandsons of Liverymen or past Liverymen. There were then three honorary freemen: The Queen of the Netherlands, Viscount Montgomery and the President for the time being of the Carpenters Company of Philadelphia.[40]

The Philadelphia Carpenters Company had been founded in 1724 'for the purpose of obtaining instruction in the science of architecture and assisting such of their members as should by accident be in need of support, or their widows or minor children of members'.[41] Its Hall, built in the early 1770s, was the scene of anti-British meetings on the eve of the Revolution and later housed the Bank of the United States for a time. It is not possible to say when the link between the Philadelphia and London Companies was first made. The London Company's Court Minutes of the eighteenth and nineteenth century do not shed any light on the matter, but some early connection is suggested by the coat of arms over Carpenters Hall in Philadelphia, which includes the three compasses (though there is no motto and in place of the chevron is a square). Notices summoning Philadelphia members to meetings, however, which are printed from copper plates believed to be at least 100 years old, do show the chevron and the motto 'Honor God'. Five of the names of the early members of the Philadelphia Company are to be found in the London apprenticeship lists, but the names are not sufficiently unusual for this evidence to be conclusive.[42] The two Companies were certainly in touch with each other in the year that the second Carpenters Hall was opened, for on February 19, 1880, the Master and Clerk, acting upon a resolution of the Court, inscribed their names in a presentation copy of Jupp's History which is still kept by the recipients in Philadelphia.[43] It does not appear, however, that any regular connection was established until after the Second World War.

The Company's banquets continued to be splendid social occasions. Perhaps the most notable of them was the one held on March 22, 1933, to commemorate the six hundredth anniversary of the drawing up of the Book of Ordinances. It was attended by the Prince of Wales who made the official presentation of a new Master's badge, designed and made by Omar Ramsden. Since the Second World War menus have not been so extensive as they previously were but the tables have glittered with much more silver: the twenty years between 1940 and 1960 saw more gifts than the inter-war period had done. Within the setting of the new Hall, these treasures look even more splendid. The convivial, like the philanthropic, activities of the Company continue undiminished in the mid-twentieth century welfare state.

APPENDIX 1
LIST OF HONORARY MEMBERS

Sir John Lubbock, Bt, MP	April 12, 1888
Sir Albert K. Rollit, MP	July 30, 1894
The Very Rev Henry Wace, DD	July 30, 1894
Professor William Robert Smith, MD	July 30, 1894
Sir Joseph Fayrer, Bt, KCSI, MD	December 4, 1894
General The Rt Hon Sir Redvers H. Buller, VC, GCB, KCMG, etc.	March 26, 1901
Major General W. H. Mackinnon, CB	March 26, 1901
Colonel H. C. Cholmondeley, CB	March 26, 1901
Rt Hon The Earl of Albemarle, CB	April 23, 1901
Rt Hon Sir George Houston Reid, KCMG, KC	June 22, 1910
Thomas Wharrie, JP	June 1, 1915
Mrs Mary Woodgate Wharrie	July 3, 1917
F-M The Rt Hon The Earl Haig of Bemerside, OM, KT, GCB, etc.	July 17, 1919
The Rev Sir Montague Fowler, Bt, MA	November 7, 1922
Rt Hon The Marquess of Reading, GCB, GCIE, etc.	October 20, 1926
Rt Hon Sir Eric Drummond, GCMG, CB, subsequently Earl of Perth	October 11, 1933
F-M The Rt Hon J. C. Smuts, PC	December 2, 1941
F-M The Rt Hon The Viscount Montgomery of Alamein, KG, GCB, DSO	June 5, 1951
Her Majesty Queen Juliana of the Netherlands	May 7, 1954
Herbert Austen Hall, FRIBA	November 1, 1960

APPENDIX 2

LIST OF MASTERS AND WARDENS

(Names in italic type are of Masters or Wardens who succeeded those who died in office or did not serve a full term)

———

Year of Election	Masters	Wardens
1437		Richard Punchon, William Crofton, Thomas Coventry
1438		John Blomvile, John Tanner, Richard Aas
1439		William Sefowl, Thomas Sexteyn, Thomas Iseleon
1440		John Salisbury, William Goldington, Richard Bird
1441		Thomas Smyth, Thomas Warham, Hugh Blyton
1442		John Wyse, William Waleys, John Silkwith
1443		John Stock, Thomas Finch, William Chacombe
1444		Robert Cowper, Thomas Coventry, William Bentham
1445		William Seryll, Piers Sexteyn, William Bowle
1446		Richard Punchon, Thomas Ungyll, Thomas Winchcombe, William Carter, Simon Chacombe
1447		William Sefowl, Robert Knight

....

1451		John Silkwith, John Punchon, John Bentley

1452		John Wyse, William Waleys, John King
1453		Thomas Smyth, Robert Churchman, John Glover
1454		Thomas Coventry, Thomas Ungyll, Simon Chacombe
1455		John Wyse, Thomas Ungyll, Edward Stone, Simon Chacombe, Symon Clenchwarton
1456	Thomas Warham	Edward Stone, Robert Knight, William Brown
1457	Thomas Warham	Robert Knight, William Brown, Thomas Fenne, William Robert
1458	Thomas Warham	John Punchon, William Robert, Thomas Fenne, Walter Orchard
1459	Thomas Warham	John Punchon, John King, Walter Orchard, John Brook
1460	Thomas Sexteyn	John King, John Brook, John Hankyn, Harry Shadd
1461	Thomas Ungyll	Symon Chacombe, William Ray
1462	Edmond Gravely	Thomas Wright, John Punchon, William Warham
1463	Walter Orchard	Thomas Pert, John Forster, William Carter
1464	Walter Orchard	Robert Knight, Thomas Pert, John Shornall
1465	Robert Knight	John Shornall, John Scalton, Christopher Baker
1466	Thomas Warham	John Haynes, Roger Lee, John Sampson
1467	Thomas Warham	Thomas Ungyll, John King, William Carter
1468	William Ray	Christopher Baker, Thomas Payne, John Davy

1469	William Ray	Christopher Baker, Thomas Pert, John White
1470	Walter Orchard	Thomas Pert, John Scalton, John White
1471	Walter Orchard	John Scalton, Thomas Wilcox, Walter Constantine
1472	Thomas Ungyll	John Sampson, Thomas Wilcox, Walter Constantine
1473	Thomas Ungyll	John Sampson, John Shornall, Andrew Essex
1474	William Carter	Christopher Baker, Andrew Essex, Edmund Denys
1475	Thomas Pert	Christopher Baker, Thomas Kydd, Robert Crosby
1476	Thomas Pert	John White, Robert Crosby, Piers Baily
1477	William Carter	John White, Piers Baily, John Berns
1478	Christopher Baker	Andrew Essex, Thomas Kydd, John Berns
1479	John White	Andrew Essex, Thomas Kydd, Robert Crosby
1480	William Ray	Walter Constantine, William Chacombe, Robert Tyrell
1481	William Carter	Thomas Payne, William Chacombe, John Ruddock
1482	John White	Thomas Kydd, Robert Crosby, Walter Wilson
1483	Christopher Baker	Stephen Scales, Christopher Kechyn, John Davy
1484	Christopher Baker	Stephen Scales, Christopher Kechyn, John Davy
1485	Thomas Kydd	Robert Crosby, William Chacombe, Walter Wilson
1486	Thomas Kydd	Thomas Bynckes, Symon Birlingham, John Pope
1487	William Carter	Thomas Bynckes, John Pope, Roger Ovenell

174

1488	Robert Crosby	Christopher Kechyn, Roger Ovenell, William Barfoot
1489	William Carter	Christopher Kechyn, Thomas Bynckes, William Barfoot
1490	Thomas Kydd	Thomas Bynckes, Walter Wilson, Symon Birlingham
1491	Thomas Kydd	Walter Wilson, John Pope, John Manecke
1492	Robert Crosby	John Manecke, Thomas Mauncy, John Bird
1493	Robert Crosby	Thomas Mauncy, Roger Ovenell, John Bird
1494	William Chacombe	Roger Ovenell, John Davy, Thomas Smart
1495	Thomas Bynckes	Thomas Smart, Richard Smyth, Thomas Clement
1496	Thomas Bynckes	Symon Birlingham, Thomas Clement, Thomas Wood
1497	John Pope	Roger Ovenell, John Bird, Thomas Wood
1498	John Pope	Roger Ovenell, John Bird, Richard Smyth
1499	Thomas Kydd	Thomas Mauncy, Thomas Smart, John Wyneates
1500	Thomas Bynckes	Thomas Smart, John Wyneates, Philip Cosyn
1501	Thomas Bynckes	Thomas Wood, Philip Cosyn, William Reynold
1502	John Pope	Thomas Wood, John Bird, William Reynold
1503	John Pope	John Davy, John Bird, Richard Smyth
1504	John Davy	Richard Smyth, John Wyneates, John Jackson
1505	John Bird	John Wyneates, John Jackson, William Cony
1506	Roger Ovenell	Thomas Wood, William Cony, Humphrey Cooke

1507	Richard Smyth	Philip Cosyn, Humphrey Cooke, William Prest
1508	Thomas Smart	John Wyneates, John Jackson, William Prest
1509	Thomas Wood	William Reynold, William Cony, John Dryver
1510	Thomas Bynckes	Humphrey Cooke, ( ), Robert Isodson
1511	John Wyneates	Philip Cosyn, John Jackson, Robert Isodson
1512	Philip Cosyn	John Jackson, William Cony, Thomas Hall
1513	Thomas Smart	William Cony, Thomas Hall, Christopher Brown
1514	Thomas Bynckes	John Jackson, Christopher Brown, Robert Short

....

| 1519 | Philip Cosyn | Humphrey Cooke, Christopher Brown, Richard Madock |

....

1533	Stephen Punchon	
1534	James Nedam	
1535	James Nedam	

....

1538	Philip Cosyn	William Walker, John Russell, William Collins
1539	? William Walker	
1540	John King	John Russell, John Arnold, Thomas Gyttons
1541	John Russell	
1542	James Nedam	
1543	Richard Madock	Thomas Ellis, Wolston Wynde, William Collins

1544	William Walker	John Arnold, d., *Thomas Ellis*, John Tryll, Richard Tylton
1545	Thomas Sheres	John Abbot, William Lugg, Francis Stelecrag
1546	Richard Amrys	Wolston Wynde, Richard Tylton, George King
1547	Thomas Ellis	John Tryll, Francis Stelecrag, Lawrence Bradshaw
1548	John Abbot	Richard Tylton, Lawrence Bradshaw, George Stalker
1549	John Russell	Lawrence Bradshaw, George King, Thomas Shereman
1550	Wolston Wynde	Richard Tylton, George King, William Mortimer
1551	Lawrence Bradshaw	John Tryll, Francis Selecrag, Edward Whytwell
1552	Richard Amrys	Francis Stelecrag, Thomas Shereman, Thomas Peacock
1553	Thomas Ellis	George King, William Mortimer, John Revell
1554	John Tryll	William Mortimer, Thomas Peacock, William Wetherby
1555	Lawrence Bradshaw	Thomas Peacock, John Revell, William Hamond
1556	Wolston Wynde	John Revell, William Wetherby, d, *Thomas Shereman*, John Owtyng
1557	John Russell	Thomas Peacock, William Hamond, Christopher Riddlesden
1558	John Abbot	William Mortimer, John Owtyng, William Ruddock
1559	John Revell	John Owtyng, William Ruddock, William Buttermore
1560	William Mortimer, d., *John Tryll*	Thomas Peacock, Christopher Riddlesden, Richard More

M   177

1561	John Tryll	William Ruddock, William Buttermore, Robert Quoyney
1562	Lawrence Bradshaw	John Owtyng, Christopher Riddlesden, Richard Bradshaw
1563	Thomas Peacock	William Ruddock, Richard More, Henry Wreste
1564	Thomas Peacock	Christopher Riddlesden, Robert Quoyney, John Hawthorne
1565	John Russell, d., *Thomas Peacock*	Christopher Riddlesden, William Buttermore, John Wolmer
1566	William Ruddock	Richard More, Henry Wreste, Richard Smart
1567	Lawrence Bradshaw	Robert Quoyney, Henry Wreste, William Fisher
1568	Christopher Riddlesden	William Buttermore, John Hawthorne, Roger Reynolds
1569	John Owtyng	Richard More, Richard Smart, John Dorrant
1570	Thomas Peacock	Henry Wreste, William Fisher, William Royse
1571	Lawrence Bradshaw	William Buttermore, John Hawthorne, John Lyffe
1572	William Buttermore	Henry Wreste, Roger Reynolds, Anthony Bear
1573	Thomas Peacock	John Hawthorn, John Lyffe, Lawrence Puddle
1574	Lawrence Bradshaw	Henry Wreste, Thomas Harper, Christopher Mortimer
1575	Henry Wreste	Roger Reynolds, John Lyffe, Roger Shers
1576	William Buttermore	John Lyffe, Thomas Townson, William Sylvester
1577	Thomas Peacock	Thomas Harper, Anthony Bear, Thomas Watts

1578	Thomas Harper	Anthony Bear, Lawrence Puddle, Robert Cawsey
1579	Lawrence Bradshaw	Thomas Townson, Christopher Mortimer, Thomas Hubie, d., *John Bond*
1580	Lawrence Bradshaw	Thomas Townson, Thomas Watts, Gregory Newland
1581	May 22nd, Thomas Peacock	
1581	Thomas Townson	Roger Reynolds, Roger Shers, Gilbert Thomplinson
1582	Roger Reynolds	John Lyffe, William Sylvester, *Robert Cawsey*, William Taylor
1583	John Lyffe	Roger Shers, John Bond, John Bland
1584	John Lyffe	Robert Cawsey, Gregory Newland, Thomas Gittins
1585	Anthony Bear	John Bond, Gilbert Thomplinson, Richard Smith
1586	Thomas Townson	Thomas Watts, William Taylor, *John Bland*, John Saxby
1587	Roger Shers	Thomas Gittins, *John Bland*, Thomas Eaton, George Bowes
1588	John Bond	Gilbert Thomplinson, Richard Smith, Robert Maskall
1589	Thomas Watts	Richard Smith, John Saxby, Thomas Hasilloe
1590	John Bland	Thomas Eaton, John Evans, William Allen
1591	Richard Smith	John Saxby, George Bowes, *Robert Maskall*, Richard King
1592	Roger Shers	Robert Maskall, *John Evans*, William Allen, John Abbott

1593	John Saxby	William Allen, Robert Ledyman, d., *R. Kinge*, John Ansell
1594	William Allen	R. Kinge, J. Ansell, J. Fymby
1595	William Allen	T. Haslowe, J. Worrall, T. Payne
1596	John Bland	J. Worrall, J. Toulson, J. Abbott
1597	John Saxbye	R. Kinge, J. Abbott, P. Cobb
1598	Richard Smith	J. Awnsell, P. Streete, T. Armatroyding
1599	Richard Kinge	G. Abbott, R. Wyatt, R. Ffysher
1600	John Worrall	P. Cobbe, R. Kerbye, d., *R. Bushe*, J. Sharpe
1601	John Ansell	R. Wyatt, G. Isack, J. Petley
1602	Geoffrey Abbott	R. Bushe, J. Hedlund, J. Reeve
1603	Peter Cobbe	R. Ffysher, J. Sharpe, R. Bentley
1604	Richard Wyatt	J. Sharpe, J. Petley, E. Harwyn
1605	Richard Wyatt	G. Isack, J. Reeve, W. Wilson
1606	John Ansell	J. Petley, R. Bentley, T. Ffawcon
1607	John Sharpe	J. Hedlund, H. Harwyn, J. Joyse, *J. Cockshutt*
1608	George Isack	J. Reeve, W. Willson, E. Moore
1609	John Petley	H. Harmyn, T. Ffawcon, W. Wheatley
1610	John Reeve	W. Wilson, J. Brock, P. Thornton
1611	John Reeve	T. Ffawcon, E. Moore, W. Bonner

1612	John Worrall	J. Cockfield, P. Thornton, T. Edmond
1613	Thomas Ffawcon	E. Moore, W. Bonner, T. Haydon
1614	John Cockfield	J. Brock, T. Edmond, J. Daye
1615	Edward Moore	P. Thornton, J. Daye, A. Messenger
1616	Richard Wyatt	W. Bonner, W. Burnham, W. Kinge
1617	Peter Cobb	T. Edmond, A. Messenger, T. Rushall
1618	George Isack	J. Daye, W. King, J. Blinckhorne
1619	John Petley	W. Wheatley, T. Rushall, E. Baker
1620	William Bonner	A. Messenger, J. Bird, d. *J. Blinckhorne*, T. Blemell
1621	John Daye	William King, d., *Thomas Rushall*, E. Baker, J. Merryman
1622	A. Messenger	E. Baker, J. Blemell, T. Ffenor
1623	Thomas Rushall	J. Blinkhorne, G. Arnold, W. Guye
1624	Edward Baker	T. Blemell, J. Merryman, R. Norman
1625	John Blinckhorne	J. Merryman, T. Ffenor, T. Potham
1626	Thomas Blemell	T. Ffenor, W. Grey, R. Standish
1627	John Merryman	G. Arnold, R. Smyth, A. Forman
1628	Thomas Ffenor	T. Potham, R. Standish, J. Prestwood
1629	George Arnold	R. Smyth, A. Jarman, M. Bancks
1630	Thomas Potham	R. Standish, J. Prestwood, H. Cordwyn

1631	Ralph Smyth	A. Jarman, W. Freeman, J. Brewer
1632	Richard Standish	J. Prestwood, M. Bancks, T. Birckhead
1633	Anthony Jarman	W. Freeman, H. Cordwyn, J. Hilliard
1634	John Prestwood	M. Bankcs, J. Brewer, T. Brewer
1635	William Freeman	H. Cordwyn, T. Birkett, J. Copland
1636	Mathew Bancks	J. Brewer, J. Hilliard, T. Kinge
1637	Henry Cordwyn	T. Birkett, J. Copland, R. Sanderson
1638	John Brewer	J. Hilliard, T. Kinge, J. Hone
1639	Thomas Birkett	J. Copland, R. Sanderson, P. Petley
1640	John Hilliard	T. Kinge, J. Hone, R. Wade
1641	John Copland	R. Sanderson, P. Petley, G. Andrewes
1642	Thomas Kinge	J. Hone, R. Wade, T. Hunt
1643	R. Sanderson	P. Petley, G. Andrewes, S. Lynn
1644	Peter Petley	R. Wade, T. Hunt, H. Standish
1645	Richard Wade	G. Andrewes, J. Berrey, N. Guy
1646	George Andrewes	J. Berrey, d., *S. Lynn*, H. Standish, J. Read, sen.
1647	Samuel Lynn	H. Standish, N. Guy, T. Dorebarre
1648	Hugh Standish	N. Guy, J. Read, sen., J. Joyse
1649	Nicholas Guy, d., *Thomas Birkett*	J. Read, sen., T. Dorebarre, T. Atkinson
1650	John Read, sen., d., *John Brewer*	T. Dorebarre, W. Blunden, R. Ffrith

1651	Thomas Dorebarre	W. Blunden, J. Joyse, W. Taylor
1652	William Blunden	J. Joyse, T. Atkinson, J. Wildgoose
1653	John Joyse	T. Atkinson, R. Smith, G. Gilpin
1654	Thomas Atkinson	N. Woodgate, W. Taylor, H. White
1655	Richard Sanderson	R. Ffrith, T. Edmonds, W. Pilling
1656	Nicholas Woodgate	W. Taylor, J. Wildgoose, J. Darvoll
1657	Richard Ffrith	T. Edmonds, H. White, J. Hawkins
1658	William Taylor	J. Wildgoose, W. Pilling, J. Pitt
1659	Thomas Edmonds	H. White, J. Darvoll, S. Berry
1660	John Wildgoose	W. Pilling, J. Hawkins, W. Ligborne
1661	Henry White	J. Darvoll, J. Pitt, T. Audley
1662	William Pilling	J. Hawkins, S. Berry, J. Seagood
1663	Joseph Darvoll	S. Berry, W. Ligborne, J. Figgins
1664	John Hawkins	W. Ligborne, T. Audley, L. Blanford
1665	Samuel Berry	T. Audley, J. Seagood, W. Wildgoose
1666	Thomas Audley	J. Seagood, J. Figgins, N. Fox
1667	John Seagood	J. Figgins, J. Read, J. King
1668	John Figgins	J. Read, T. Wildgoose, T. Charman
1669	John Read	T. Wildgoose, N. Fox, J. Marshall
1670	John Seagood	N. Fox, J. King, W. Pope

183

1671	Nathaniel Fox	J. King, T. Charman.
		E. Buckley
1672	John King	T. Charman, J. Marshall,
		S. Linn
1673	Thomas Charman	J. Marshall, W. Pope,
		W. Willis
1674	Joseph Marshall	W. Pope, E. Buckley,
		T. Brockwell
1675	William Pope	E. Buckley, T. Brockwell,
		A. Attwell
1676	Edward Buckley	T. Brockwell, T. Attwell,
		R. Jarman
1677	Edward Buckley	T. Attwell, I. Knowles,
		O. Lyde
1678	Thomas Attwell	I. Knowles, B. Spencer,
		B. Lipscombe
1679	Israell Knowles	B. Spencer, H. Wilkins,
		P. Barber
1680	Thomas Brockwell	O. Lydd, B. Lipscombe,
		W. Young
1681	Ben. Spencer	H. Wilkins. N. Kilby, T. Cass
1682	Henry Wilkins	N. Kilby, H. Peirson,
		R. Horton
1683	William Young	H. Pierson, J. Deane,
		C. Stanton
1684	Phillip Barber	J. Deane, R. Horton, J. Chitty
1685	Phillip Barber	J. Deane, R. Horton, J. Chitty
1686	John Deane	T. Cass, W. Gray, W. Peacock
1687	Henry Peirson	R. Horton, C. Stanton,
		T. Buttamore
1688	Thomas Cass	W. Gray, E. Clarke,
		J. Warren
1689	William Gray	T. Kentish, J. Haynes,
		S. Tovey
1690	Robert Horton	E. Clarke, J. Chitty,
		W. Champion
1691	Thomas Kentish	C. Stanton, J. Warren,
		T. Haynes

1692	Edmond Clarke	J. Chitty, S. Tovey, T. Scott
1693	Charly Stanton	J. Warren, W. Champion H. Joyce
1694	Joseph Chitty	H. Pottinger, E. Withers, J. Rawlins
1695	John Warren	E. Withers, W. Miller, W. Biggs
1696	Edward Withers	T. Scott, H. Joyce, S. Knapp
1697	Thomas Scott	H. Joyce, T. Buttamore, T. Donning
1698	Mathew Banckes	W. Champion, J. Rawlins, W. Attwell
1699	Henry Joyce	W. Mills, S. Knapp, R. Norman
1700	William Champion	T. Buttamore, J. Collyer, J. Freeman
1701	Thomas Buttamore	J. Rawlings, E. Rainsford, W. Lawe
1702	Jasper Rawlins	Capt. Knapp, R. Norman, E. Calcutt
1703	Samuel Knapp	E. Rainsford, J. Greene, A. Arlidge
1704	John Foltrop	R. Norman, J. Freeman, A. Jordan
1705	Edward Rainsford	J. Greene, T. Lockwood, T. Dennett
1706	Richard Norman	J. Freeman, R. Calcutt, G. Faulkner
1707	John Greene	T. Lockwood, A. Arlidge, J. Abbott
1708	John Freeman	R. Calcutt, R. Andrews, S. Rickward
1709	Thomas Lockwood	A. Arlidge, T. Howes, T. Bowcher
1710	Robert Calcutt	R. Andrews, G. Faulkner, R. Hedges

1711	Sir John Cass	A. Jordon, S. Rickward, T. Arnold
1712	Abraham Arlidge	T. Dennett, J. Brydon, P. Rogerson
1713	Robert Andrews	G. Faulkner, J. Chamberlen, H. Stevenson
1714	Thomas Dennett	S. Rickward, J. Moore, J. Walker
1715	George Faulkner	J. Chamberlen, J. Brittaine, J. Headland
1716	Samuel Rickward	J. Moore, T. Bowcher, T. Dawson
1717	John Chamberlen	J. Brittaine, d., *T. Bowcher*, T. Arnold, T. Arlidge
1718	James Grove	T. Arnold, P. Rogers, E. Cordwell
1719	John Moore	P. Rogerson, W. Abby, S. Boughton
1720	Thomas Bowcher	W. Abby, J. Headland, T. Boddell
1721	William Abby	J. Headland, T. Dawson, E. Oliver
1722	John Headland	T. Dawson, W. Ogborne, W. Hazard
1723	Thomas Dawson	W. Ogborne, J. Edden, R. Grasswell
1724	William Ogborne	J. Edden, T. Arlidge, J. Buckland
1725	John Edden	T. Arlidge, S. Boughton, W. Smith
1726	Sir William Ogborne	S. Boughton, T. Boddell, E. Littlefoild
1727	Samuel Boughton	T. Boddell, T. Willmore, T. Davis
1728	Thomas Boddell	T. Willmore, J. Spencer, J. Brittan
1729	Thomas Willmore	J. Spencer, E. Bowcher, Capt. B. Osgood

186

1730	Joseph Spencer	E. Bowcher, M. Deane, B. Barlow
1731	Edward Bowcher	M. Deane, J. Meard, J. Williams
1732	Matthew Deane	R. Norman, J. Prater, J. Russell
1733	Richard Norman	J. James. J. Chitty, T. Haddon
1734	John James	J. Meard, B. Osgood, N. Ward
1735	John Meard	S. Burgin, B. Barlow, N. Benbridge
1736	Samuel Burgin	J. Prater, Col. J. Williams, S. Horton
1737	John Prater	J. Chitty, d., *Maj. B. Osgood*, T. Haddon, R. Plimpton
1738	Major B. Osgood	Col. J. Williams, N. Ward, S. Hawkins
1739	Colonel J. Williams	T. Haddon, N. Benbridge, J. Brookes
1740	Thomas Haddon	N. Ward, T. Ripley, T. Keene
1741	Nat. Ward, d. *Nat. Benbridge*	T. Ripley, G. Newland, J. Bush
1742	Thos. Ripley	G. Newland, R. Plimpton, J. Cordwell
1743	George Newland	R. Plimpton, S. Hawkins, W. Champion
1744	Robert Plimpton	S. Hawkins, J. Bush, J. Stedman
1745	Samuel Hawkins	J. Cordwell, W. Champion, B. Sparruck
1746	John Cordwell	W. Champion, J. Stedman, A. Mason
1747	W. Champion, d., *James Stedman*	J. Stedman, *B. Sparruck*, B. Sparruck, *R. Boulton*, A. Natt
1748	Barth. Sparruck	R. Boulton, T. Moore, Col. J. Steere

1749	Richard Boulton	T. Moore, R. Langton, H. Denning
1750	Thomas Moore	R. Langton, J. Lamborne, J. Dutton
1751	Richard Langton	J. Lamborne, J. Price, W. Robinson
1752	James Lamborne	J. Price, A. Russell, J. Lawrence
1753	John Price	A. Russell, R. Sparkes, T. Bates
1754	Augustus Russell	R. Sparkes, T. Funge, E. Johnson
1755	Richard Sparkes	T. Funge, T. Radcliffe, A. Pullen
1756	Thomas Funge	T. Radcliffe, A. Mason, R. Plimpton
1757	Thomas Radcliffe	A. Mason, W. Reynolds, W. Alingham
1758	Anthony Mason	W. Reynolds, S. Chitty, R. Jupp
1759	William Reynolds	S. Chitty, W. Robinson, J. Holden
1760	Samuel Chitty	W. Robinson, R. Mount, S. Oliver
1761	William Robinson	R. Mount, E. Johnson, d., *I. Ware*, J. Spencer
1762	Richard Mount	I. Ware, A. Pullen, R. Day
1763	Isaac Ware	A. Pullen, W. Bigg, J. Read
1764	Abraham Pullen	W. Bigg, R. Plimpton, W. Witcher
1765	William Bigg	R. Plimpton, W. Allingham, d., *W. Dermer*, A. Atterbury
1766	Robert Plimpton	W. Dermer, R. Jupp, G. Bellas
1767	William Dermer	R. Jupp, J. Biddlecom, W. Jones

1768	Richard Jupp	J. Biddlecom, S. Oliver, J. B. Turner
1769	Joseph Biddlecom	S. Oliver, J. Spencer, T. Whittaker
1770	Sanders Oliver	J. Read, W. Witcher, T. Steedman
1771	John Read	W. Witcher, d., *A. Atterbury*, A. Atterbury, *G. Ballas*, R. Withers
1772	Abraham Atterbury	G. Ballas, W. Jones, R. Fawson
1773	William Jones	J. B. Turner, T. Whittaker, M. Fairless, d., *T. Jernegan*
1774	John B. Turner	T. Whittaker, T. Steedman, J. Payne
1775	Thomas Whittaker, d., *J. Biddlecom*	T. Steedman, R. Withers, J. Buckland
1776	Thomas Steedman	R. Withers, T. Jernegan, d., *S. Hanning*, C. Mills
1777	Robert Withers	S. Hanning, R. Jupp, Jnr., E. Gibbs
1778	Samuel Hanning	R. Jupp, Jnr., J. Taine, T. Russell
1779	Richard Jupp	J. Taine, J. Buckland, T. Hudson
1780	John Taine	J. Buckland, T. Flight, J. Johnson
1781	James Buckland	W. Dermer, John Jordon, W. Jupp
1782	Thomas Flight	J. Jordan, C. Mills, W. Palmer
1783	John Jordan	C. Mills, E. Gibbs, T. Edgerton
1784	Charles Mills	E. Gibbs, T. Russell, W. Higgins
1785	Edward Gibbs	T. Russell, T. Hudson, S. Parker

1786	Thomas Russell	T. Hudson, P. Thompson, J. Webb
1787	Thomas Hudson	P. Thompson, J. Johnson, J. Brayne
1788	Peter Thompson	J. Johnson, T. Edgerton, W. Lawrence
1789	Joel Johnson	T. Edgerton, W. Higgins, T. Mutter
1790	Thomas Edgerton	W. Higgins, G. Shakespear, J. Suter
1791	William Higgins	W. Lawrence, W. Staines, E. Wells
1792	William Lawrence	Ald. Staines, R. Woodyer, W. Arrow
1793	Ald. Staines	R. Woodyer, J. Suter, J. Tappen
1794	Richard Woodyer	J. Suter, T. Hardy, J. Yellowley
1795	John Suter	T. Russell, R. Hunt, W. Ayscough
1796	James Wheeler	W. Arrow, P. Dunkley, J. Rosher
1797	William Arrow	P. Dunkley, J. Yellowley, N. Wright
1798	Peter Dunkley, d., *Richard Jupp, d., Sir William Staines*	J. Yellowley, W. Ayscough, T. Taylor
1799	Joseph Yellowley	J. Sutter, N. Wright, C. Iliffe
1800	Nathaniel Wright	T. Taylor, R. Golden, J. Golden
1801	Thomas Taylor	R. Golden, C. Iliffe, T. Flight
1802	Robert Golden	C. Iliffe, d., *Sir W. Staines*, J. Golden, J. Vickerman
1803	John Golden	P. Norris, T. W. Preston, J. Taylor
1804	Thomas W. Preston	W. Smith, J. Champion, T. Russell

1805	William Smith	J. Champion, W. Norris, S. Cosser
1806	William Norris	B. Flight, T. Flight, J. Champion
1807	Banister Flight	T. Flight, J. Vickerman, R. Porter
1808	Thomas Flight	J. Vickerman, J. Spencer, W. Hawksworth
1809	John Vickerman	J. Spencer, J. Taylor, A. Creaton
1810	John Spencer	J. Taylor, T. Russell, D. Westbrook
1811	John Taylor	T. Russell, D. Schofield, J. F. Buhl
1812	Thomas Russell	J. Schofield, R. Porter, W. Lumley
1813	John Schofield	R. Porter, A. Creaton, R. Field
1814	Robert Porter	A. Creaton, D. Westbrook, J. Wilkinson
1815	Albon Creaton	D. Westbrook, J. F. Buhl, J. Flight
1816	David Westbrook	J. F. Buhl, W. Lumley, E. Trimmer
1817	John Frederick Buhl	W. Lumley, R. Field, J. Rosher
1818	William Lumley	R. Field, J. Wilkinson, R. Ashton
1819	Richard Field	J. Wilkinson, J. Flight, T. Lett
1820	John Wilkinson	J. Flight, E. Trimmer, J. Bury
1821	Joseph Flight	E. Trimmer, J. Rosher, H. Hurle
1822	Edward Trimmer	J. Rosher, R. Ashton, T. Reid
1823	Jeremiah Rosher	R. Ashton, T. Lett, J. Simmons
1824	Robert Ashton	T. Lett, J. Bury, d., J. Yellowley, Jnr.
1825	Thomas Lett	J. E. Cook, T. Long, d., W. Woodyer

1826	John E. Cook	H. Hurle, J. Yellowley, Jnr. J. Richardson, d., *P. J. Harrison*
1827	Henry Hurle	J. Yellowley, Jnr, W. Woodyer, W. Jupp
1828	J. Yellowley, d., *Banister Flight*	W. Woodyer, P. J. Harrison, C. Maxey
1829	William Woodyer	P. J. Harrison, W. Jupp, R. Hillcock
1830	P. J. Harrison	W. Jupp, C. Maxey, W. Payne
1831	W. Jupp	C. Maxey, R. Hillcock, M. Warton
1832	Charles Maxey	R. Hillcock, W. Payne, W. P. Ulgate
1833	Mat. Warton	W. P. Ulgate, J. Taylor, J. Kershaw
1834	W. Phil. Ulgate	J. Taylor, J. Kershaw, T. W. Snelson
1835	T. W. Snelson	T. Wright, J. Watts, T. Long
1837	Thomas Flight	J. Watts, T. Long, W. F. Pocock
1838	J. Wilkinson	T. Long, W. F. Pocock, E. Staple
1839	Thomas Long	W. F. Pocock, E. Staple, T. Ayscough
1840	William F. Pocock	E. Staple, T. Ayscough, T. Flight, Jnr.
1841	Edward Staple	T. Ayscough, T. Flight, Jnr., W. Churchill
1842	Thomas Ayscough	J. Flight, Jnr, W. Churchill, J. Harvey
1843	Thomas Flight, Jnr	W. Churchill, J. Harvey, J. Fleetwood
1844	William Churchill	J. Harvey, J. Fleetwood, T. W. Browne
1845	Thomas Long	J. Fleetwood, T. W. Browne, M. Savory

1846	John Fleetwood	T. W. Browne, M. Savory, J. Foot
1847	R. W. Kennard	J. Foot, J. Taylor, J. Browne
1848	Ald. W. Lawrence	J. Taylor, J. Browne, R. S. Jupp
1849	John Foot	J. Browne, R. S. Jupp, T. Martyr
1850	James Browne	R. S. Jupp, T. Martyr, C. Rosher
1851	Richard Samuel Jupp	T. Martyr, C. Rosher, J. Hurst
1852	Charles Rosher	J. Hurst, J. Allen, H. Rosher
1853	William Churchill	J. B. Rosher, H. Rosher, R. Waylat
1854	Henry Rosher	J. Allen, R. Waylat, J. F. Bury
1855	James F Bury	T. Lett, J. Atkinson, E. Ward
1856	Ald. W. Lawrence	E. Ward, F. W. E. Jowers, T. G. Smith
1857	Thomas Lett	F. W. E. Jowers, T. G. Smith, T. Finden
1858	Edward Ward	T. G. Smith, T. Finden, G. Faith
1859	F. W. E. Jowers	T. Finden, G. Faith, T. A. Brew
1860	Thomas G. Smith, d., *Thomas Finden, d., Sir J. C. Lawrence*	G. Faith, T. A. Brew, J. Archer
1861	George Faith	T. A. Brew, J. Archer, d., *R. Warton*, J. C. Smith
1862	Thomas A. Brew	J. C. Smith, d., *W. Biggerstaff*, R. Warton, R. J. Stuckey
1863	Robert Warton	R. J. Stuckey, W. Biggerstaff, J. Blyth
1864	R. J. Stuckey	W. Biggerstaff, J. Blyth, G. Rosher
1865	William Biggerstaff	John Blyth, W. Rosher, E. Rosher

1866	John Blyth	W. Rosher, E. Rosher, J. M. Morris
1867	Edward Rosher	J. M. Morris, G. Hensman, W. H. Warton
1868	Edward Ward	G. Hensman, W. H. Warton, W. Robertson
1869	George Hensman	W. H. Warton, W. Robertson, B. Jacob
1870	W. H. Warton	W. Robertson, B. Jacob, J. T. Preston
1871	William Robertson	B. Jacob, J. T. Preston, R. S. Faulconer
1872	Benjamin Jacob	J. T. Preston, R. S. Faulconer, S. W. Preston
1873	Joseph T. Preston	R. S. Faulconer, S. W. Preston, J. Foot
1874	R. S. Faulconer	S. W. Preston, J. Foot, G. H. Ellis, d., *T. D. D. Robertson*
1875	Stanley W. Preston	J. Foot, T. D. D. Robertson, R. Grace
1876	John Foot	T. D. D. Robertson, R. Grace, J. P. Long
1877	T. D. D. Robertson	R. Grace, J. P. Long, S. Gibbins
1878	Richard Grace	J. P. Long, S. Gibbins, J. W. Browne
1879	J. Pollock Long	S. Gibbins, J. E. Cook, A. Preston
1880	Samuel Gibbins	J. E. Cook, A. Preston, T. W. Long
1881	Alfred Preston	T. W. Long, W. W. Pocock, F. P. Keysell
1882	Thomas W. Long	W. W. Pocock, F. P. Keysell, F. Rosher
1883	W. W. Pocock	G. S. Nottage, F. Rosher, H. J. Kennard
1884	G. S. Nottage, d., *John E. Cook*	F. Rosher, H. J. Kennard, H. C. Smith

1885	F. P. Keysell	H. J. Kennard, H. C. Smith, A. Rosher
1886	H. J. Kennard	H. C. Smith, A. Rosher, B. Fletcher
1887	H. C. Smith	A. Rosher, B. Fletcher, W. Robertson
1888	A. Rosher	B. Fletcher, W. Robertson, T. Robertson
1889	Banister Fletcher	W. Robertson, T. Robertson, B. J. Jacob
1890	J. W. Browne	T. Robertson, B. J. Jacob, W. Faith
1891	T. Robertson	B. J. Jacob, W. Faith, N. Smith
1892	B. J. Jacob	W. Faith, N. Smith, Edward Smith
1893	H. Harben	N. Smith, E. Smith, J. Jacob
1894	N. Smith	E. Smith, J. Jacob, J. H. Gibbins
1895	Edward Smith	J. Jacob, J. H. Gibbins, J. C. Preston
1896	Jesse Jacob	J. H. Gibbins, J. C. Preston, A. Jacob
1897	J. H. Gibbins	J. C. Preston, A. Jacob, T. R. Smith
1898	J. C. Preston	A. Jacob, T. R. Smith, J. Willson
1899	A. Jacob	T. R. Smith, J. Willson, W. Smith
1900	T. R. Smith	J. Willson, W. Smith, P. Preston
1901	J. Willson	W. Smith, P. Preston, E. Field
1902	W. Smith	P. Preston, E. Field, F. A. Crisp
1903	P. Preston	E. Field, F. A. Crisp, G. R. B. Drummond. F. A. Crisp, A. B. Hammond (October)

1904	F. A. Crisp	G. R. B. Drummond, A. B. Hammond, W. Robertson
1905	G. R. B. Drummond	A. B. Hammond, W. Robertson, A. C. Preston
1906	A. B. Hammond	W. Robertson, A. C. Preston, M. H. Pocock.
	W. Robertson (October)	A. C. Preston, M. H. Pocock, C. B. Bartlett (October)
1907	A. C. Preston	M. H. Pocock, C. B. Bartlett, R. Cobay
1908	M. H. Pocock	C. B. Bartlett, R. Cobay, W. R. Cobay
1909	Reverend C. B. Bartlett	R. Cobay, W. R. Cobay, S. W. Morris
1910	R. Cobay	W. R. Cobay, S. W. Morris, J. Hook
1911	W. R. Cobay	S. W. Morris, J. Hook, F. Preston
1912	S. W. Morris	J. Hook, F. Preston, M. Smith. M. Smith, W. W. Pullein (April)
1913	J. Hook	M. Smith, W. W. Pullein, F. G. Fitch
1914	M. Smith	W. W. Pullein, F. G. Fitch, F. Sutton
1915	W. W. Pullein	F. G. Fitch, F. Sutton, E. T. Pullein
1916	F. G. Fitch	F. Sutton, E. T. Pullein, W. T. Birts
1917	F. Sutton	E. T. Pullein, W. T. Birts, W. J. Minn
1918	E. T. Pullein	W. T. Birts, W. J. Minn, E. S. Preston
1919	W. T. Birts	W. J. Minn, E. S. Preston, C. Denny
1920	W. J. Minn	E. S. Preston, C. Denny W. H. Evans

1921	E. S. Preston	C. Denny, W. H. Evans, J. H. Browne
1922	C. Denny	W. H. Evans, J. H. Browne, F. Barnes
1923	W. H. Evans	J. H. Browne, F. Barnes, D. W. Stable
1924	J. H. Browne	F. Barnes, D. W. Stable, H. W. Preston
1925	D. W. Stable	H. W. Preston, F. A. Smith, W. Jacob
1926	H. W. Preston	F. A. Smith, W. Jacob, G. D. Minn
1927	F. A. Smith	W. Jacob, G. D. Minn, C. A. Robertson
1928	W. Jacob	G. D. Minn, C. A. Robertson, L. Jacob
1929	G. D. Minn	C. A. Robertson, L. Jacob, R. E. Smith
1930	L. Jacob	R. E. Smith, F. O. Keysell, F. S. Punnett. F. O. Keysell, F. S. Punnett, R. H. Smith (January)
1931	F. O. Keysell	J. R. Lancaster, H. C. Preston, F. M. Smith
1932	J. R. Lancaster	H. C. Preston, F. M. Smith, A. Roberts
1933	H. C. Preston	F. M. Smith, A. Roberts, F. S. Sutton
1934	F. M. Smith	A. Roberts, F. S. Sutton, F. Hugh Smith
1935	J. H. Freeman	F. S. Sutton, F. Hugh Smith, G. Smith
1936	B. F. Fletcher	F. Hugh Smith, G. Smith, A. E. Robertson
1937	F. Hugh Smith	G. Smith, A. E. Robertson, R. Jacob
1938	G. Smith	A. E. Robertson, R. Jacob, A. E. Bernays

197

1939	A. E. Robertson	R. Jacob, A. E. Bernays, W. T. W. Birts
1940	R. Jacob	A. E. Bernays, W. T. W. Birts, H. W. Morris
1941	A. E. Bernays	W. T. W. Birts, H. W. Morris, R. H. Smith
1942	A. E. Bernays	H. W. Morris, R. H. Smith, H. U. Fletcher
1943	H. W. Morris	H. U. Fletcher, J. G. King, A. B. Rosher
1944	H. U. Fletcher	J. G. King, A. B. Rosher, G. M. Hamilton
1945	J. G. King	A. B. Rosher, G. M. Hamilton, A. J. M. Binny
1946	G. M. Hamilton	A. J. M. Binny, F. R. Freeman, A. Faith
1947	A. J. M. Binny	F. R. Freeman, A. Faith, Ald. Sir Leslie Boyce
1948	F. R. Freeman	A. Faith, Ald. Sir Leslie Boyce, R. C. Barnes
1949	A. Faith	R. C. Barnes, J. B. Rosher, Ald. C. L. Ackroyd
1950	R. C. Barnes	J. B. Rosher, Ald. C. L. Ackroyd, K. M. Roberts
1951	J. B. Rosher	Ald. C. L. Ackroyd, K. M. Roberts, W. W. Dove
1952	Ald. C. L. Ackroyd	K. M. Roberts, W. W. Dove, G. W. Ridley
1953	K. M. Roberts	W. W. Dove, G. W. Ridley, A. M. D. Robertson
1954	W. W. Dove	G. W. Ridley, A. M. D. Robertson, A. W. Preston
1955	G. W. Ridley	A. M. D. Robertson, A. W. Preston, H. M. Merriman
1956	A. M. D. Robertson	A. W. Preston, H. M. Merriman, R. W. Gordon Dill

1957	A. W. Preston	H. M. Merriman, R. W. Gordon Dill, B. J. Nicholson
1958	H. M. Merriman	R. W. Gordon Dill, B. J. Nicholson, G. Lewis, F. Grece
1959	R. W. Gordon Dill	B. J. Nicholson, G. Lewis, F. Grece, Ald. Sir Edmund Stockdale
1960	B. J. Nicholson	G. Lewis F. Grece, Ald. Sir Edmund Stockdale, F. Halliburton Smith
1961	G. Lewis F. Grece	F. Halliburton Smith, D. L. Jacob, H. F. Groves
1962	F. Halliburton Smith	D. L. Jacob, H. F. Groves, H. M. Mace
1963	D. L. Jacob	H. F. Groves, H. M. Mace, K. B. Jacob
1964	H. F. Groves	H. M. Mace, K. B. Jacob, F. Morton-Smith
1965	H. M. Mace	K. B. Jacob, F. Morton-Smith, F. C. Braby

LIST OF CLERKS AND BEADLES*

<hr>

Date of
Appointment

1438–(1448)	William Mendham
1452–(1463)	'Thomas'
1482	'Hugh'
1483	John Braban (Clerk)
1483	Thomas Batman
1487	( ) Banaster
1489	Robert Pert
1490	John Forster (Clerk)
1500	Harry Bagott
1510	Thomas Cutler
1515	'Wayter' (March–June)
1515	George Maxwell
1541	Bartholemew Sampson
1543	Henry Townson
1544	Richard Burdon
1561	Richard Sowthye
1563	Robert Armstrong
1566	John FitzJohn

CLERKS

1573	John FitzJohn
1595	Thomas Bowes
1602	Thomas Tanner
1636	Peter Hodgson
1642	Andrew Baker
1652	Roger Goodday
1674	Thomas Ley
1683	John Smalley
1685	James Stone

* Until 1573 Clerks and Beadles are not clearly distinguished.

1709	Joseph Knapp
1712	Richard Hutton
1723	John Michell
1728	Nathaniel Poole
1750	R. Prater
1757	Thomas Wall
1778	Hawkins Wall
1798	Richard Webb Jupp
1852	Edward Basil Jupp
1878	Stanton William Preston
1902	Joseph Hutton Freeman
1935	Henry Carl Osborne, MC
1960	George Baillie Barstow [Capt. RN (Ret'd)]

BEADLES

1608	John Adams
1629	Samuel Taleford
1632	John Walter
1657	Thomas Heake
1665	Joseph Hutchinson
1687	Samuel Hughes
1699	Edmund Clarke
1703	John Manuell
1731	Thomas Barnard
1738	Benjamin Barlow
1739	Richard Danes
1741	Richard Vestille
1767	Richard Young
1771	William Bigg
1810	William Lewis
1843	Thomas Standage
1856	Thomas Carter
1895	Frank Carter
1928	Frederick William Powell
1964	William Henry Hopkins

APPENDIX 4

THE PLATE AND JEWELS
AND THEIR HISTORY

by Charles Oman

It is unlikely that the Carpenters had any plate before they had a hall since its care would have been an embarrassment to the officer in whose charge it would have had to be placed. The first piece, however, must have arrived soon after the erection of the Hall, since its donor, Thomas Moysaunte, is mentioned in 1439. The possession of plate was much more than a status symbol since in difficult times it could always be pledged or sold—a fact of which the Carpenters were fully aware.

Previous writers on the Company's history discovered three early lists of plate but made no serious attempt to analyse them. The earliest is headed:

'Theis ben the names und Writen Which have yeven certyn Jewelles to the crafte of Carpenters for the honoure and waship of the Felashipe of the same crafte to the use of theire Feste and quater daies in theire common halle holden'.[1]

The first nine items were written by the same hand and from the information which we have about their donors, it is possible to date the document about 1480. At the bottom of the page are written two more items by another hand which also wrote the first six on another sheet (bound up earlier).[2] These are followed by twenty further items added probably by three other hands and taking the list down to about 1520.

The original collection lists five masers and nine spoons. Of the masers Thomas Moysaunte's alone had a cover and was evidently the largest. The others were of varying sizes and we are able to pick up some details regarding them from later descriptions, which usually distinguish them by the device on the enamelled silver medallion in the middle of the bowl, which was described variously as a boss, flower or print. Thus Thomas Sexteyn's maser had a 'blew Rosse' and Symon Jacombe's 'a figur of iiij' (doubtless his mark). Thomas Warham (Master 1457–60) gave 'half a dosen of spones' but they are not described nor are the three other spoons which had arrived separately. The two other early lists[3] are contemporaneous and have been dated to 1513. Both are much damaged but combine to give us an idea as to how the collection was developing. Though the Wardens' accounts make several references to repairs to the masers nothing had been sold since 1480. In 1512 had been bought 'ij salltes wyth a Cov̄ pcellgylt weying xlix hounsys' since no benefactor had seen good to provide this essential feature of an English medieval dinner table. The most important gift had been a standing cup from William Godfrey but the description is both meagre and defective. Five more masers had come in. Nothing comparable to the 'masser wt iij corners' of John Darvallde is now known but the rest appear to have belonged to familiar types and are distinguished by the motif on the print, thus Robert Crosby's had 'a peycokke tell [tail] yn the bosse' whilst William Prest's had 'a ymagg of seynt thomas yn the bosse and a spyer [spear] in his hand'. The number of spoons had grown to twenty-seven. Six 'wt lyons' had come from John White (d. 1485) but the remainder were mainly the proceeds of a new regulation, dating apparently from 1505, which exacted a piece of plate from each successive Junior Warden. Its form was not prescribed but at this period it was nearly always a spoon. The designs of the spoons are not usually mentioned though William Cony gave one with a maidenhead in 1503. From the additions to the end of the lists we learn that in 1513 it was decided to collect a set of apostle spoons on an instalment plan.

The lack of documents covering the years 1516–33 makes it impossible to trace in detail the growth of the collection. Two important additions are recorded in the *Calendar of the Wills in the Court of the Hustings*.[4] In his will dated September 1, 1517, William Cony (Warden 1506–7) left a silver cup with covercle parcel gilt, commonly called 'a Goblett', having a silver gilt coney on the top, whilst Thomas Smart in his will of March 12, 1519, gave a silver-gilt cup 'with my name & my Timber marke'. Hitherto we have had mention only of acquisitions and of repairs but from henceforth we shall have records of the sale and pledging of plate. Owing to the deficiencies of the records we sometimes find references to the disposal of pieces which have not previously been mentioned. It would seem, however, that down to about 1550 the collection was growing regularly.

The Court Minutes give no direct indication as to why it was suddenly decided to realize on most of the plate in the spring of 1558 but it was clearly the cumulative result of a series of demands for money from the Government. The money was raised partly by means of private agreements with members of the Company and partly by sale to the 'goldsmith at the star in Chepe' (John Clerke) who on March 11th bought[5]—

'a flat bowll all gylt w^t owte a cov̄
a goblett wyth a cov̄ ꝑcell gylt
xij spoones wyth gylte emages on ther endes [the apostle spoons] xxiij spones'

Five days later he took—

'a blake nott wyth a fotte and a band and a cov̄ all gylt and ij lytyll masers'

Four spoons had been bought by Warden Howttyng and five senior members took in pledge for £44 os od—

'iiij dossen of spones, a standyng cup w^t a cov̄ ꝑsell gylt, a flatt pece ꝑcell gylt vij sylv̄ pottes, a goblett w^t a cov̄ ꝑcell gylt, a salt ꝑcell gylt'.[6]

Whereas the pieces taken to John Clerke at *The Star* were sold outright, those taken by members of the Company were probably held with an option to re-purchase, but it seems likely that much was never redeemed. When the Company was once more in funds there was always the alternative of buying something in the latest fashion. Thus the next reference to the plate is the record of the acquisition in 1560 of a nest of goblets with a cover, weighing 73 ounces.[7] Purchases were unusual and additions came mostly from the annual gift from the junior warden supplemented occasionally by fines paid in kind. An instance of the latter was the receipt in 1558 of a parcel-gilt pot, weighing 8½ ounces, received from Mistress Ellis, a 'turned over' apprentice. By this date the customary gift from the Junior Warden had ceased to be a spoon. It was commonly some sort of drinking vessel but not usually of much prestige value. For important pieces the Company had to rely on the generosity of Masters or on exchanges. Thus on October 31, 1615, the Court decided to add to the money for the annual gifts from the Junior Warden and his predecessor the proceeds of the sale of certain cups from the collection and £1 11s 11d of petty cash and purchase a silver parcel-gilt ewer and basin.[8] It was delivered on January 22, 1616. The Company is fortunate in the possession of three prestige pieces dating from the reign of James I. They are standing cups of silver-gilt of the most fashionable design of the period. Their covers are surmounted by what was described at the time as a 'pyramid'.[9] They came to be known as the *Election Cups* as they figured prominently at the ceremonial inauguration of the new master and wardens. The collection was built up over the years 1611–13. The first two appear to have arrived in 1611 and were made by a goldsmith whose mark was F and who was a specialist in this type of cup—twenty-three other examples from his shop still survive.[10] They are of almost identical design but the cup given by John Reeve, Master 1610 and 1611, is 24 inches high and is surmounted by the figure of a warrior (Cat. No. 1, Pl. 10), whereas that given by John Ansell, Master 1601 and 1606, is only 19¼ inches high and has only a turned finial at the top of its 'pyramid' (Cat. No. 2, Pl. 10). He may have used it for a short time before passing it to the Company since it bears the hall-mark for 1609–10 whereas the Reeve Cup bears the hall-mark for the current year 1611–12. A third cup, which was sold in 1627, was provided from the Company's funds but it was not until 1613 that Thomas Edmones, Junior Warden 1612, provided a cup for his sucessors in that office (Cat. No. 3, Pl. 10). He evidently bought it from the stock of another goldsmith since it bears a different maker's mark and only superficially matches the others.

An inventory which can be dated to the year 1625[11] gives us an exact account of the collection shortly before it was pruned in order to provide £300 for a forced loan to the King in 1627. The extent of the reduction then made can be gathered from the repetition of the word 'sold' in the margin.

An Inventorye.of all the plate belonginge unto the Companie of Carpenters, London

in domo	Inprimis ffower Garlands given by Mr Trull, Mr Ansell, Mr Thornton and Mr Wheatley.
in domo	ffower Standinge Cupps one given by Mr Ansell another by Mr Edmunde and one [*two* erased] made by Nobles in Mr Reeves tyme [*one sold* in a later hand].
sold	One Bason and Ewer pcell gilt towarde wh. Mr Daye gave vij[li] and Mr Messenger vj[li].

in domo	One Goblett pcell guilt.
sold	ffower dozen and one Spoone.
sold	three stoops guilt.
sold	three saltes pcell guilt w^t their cover.
in domo	ffower Saltes guilt of the guift of Mr Petley, Mr Hedlund, Mr Reeve and Mr Harwyn.
in domo	One Trencher all guilt.
sold	One Neast of guilt broad Boles.
sold	One Neast of Boles pcell guilt given by Mr Condall & Mr Cobb and Mr Messenger.
sold	One Bole pcell guilt given by Mr Fryer.

sould all {
One Neast of Tankards pcell guilt.

One Neast of white potts w^t out knobbs.

One Neast of white potts w^t knobbs given by Mr Wyatt, Mr Abbot & Mr Sharp.

Five deepe Bolles pcell guilt of the guift of Mr Willson, Mr Flower, Mr Cockshutt and Mr Joyce and Mr Moore.

One white cupp of the guift of Mr Bentley.

One guilt Cupp of the guift of Mr Sharpe.

One guilt Cupp of the guift of Mr Wheatley.

One Nest of Guilt Cupps.

One Nest of white Beakers.

One Nest of white ffrench Boles.

One Haunse potte[12] pcell guilt.

One Hanspott all guilt.

One Oxeye[13] pcell guilt.

One Nest of pounced guilt boles two of them given by Mr Thornton.

One Nest of White Bolles given by Mr Bonner.

One Nest of white cupps w^t ffeathers given by Mr Burman.

One Nest of white cupps without ffeathers given by Mr Rushall.

One Nest of Wine bolles pcell guilt given by Mr Baker.

Two guilt cupps venice ffacon given by Mr Blinkhorne.

Two plane white bolles w^t ffeathers of the guift of Mr Bloumell.

Two small white bolles of the guift of Mr Merriman.

One white Beerbolle of the guift of Mr ffenor.
}

sould all {
One white Beere Bolle of the guift of Mr Arnold being second warden.

One white salt w^t out a cover ex dono Gulielmi Guy he being youngest warden.
}

Though the descriptions are meagre several facts are evident. Firstly it will be noticed that not only did nothing survive from the earliest lists but that the oldest pieces dated only from the latter years of Elizabeth I. The weeding was extremely drastic and included pieces which had been held in high estimation such as the fourth Election Cup and the ewer and basin bought in 1615. There is no hint that plate was pledged to members of the Company on this occasion and when Anthony Jarman, Middle Warden, replaced the fourth Election Cup in 1628, it was specially made. It was copied from the Ansell Cup (Cat. No. 4, Pl. 10) by a different goldsmith, though the one who had made the original two was still at work.

The rebuilding of the collection started from the date of the sale by means of the customary gifts from the Junior Wardens, which arrived, though sometimes not punctually, throughout the reign of Charles I and the Commonwealth and were not affected by the recurrent financial crises suffered by the Company. The first of these was occasioned by the need to find the Company's share of the levy imposed on the City by the King and Parliament in 1640–3. On May 17th there was a discussion at the Hall as to the advisability of selling the plate and on the 22nd it was later noted that £90 5s 0d[14] had been received for the pieces sold. This was a very substantial inroad although some of the pieces were sold to members of the Company and eventually returned only to be sold on a later occasion.

The next emergency arose at the beginning of December 1648, when there was a threat that the Hall would be required for billeting troops drafted into the city to suppress any expression of disapproval at the execution of the King and the abolition of the monarchy. On the 15th it was 'ordered that all the plate belonginge unto this Company shalbe sould (excepting the guifts of the assistants of the said Company that are living) and the ffower great standing guilt cuppes & the twoe guilt gobletts that are used to gather quarteridge, and all the plate remaininge unsould, is to be disposed of, by the Master & Wardens as they thinke fitt, for the best safetey & securitie of it for the said Company'.[15] It would seem that it was intended that the Master,

Wardens and Assistants would be personally responsible for the main pieces and for those which they had presented. These appear mostly to have remained at the Hall whilst it was uncertain whether the danger would become actual. The remainder of the plate which was 'sold' (which often meant pledged to a member of the Company) provided a fund some of which was used in gratuities to the billeting officer and to 'severall men of quallitie' who arranged that soldiers should not be quartered in the Hall.[16]

The following years would appear to have passed without incident but another crisis appears to have arisen in 1659, the origin of which remains obscure. We have a list, dated September 13th, headed 'Plate left remaining in the house after the Company had sold some'. It is not clear whether this was a genuine sale or another instance of pledging to members but sixteen pieces were involved, weighing 199½ ounces.[17] After this additions continued to be made until 1666. These included the tankard bearing the hall-mark for 1653–4, due from John Hawkins who was Junior Warden in 1657, but actually received on September 11, 1660.

Had the Great Fire reached Carpenters' Hall the Company would have been doubly unfortunate since in 1664 it had authorized an expensive addition to the structure. To pay for this recourse was made to the sale of the plate on October 26, 1666.[18] Since the money had to be raised just over a month after the Great Fire the pruning had to be drastic as there could be no question of members of the Company taking pieces in pledge. All that was left was the four Election Cups, the Hawkins tankard, one salt, seven drinking vessels of various sorts, and 'six gold chains in a box'. At the end of this list are added the customary gifts of the Junior Wardens for the years 1667–74. Amongst these were:

'1 Aug., 1667 It. 1 silver Beere Bowl of the guift of Mr Figgon.[19]
19 Sept., 1672 It. one silver bowle of the guift of Mr Charman.' These are the two cups on baluster stems, almost a pair, which have survived (Cat. Nos. 7 & 9, Pl. 12).

It is unfortunate that the Court Books generally record only decisions and only occasionally throw light on the previous discussions. The reign of Charles II was of great importance in English financial history and it is clear that the new thinking affected the policy of the Court towards the plate. Since 1558 each financial crisis had been followed by a sale of some of the Company's silver. Though some of it had been pledged to members there had been a continuous turn-over of the collection. It is understandable that the senior members should have resented the unwritten obligation to provide temporary accommodation to the Company, whilst the more junior must have regarded with a certain cynicism the speedy sale of their customary gifts.

The first move towards a purely monetary backing for the Company came as the result of a protest from Mr Lyde, who had served as Junior Warden in 1677, who defaulted on his customary gift of plate and brought up the whole question as a matter of policy at a court held on August 10, 1680, when it was decided as follows:

'On a moson of Mr Lyde it is agreed & Ordered that the sume of fifty shillings shall be accepted in loiu [*sic*] of the Plate wch ye members of this Comp. that serve as Renter warden have used to psent'.[20]

It was not until June 1, 1697, that the next move was made when the minute reads as follows: 'Ordered that such of the Plate as is in the Chest & thought least usefull be sold by ye Ma. & Wardens'.[21] Ever since the Restoration the Government had been disturbed by the knowledge that the supply of silver currency was inadequate and that it was being constantly diminished by conversion into plate. Eventually Parliament produced in 1696–7 a statute (8 & 9 Will. 3, c. 8) entitled *'An Act for the encouraging the bringing in of wrought plate to be coined'.* We are not concerned with the attempt to discourage the manufacture of plate by raising the standard of its silver content (which is generally held to have been unsuccessful), but it is clear that it did give a fillip to those who were already thinking of abandoning plate as a form of investment in favour of a deposit at the newly founded Bank of England.

There is no record of what the Masters and Wardens sold in 1697 beyond that it weighed 100 ounces and fetched £26 10s 0d.[22] But an inventory dated September 27, 1711, shows that there was little left. It reads:

'The Companys Iron Chest is D^r to ye following plate & lockt up this day vizt.

4 Gilt Cupps & Covers	four
1 large silver Cupp puncht round with figures	one

1 silver Tankard   one
2 silver Cupps with feet   two
4 Embroidered Capps for yᵉ Master & Wardens
All yᵉ above pticulars made use of on Election day'.[23]

All the above survive with the exception of the second item the dates of whose arrival and loss are equally unknown. It is not entirely obvious how the decision was reached as to which pieces should be retained when the reduction was made in 1697. The four gilt cups, of course, figured prominently on Election day, when they were first carried in procession and then used by each of the new officers to toast his fellows. They were prestige pieces and, unlike the rest of the plate, had been furnished with cases. The tankard and the two beer bowls do not appear to have served any special function and probably differed little from others in the collection.

The decision not to invest in plate was adhered to throughout the eighteenth century. A list of plate taken 1756 (reproduced on page 130)[24] records merely the same pieces of plate as in 1711 except that the silver standing cup is wanting, but the little posset cup with the hall-mark for 1664–5 (Cat. No. 8, Pl. 12) appears as 'A Wrought Cup of Mrs Purifoy's Gift'.

For the first time the silver head of the Beadle's staff is listed amongst the plate. This is probably because it was now detachable whereas the previous one may have been permanently attached to its staff. On October 30, 1657, Mr Blackwell, goldsmith,[25] had been paid £6 10s od for the latter but by 1725 it had come to be regarded as inadequate. The present one (Cat. No. 10, Pl. 13) is a delightful baroque fantasy but it has no marks and the records about it are ambiguous. On February 6, 1725, the Renter Warden was ordered to 'pay the person who drew the plan of the Beadle's staff two guineas for his Care & trouble therein'.[26] About the same time two payments, totalling £48 19s 3d, were made to Mr Richard Langton, goldsmith. This sum seems rather a lot for the repair of the Company's plate which had been entrusted to him on September 1, 1724,[27] so that it may have included the making of the staff head. On July 7, 1747, it was ordered that the pineapple on the top should be gilded. After this the collection stagnated for more than 100 years, though it was well maintained, and on January 1, 1754,[28] the Master was instructed to have the Company's arms engraved on the plate. The name of the engraver who executed the delightful little rococo shields on some of the pieces is not recorded.

The modern period of the collection began inauspiciously in the 1870s with the presentation of three large loving cups engraved with the inevitable lines of Burns, and a pair of large rosewater dishes. A better standard was attained by a pair of massive ewers (Cat. No. 15), made by Carringtons in 1899 though their design looks half a century earlier. Two trends are noticeable after the opening of the present century. Frederick Arthur Crisp was a distinguished antiquary and celebrated his service as Master in 1904 not only by the presentation of a splendid Regency silver-gilt tray, but by the issue of a *Catalogue of the Plate belonging to the Worshipful Company of Carpenters* printed by his private press two years later. This set a fashion for gifts of antique plate a selection of which are included in the present catalogue. By far the most important of these is a pair of small gilt tankards with the hall-mark for 1621–2, bequeathed by the descendant of a former Master and benefactor of the Company (Cat. No. 5, Pl. 11). Before World War I donors who decided to give modern plate tended either to choose replicas of antiques or to leave the selection to some well-known firm. Gradually it was realized that the customer should take a greater care to see that his gift was designed by a good artist who might or might not be a practical goldsmith. At the time Omar Ramsden was the most popular artist in this field and executed the Master's Jewel (Cat. No. 25, Pl. 14) and several pieces of plate presented to the Company. In recent years have been added a series of pieces (five standing cups and one salt), each surmounted by a finial inspired by the tower or steeple of one of the city churches (Cat. Nos. 18–23, Pl. 16). The work has been distributed between a number of artists who have all produced interesting interpretations of the common theme.

CATALOGUE OF THE PRINCIPAL PIECES OF PLATE ARRANGED CHRONOLOGICALLY

Abbreviations

South Kensington Museum, Special Loan Exhibition of Works of Art, 1862=S.K.M., 1862; *Victoria & Albert Museum, Works of Art of the Livery Companies of the City of London,* 1927=V. & A.M., 1927; *Goldsmith's Hall, Historic Plate of the City of London,* 1951=G.H. 1951.

1. STANDING CUP AND COVER, silver-gilt.

Maker's mark, *FT monogram.*

London hall-mark for 1609–10. H. 19¼ inches.

Egg-shaped bowl embossed with conventional flowers and foliage and with two escutcheons engraved, respectively, with the arms of the Company and the donor's mark; baluster stem surrounded by three cast brackets; tall spreading foot. Domed cover with applied decoration similar to that on the bowl, surmounted by three cast brackets supporting a triangular openwork 'pyramid'. Around the lip of the cup is pounced: *John Ansell having been Mʳ of yᵉ Comp of Carpenters gave this to the Mʳ Wardens & Comlty of yᵉ mistery of fremen of yᵉ Carpenters of yᵉ Cittye of London.* S.K.M., 1862, No. 5407; V. & A.M., 1927, No. 407.

2. STANDING CUP AND COVER (The Master's Cup), silver-gilt.

Maker's mark, *FT monogram.*

London hall-mark for 1611–12. H. 24 inches.

Shape and decoration similar to the last but without the escutcheons with the donor's mark, the cover surmounted by three brackets supporting a triangular openwork 'pyramid' with finial in the form of a warrior holding a shield engraved with the Company's arms. Around the lip is pounced: *John Reeve being yᵉ Second tyme made me For y use of y Mʳ Wardens & Coi-altye of y Mistery of Freemen of yᵉ Carpentry of yᵉ Citty of London for ever wᵗʰ out charging y Coi-altye then being,* and on the rim of the foot: *Wardens Tho Fawcon, Edward More & William Bonner.*

The wording of the inscription makes a covert allusion to the companion cup which was paid for by the Company but was sold in 1627.

S.K.M., 1862, No. 5407; V. & A.M., 1927, No. 408; G.H., 1951, No. 73.

3. STANDING CUP AND COVER, silver-gilt.

Maker's mark, *R S with a pellet above and below.*

London hall-mark for 1613–14. H. 19½ inches.

Shape and decoration generally similar to No. 1. The escutcheons on the bowl and cover pounced with the arms of the Company and the initials of the donor. Around the lip is pounced: + *This Cup is y Gift of Thomas Edmones yongest warden of y Company of Carpenters & Mᵣ Carpenter of yᵉ Chamber of London & one of yᵉ fower vewers of yᵉ same Cyttye Anno Dom 1612.*

S.K.M., 1862, No. 5407; V. & A.M., 1927, No. 409.

4. STANDING CUP AND COVER, silver-gilt.

Maker's mark, *B P with a mullet below.*

London hall-mark for 1628–9. H. 19⅛ inches.

Shape and decoration similar to No. 1. The escutcheons pounced, respectively, with the arms of the Company and with his mark flanked by his initials and with three compasses below. Around the lip is pounced: *The Guift of Anthony Jarman Yonger Warden of the Carpenters and Mᵣ to the Chamber of London and one of the foure vewers of the same Cyttye Aug 12 1628.* The arms of the Company on the rim of the cover were evidently added in 1754.

S.K.M., 1862, No. 5407; V. & A.M., 1927, No. 410.

5. PAIR OF TANKARDS, silver gilt.

Maker's mark, *I C above a mullet.*

London hall-mark for 1621–2. H. 6⅞ inches.

Cylindrical, with low skirted base, slightly domed cover with billet thumb-piece and scroll handle. On the front is engraved a cartouche in the style of the early eighteenth century enclosing the arms of Wyatt. Underneath is engraved: *Richard Wyatt Citizen and Carpenter of London in the yeare 1619.*

Bequeathed by Stewart C. Wyatt in 1946.

As Richard Wyatt died in 1619 these can only have been made out of the proceeds of a bequest.
G.H., 1951, No. 85.

6. TANKARD, silver.
Maker's mark, *H G above a mullet.*
London hall-mark for 1653–4.   H. 6 inches.
Cylindrical with skirted base, single-stepped lid, double plume thumb-piece and scroll handle. On the front are engraved the arms of the Company and *The Gift of John Hawkins second warden.* John Hawkins was Middle Warden in 1660 but had been Junior Warden in 1657.
V. & A.M., 1927, No. 411; G.H., 1951, No. 106.

7. CUP (Beer Bowl), silver.
Maker's mark, *D R, a pellet above and below.*
London hall-mark for 1655–6.   H. 7½ inches.
Bell-shaped bowl, baluster stem and round foot. Engraved on the bowl: *August 67 The Gift of John Jegens second warden* and the arms of the Company in a rococo cartouche (added in 1754). In the *Court Book 1659–76* (Ms 4329/7) the gift is recorded thus— 'Aug. 1667. It. one silver Beere Bowle of the guift of Mr Figgon'. John Figgins was Second Warden in 1666 and no one of the name of Jegens is mentioned in the records.
V. & A.M., 1927, No. 412.

8. POSSET CUP, silver.
Maker's mark, *O S, a pellet above and a trefoil below.*
London hall-mark for 1664–5.   H. 4¼ inches.
Bulging body, the lower part embossed with flowers and foliage, two cast scroll handles. On the plain upper part of the body is engraved on one side within two plumes *The guift of Mary Purifoy* and on the other the arms of the Company in a rococo cartouche (added in 1754).
Nothing is known of the donor nor of the manner in which the piece reached the Company. It is first mentioned in 1756 but it had evidently arrived in time to be engraved with the other pieces in 1754.

214

S.K.M., 1862, No. 5409; V. & A.M., 1927, No. 413; G.H., 1951, No. 120.

9. CUP (Beer Bowl), silver.
Maker's mark, *R M, two rosettes above and four pellets below, in a heart.*
London hall-mark for 1665–6.   H. 7⅛ inches.
As No. 7, the bowl pounced: *The guift of Thomas Charman Second Warden Sept. 1671.* and engraved with the arms of the Company in a rococo cartouche (added in 1754).
Recorded in the *Court Book 1659–76* (Ms. 4329/7) as follows: '19 Sept. 1671 It. one silver bowle of the guift of Thomas Charman'.
V. & A.M., 1927, No. 414.

10. HEAD OF BEADLE'S STAFF, silver, parcel-gilt.
No marks.
1725.   H. 15 inches.
Socket in the form of the top of a Corinthian column on which rest a four-sided plinth engraved *1st William Ogborne Master 1725, 2nd Mr John Edden Upper Warden, 3rd Mr Thomas Arlidge Middle Warden, 4th Mr James Buckland Renter Warden.* The sides of the plinth are masked by four baroque cartouches with the arms and motto of the Company and on the top are four broken scrolls supporting a gilt pineapple.
The history of this piece has been given above.

11. BEAKER, silver, parcel-gilt.
Maker's mark of Petter Sundelius.
Swedish: Visby mark for 1794.   H. 8 inches.
Trumpet-shaped with spreading domed base. Decorated with wriggle engraving showing a crowned shield with *L L S C A D 1794,* flanked by crossed branches; above are *P P S S: A M L D.* Around the lip is engraved: *Presented to the Carpenters' Company by the Master William Herbert Evans 1923–4.* Inside is engraved: *A gift from an old friend to William Herbert Evans and his wife on the occasion of their Silver Wedding Sept. 10, 1909.*

215

12. TRAY, silver-gilt.
Maker's mark of Benjamin Smith.
London hall-mark for 1807–8. W. 31 inches.

Oval, with cast openwork border of vine scroll, two handles each formed by a lion mask between two goat's legs and four feet each formed by a human mask between two goat's feet. The bottom engraved with an acanthus scroll enclosing the arms of Adolphus Frederick, Duke of Cambridge, seventh son of George III and on the underneath is engraved: *This silver-gilt tea tray formerly belonged to H.R.H. The Duke of Cambridge and was bought at the sale of his plate (lot 106) at Christie, Manson & Woods, June 6th, 1904. The Gift of Frederick Arthur Crisp, Master, 1904*, together with the arms of the Company and of the donor. Underneath the rim is inscribed: *Rundell, Bridge & Rundell Aurifices Regis et Principis Walliae Londini Fecerunt.*

The firm of Rundell, Bridge & Rundell received the Lord Chamberlain's warrant of appointment as Royal goldsmiths on March 15, 1797. They did not at first run a workshop of their own although they controlled the designs of the plate which they sold. At the period in question they were handing out their work mainly to two working goldsmiths, Benjamin Smith and Paul Storr.

13. CUP AND COVER, silver-gilt.
Maker's mark of Emes & Barnard.
London hall-mark for 1812–13. H. 15 inches.

Vase-shaped with band of vine-scroll round the top and palm leaves round the lower part of the body; round base with wreath of acanthus ornament. Concave domed cover with flame knob. Engraved underneath: *The Worshipful Company of Carpenters George Robinson Drummond Master 1906*.

14. SIX GOBLETS, silver, gilt inside.
Maker's mark of William Elliott.
London hall-marks for 1814–15 (five)
and 1816–17 (one). H. 6 inches.

Thistle-shaped bowl, the lower part gadrooned; spreading foot

Beadle's Staff Head (1725)
(See Appendix 4)

14. The Master's and Wardens' Badges
(See Appendix 4)

Three Modern Silver-Gilt Steeple Cups
Left to right: Jacob Cup, Dill Cup, Bernays Cup
(See Appendix 4)

16. Two Modern Silver-Gilt Steeple Cups and a Salt
Left to right: Hugh Smith Cup, Barnes Salt, Rowden Cup
(See Appendix 4)

with band of gadrooning. Engraved with the crest of Colonel
W. W. Dove who gave them in 1964.

15. PAIR OF EWERS, silver.
Maker's mark of J. B. Carrington.
London hall-mark for 1899–1900.   H. 16 inches.
Vase-shaped body with applied vine wreath round the top and
gadrooning round the lower part which is supported on a fluted
stem on a square base. Behind the spout is crouched a satyr;
curved handle. On the front are engraved the arms of the Company and MDCCCC.

16. ROSEWATER DISH, silver.
Maker's mark of Omar Ramsden.
London hall-mark for 1917–18.   Diam. 21 inches.
Raised centre embossed with an archery scene, the rim embossed
with a rose garland divided by five shields with the arms of the
City of London, the Company and of the donors. Around the
edge is inscribed: *I was wrought in the year of Our Lord 1918
for the Worshipful Company of Carpenters by command of Sir
William John Lancaster, J.P.; David Wintringham Stable, L.L.B.,
J.P., and John Hooke, P.M., that there may be brotherly love of their
sons, Utten Lamont Hooke, Lieut. Colonel; Loscombe Law Stable,
Captain; and Robert Lancaster 2nd Lieut.; who gave their lives
fighting for King and Country in France during the Great War.*
On the bottom is inscribed *Omar Ramsden me fecit.*
In 1925 D. W. Stable presented a large four-handled cup and
cover in the late gothic style also made by Omar Ramsden.

17. ROSEWATER DISH, silver.
Maker's mark of H. G. Murphy.
London hall-mark for 1936–7.   Diam. 15¼ inches.
The arms of the Company are engraved in the centre, the rim
pierced with seven tulip sprays. Engraved: *Presented to the
Worshipful Company of Carpenters on the tenth day of March
1936 to commemorate the centenary of the birth of Benjamin Joseph
Jacob (master 1892) by Walter Louis & Reginald Jacob (sons)*

& Kenneth Douglas, John and Leslie Jacob & Roy Freeman (grandsons) all members of this Company.

18. STANDING CUP, silver-gilt.
Unmarked.
1941.   H. 19 inches.
Egg-shaped bowl on baluster stem and round foot. The domed
cover surmounted by a replica of the spire of St Martin within
Ludgate. The cover, the lower part of the bowl and the foot
chased with London Pride. Around the lip is engraved: *The gift
of Reginald Jacob Master of the Carpenters' Company made in the
year of the destruction of Carpenters' Hall, 1941.* Inscribed underneath the foot: *Designed by Mr Gleadowe, Citizen Goldsmith and
wrought by Messrs. Wakely & Wheeler, Goldsmiths of London.*

19. STANDING CUP, silver-gilt.
Maker's mark of Wakely & Wheeler (designed by R. M. Y.
Gleadowe).
London hall-mark for 1947–8.   H. 19 inches.
Egg-shaped bowl on baluster stem and round foot. The domed
cover surmounted by a replica of the spire of St Bride, Fleet
Street. The cover, lower part of the bowl and foot chased with
acorns and oak sprays. Around the lip is engraved: *The Gift of
Evan Bernays, twice Master of the Carpenters' Company, 1941
and 1942.*

20. STANDING CUP, silver-gilt.
Maker's mark of Leslie Durbin.
London hall-mark for 1949–50.   H. 19 inches.
Egg-shaped bowl on baluster stem and round foot. The domed
cover surmounted by a replica of the tower and spire of St Mary-
le-Bow and set with applied columbine flowers. The bowl engraved
round the lip with: *The Gift of Frederick Hugh Smith Master of the
Carpenters Company, 1957,* and with applied shield charged with
the arms of the Borough of Wigan, columbine flowers and sprays.
The foot decorated with pea pods.

THE PLATES AND JEWELS AND THEIR HISTORY

21. STANDING CUP, silver-gilt.
Maker's mark of Leslie Durbin.
London hall-mark for 1949–50.   H. 19 inches.
Egg-shaped bowl on baluster stem and round foot. The domed
cover surmounted by a replica of the tower of St Stephan Wal-
brook and set with eight daisy heads. The bowl engraved round
the lip: *The Gift of Tom Sowerby Rowden, Eric Englefield Rowden,
his son and another '1948.* and with two baroque cartouches, one
filled with the arms of the Company.

22. STANDING SALT, silver.
Maker's mark of Leslie Durbin.
London hall-mark for 1951–2.   H. 8¼ inches.
Octofoil container on a round base; four branches support a
replica of the spire of St Dunstan-in-the-East. Round the bowl
are engraved (1) the arms of the Company; (2) *The Gift of Robert
Cecil Burnes, Master 1950–1;* (3) the arms of the donor; (4) a garter
inscribed: ΦΙΛΑΔΕΛΦΙΑΜΕΝΕΤΩ
Salt spoon with finial in the form of a shield engraved on one side
with the arms of the Company and on the other with those of the
donor.

23. STANDING CUP, silver-gilt.
Maker's mark of Louis Osman.
London hall-mark for 1962–3.   H. 19 inches.
Trumpet-shaped body formed by twelve vertical struts bound
together at the bottom by a beaded ring and then expanding to
join the flat circular base. The bowl is roughly frosted and is
decorated with a triangular shield with the arms of the Company.
The cover is formed by twelve struts conjoined at the top by a
beaded ring and supporting a replica of the turret of All Hallows,
London Wall. The cover is inscribed outside: *Richard Wale
Gordon Dill, M.C., Master, 1959–60,* and inside *All Hallows,
London Wall, George Dance, 1765.*

219

BADGES AND JEWEL

24. BADGES FOR THE THREE WARDENS, gold with enamel.
1875.   H. $2\frac{1}{4}$ inches.
Arms of the Company on a heater-shaped shield, with motto
below and cherub above. On the back is engraved: *A.D. 1477, The
Gift of Robert Stephan Faulconer, Master, 1875.*

25. THE MASTER'S JEWEL, gold, set with diamonds and semi-
precious stones.
Maker's mark of Omar Ramsden.
1933.   H. $5\frac{1}{2}$ inches.
The arms of the Company supported by two winged female
figures surrounded by cherubs. On the back is inscribed: *I was
wrought for the worshipful Company of Carpenters to commemorate
the 600th year of the making of the 'Boke of Ordinances' in 1333,
and delivered into the keeping of the Master H.R.H. Edward Prince
of Wales at a banquet on March 22nd, 1933.* With fourfold gold
chain.

NOTES

The Company's records are deposited in the Guildhall Library. The
references to the Wardens' Accounts are here abbreviated to W.A.
followed by the manuscript number and those to the Court Books are
similarly abbreviated to C.B. with the manuscript number.

1. W.A., MS. 4326/1, f. 206.
2. Ibid., f. 203.
3. Ibid., ff. 333 & 346.
4. 1890, pt. 2, p. 692.
5. W.A., MS. 4326/2, f. 167.
6. C.B., MS. 4329/1, f. 93.
7. W.A., MS. 4326/2, f. 185.
8. C.B., MS. 4329/3, f. 368 & W.A., MS. 4326/7, f. 24.
9. The name 'Steeple Cup' seems to have been invented in the
   nineteenth century.

10. 'An Index of English Silver Steeple Cups', in *Proceedings of the Society of Silver Collectors*, 1966.
11. C.B., MS. 4329/7, f. 3.
12. *Hansepots* were flagons with cylindrical bodies and took their name from the Hanseatic towns.
13. *Oxeye cups* have bulbous bodies and two ring-handles. They were also known as *College cups*. Nearly all surviving examples belong to Oxford colleges.
14. W.A., MS. 4326/8, April 27, 1643.
15. W.A., MS. 4326/9 & 4326/10.
16. Ibid., March 21, 1649.
17. C.B., MS. 4329/7, f. 1.
18. Ibid., f. 2v.
19. These cups on baluster stems were usually described as *Beer Bowls*. For the donor's name see the Catalogue entry.
20. C.B., MS. 4329/8. Mr Lyde paid up immediately as did Mr Wilkins who had been Middle Warden in 1679. In the past Middle Wardens who had escaped service as Junior Wardens had usually made gifts but the wording of the 1680 resolution was ambiguous and their liability was later specifically ended by a resolution on October 20, 1694 (C.B., MS. 4329/11).
21. C.B., MS. 4329/11, f. 6v.
22. W.A., MS. 4326/11.
23. C.B., MS. 4329/13.
24. C.B., MS. 4329/16, fly-leaf.
25. Richard Blackwell had taken his oath at Goldsmith's Hall in 1646. Edward Basil Jupp and William Willmer Pocock, *An Historical Account of the Worshipful Company of Carpenters* (1889), pp. 488, 576, confuse him with his eminent contemporary, Alderman Edward Backwell, the banker.
26. C.B., MS. 4329/15.
27. Ibid.
28. C.B., MS. 4329/16.

APPENDIX 5

THE CROWNS, PAINTINGS AND FURNITURE

by John L. Nevinson

I. THE CROWNS OF THE MASTER AND WARDENS

As the Company possesses the oldest dated crown of embroidered velvet (No. 26) something needs to be said about the custom and ceremonies of crowning the Master and Wardens after their election. These are not set out clearly until 1656 when Roger Goodday, the Clerk, records:

> 'After dinner the said election was openly published in the hall and their election cupps & garlands particularly presented to them that were present according to the usual customs. But forasmuch as Mr Hawkins the youngest Warden elect was now absent, his garland was presented at the upper end of the table where his usuall place hath been, & he was drunk to & openly published. . .'.[1]

The official livery of the Company from medieval times was the gown and hood, the materials, colours and trimmings of which varied. These were provided on admission or when the Livery was clothed or habilled.[2] When the hood had gone out of fashion in the sixteenth century, the flat cap replaced it for ordinary wear. In the early seventeenth century the cap in its turn had been replaced by the hat, but remained obligatory wear for Court. In 1628 the Court fined Mr George Arnold, Warden, twelve pence, 'for sitting in Court in his Hatt, and leaving the keyes of the Cubbard behind so that others could not come at their Capps'.[3]

The medieval hood, when not pulled over the head in Balaclava helmet style, was sometimes worn on the head with the face-ring in a roll about the top of the head and the streamers and neck-flaps hanging down behind; an example was seen on a corbel-head in the Company's old hall.[4] At first sight it might be held that this could have developed into the Master's crown or garland, but in fact the garland or chapelet was of an earlier date than 1400, and took a different form, perhaps adapted from a garland of flowers.

The crowning ceremony is first mentioned in the Ordinances of the Grocers' Company, 1345,[5] in old French, to the effect that:

'. . . the wardens after dinner done shall come with chapelets and choose two other wardens for the next year ensuing upon whom the said chapelets shall be set . . .'.

In each Company the crowning of the Master and Wardens was not a formal ceremony performed after election in Court, but something of a festive interlude at the Election Dinner, as described above.

The Grocers Company accounts show that the medieval chapelets were not expensive, but by the sixteenth century the chapelet had been formalized into an embroidered band of velvet or leather, handed down from year to year. In 1550 the Girdlers Company had crowns of gold and blue with a figure of St Lawrence, and the first specification for a crown is for that given by their Master, Cuthbert Beeston, in 1575:

'One Crowne Garland of black velvett imbrodered with the letters of his name, a Towne (i.e., a "tun" rebus) and a gredyron of gold and the girdle with the buckles of brodered gold lace compassinge the said garland . . .'.[6]

This confirms that the Master's crown (No. 26) with its silver shields dated 1561 is not only the oldest surviving crown but is in its original form as given by John Tryll, although, as mentioned below, the velvet may have been renewed. It is authenticated by the Inventory of 1625 (see p. 205) which lists the garlands before the cups. This inventory clears up the old difficulty about the initials on No. 28, P.T., which are now shown to stand for Peter Thornton, and not to be those of Thomas Pecock.[7]

Repairs must have been frequent since the silver thread would cut the silk which stitches it down. In 1760 the Court ordered payment for substantial repairs:

'. . . that the Embroiderers Bill of £14 14s. od for Repairing the Master and Wardens Wreaths be paid, and that Mr Warden Robinson be desired to prepare Four Boxes to keep them in'.[8]

At this date, if not before, the velvet of No. 26 may have been replaced. The silk lining and ribbons, being most exposed to harder wear, would certainly have needed both earlier and later renewals.

In the reign of Charles II, Mr William Levett, the Company's cook, was evidently a prominent organizing character and took charge at feasts; in 1688 the Court allowed him forty shillings 'for a lached Capp with the Company's arms, to be worn and used by him upon all public dinners', and two years later an apron with lace was bought for him at a cost of thirty-six shillings.[9]

It was not to be expected that the Cap and Apron would have survived any more than the Company's streamers and banners, which, as the accounts show, were frequently repaired and replaced. New banners had obviously to be provided for Lord Mayor's day 1660, but in 1663 the Company, seeing that the fabric was good, paid forty shillings for altering an old banner of the State's (i.e. Commonwealth) Arms into the Company's Arms.[10]

Another loss has been the Company's pall or hearsecloth, which was used at funerals of all members of the Livery. It is not mentioned in inventories after 1649, but had been made, replacing an earlier pall, in 1591 by John Ellidge, the embroiderer, at a cost of £13 9s 6d including nearly £5 for the velvet.[11]

Until after 1660 the Company possessed a quantity of table linen, probably plain damask, but all marked with the Company's mark and kept in the 'great Danscik Cheste' bought for 8s 4d in 1598.[12] The inventory of 1572 has been printed[13] and in 1622 Mr Daye, late Master, brought in a new supply all inked with the Carpenters' mark and a capital 'D'.[14] As late as 1632 there is an entry for the 'Foole's cloth'; this was a towel, apparently for a table and not worn by the Fool as an Apron.[15]

(*Abbreviations are the same as used in the previous Appendix—see p. 212.*)

26. MASTER'S CROWN.

Dated 1561.   Diam. 10 in.   H. 3 in.

Red velvet, probably of later date, with couched embroidery, and engraved silver plates. Two escutcheons with the Arms of the Company and of the City of London in enamel inlay. Engraved silver-gilt initials, I. T. (for John Tryll, Master 1561), and his mark. The embroidery in couched cord and silver twist has been repaired; two flowers in long and short stitch added in late seventeenth century. New lining silk and ribbons.[16]

S.K.M., 1862, No. 5408; V. & A.M., 1927, No. 415.

THE CROWNS, PAINTINGS AND FURNITURE

27, 28, 29. THREE WARDENS' CROWNS.

Early seventeenth century.   Diam. 9¾ in. H. 3 in.
Silver-gilt and silver thread embroidery on red velvet, couched
and padded work, purl and silver twist.
Escutcheons of arms, vases, No. 27 with initials I. A. for John
Ansell (Master 1601, 1606); No. 28 with initials P. T. for Peter
Thornton (Warden 1610, 1612, 1615); No. 29 with initials W. W.
for William Wheatley (Warden 1609, 1619).
The red silk lining and ribbons have been replaced.
S.K.M., 1862, No. 5408; V. & A.M., 1927, No. 416.

II. PAINTINGS FROM THE OLD HALL OF THE COMPANY[17]

For some reason, perhaps because of their disagreements with the
Joiners Company, the Carpenters Company seem to have preferred
painting rather than Elizabethan panelling or carving in their hall
and other rooms. During the 1561 redecoration, gifts were received
from members of the Livery:
    '. . . Item, Mr Tryll did gyve ye payntinge of ye said baye, & also
    he gave a garland to ye choysing of ye Mr & a new cloth for ye
    table in ye parler.
    Item, Wyllam Ruddocke, Wyllm. Buttermore & Robert Quonye
    dyd gyve ye painting of ye other ij bayes & a storye [i.e. a historical
    picture] over ye skrenes and payntinge of ye skrenes. . .'.[18]
The painter's name is not given but in 1571 Baker the painter was
allowed eleven yards of canvas and received fifty-three shillings for
making the story in the parlour.[19] In 1573 another painter, John
Knight, painted the roof of a window and a 'piece of Antykes' or
grotesque upon the transome, and also a piece of the wall to look like
glass.[20] He was succeeded by yet another painter Coldaill, Coldwill,
or Cowdall.[21]
    Paintings on canvas nailed to a wall are short-lived, and may have
perished or been covered over even before the hall was panelled,
wainscoted, and gained a new coffered ceiling in 1667–70[22] when the
prejudice against carving was probably less. Nothing more is heard
of the paintings until December 19, 1845, when C. Roach Smith, the
antiquary, wrote a hurried note to F. W. Fairhold, the artist:
    'This p.m. the workmen repairing Carpenters Hall have uncovered

P   225

a border of paintings about 14 feet long by two of the time of Henry VIII in good preservation'.[23]

The sequel is recorded in the Court minutes for January 6, 1846:[24] 'The Clerk reported . . . that one of the Workmen engaged in repairing the Great Hall having driven a nail through some old Canvass into the Western Wall . . . discovered an old Painting three feet in height . . . [which] extended the entire length of the western side . . . the clerk informed the Master and the estate committee . . . and issued a circular to the whole Livery. . . . The Committee of the Archaeological Society inspected the painting and made a tracing'.

As the estimate for repairing the painting was no less than £70, the Company were no doubt relieved to hear that it would be imprudent to restore the original writing. Instead, the painting was framed and glazed, and Mr Fairholt, who had made watercolour sketches, now in the British Museum,[25] painted for the Company at the cost of £12 10s 0d a full-scale facsimile now kept on a roll.[26] An account of the discovery appeared in the *Illustrated London News* for January 3, 1846, with a picture of the end of the hall, and a paper was printed by the Archaeological Society.[27] An effort to preserve the colours which faded as the plaster dried was not successful. When the old hall was demolished in 1873 the frescoes were lifted, cut down and reframed in three sections, one of which has since disintegrated (Nos. 30, 31).

The story originally consisted of four scriptural scenes chosen for their relationship to the mystery of the Carpenters. These were:

(a) *Noah and the Building of the Ark.*

On the left Noah with his adze kneels before the figure of the Almighty in the clouds; on the right his three sons are busied with saw and hammer about a sturdily built but none too roomy Ark.[28] The inscription based on Genesis VI, verse 13, in black letter was read as ' . . . the earth is full of lyve [a mistake for "vyolence"] and I shall destroy them'. This panel has now perished.

(b) *King Josiah rebuilds the Temple in Jerusalem* (No. 30).

This is a less familiar scene based on 2 Kings, XII, verses 5 to 7, showing on the left King Josiah enthroned and attended by two courtiers dressed in the style of Henry VIII's reign; he is instructing Shaphan the Scribe, who as a Court officer holding a white staff has not taken off his Tudor cap; on the right the Clerk of the Works (or perhaps the High Priest Hilkiah), in a long Kaftan gown and high Jewish hat, hands out bags of money to a group of bareheaded carpenters (there should be masons present also) who were judged capable of buying materials and carrying out work without submitting reckonings and estimates of accounts. The inscription read 'King Josyas commandyd yt ye hye prest yt. ye money wch. was . . . house of the Lord should be delyvered to ye carpynters wt. out any . . .'.

(c) *Christ in the Carpenter's shop* (No. 31).

In the centre Joseph is trimming a beam; on the right, the Virgin Mary, who is fashionably dressed in German-style clothes with a roll head-dress, sits with her distaff spinning wool from a silver urn; in the background is the defaced figure of the Child Christ with wood splinters in a basket. On the left stands a commanding figure in a livery gown, flat cap and Tudor dress with a new fashioned ruff. The Elizabethans would have seen nothing incongruous in introducing a portrait of the Master of the Company or a donor into this scriptural scene. The inscription reads: 'Chryst at ye age of xij yeres syttynge among the teachers in the temple, his father and his mother were come to seke him, he went wyth them to Nazarethe and was obedyent unto them. . . . Lueke ii'.

(d) *Christ teaching in the synagogue* (No. 31).

This is based on Matthew XIII, verses 54–5, and Mark VI, verse 3, and shows the Child Christ seated at a high desk preaching to an audience of citizens in contemporary dress with cloaks; one carries a book, but none has the appearance of a Doctor of the Law. They are probably intended to represent a Jewish congregation, even though only two wear hats. The inscription read: 'Chryst teachynge in ye synag . . . ; . . . wysdom is thys, is not thys that carpynters [son . . .]'.

The illustrated bible or prints on which these scenes are based have not yet been traced. The designer, perhaps a refugee from the Low Countries, would seem to have worked from models showing figures in rather more contemporary styled dress than in engravings by Martin van Heemskirk or M. Vos; many of the men wear coats with a distinctive slit and button above it on the upper arm. The figure of Joseph and the pose of the Virgin remotely resemble one of Dürer's Life of the Virgin woodcuts, but in the woodcut Christ still a child lies in the cradle, and winged cherubs collect the wood splinters.

In a scurrilous letter to William Cotton in 1596, Thomas Nashe, the pamphleteer, mentions the paintings.[29] His enemy, Thomas Churchyard, was about to publish a miscellany under the title 'the second part of Churchyard's Chips'; Nashe thought it would not sell even if the chips were given out to be 'the very same which Christ in Carpenters' Hall is paynted gathering up as Joseph his father stands hewing a piece of timber'.

30, 31. TWO FRAGMENTS OF WALL PAINTINGS.

English; second half of the sixteenth century. Plaster on canvas.

No. 30.   L. 69 in.   D. 35 in.   Scene (b).

No. 31.   L. 110 in.   D. 35 in.   Scenes (c) and (d).

The colours of the tempera painting are very much faded, as will be seen by reference to Fairholt's watercolours mentioned above.[30]

III. THE FURNITURE

Before 1600 the hall would have appeared rather bare with its painted walls and roof; there was some plain wainscoting, but probably the parlour alone had carved panels (No. 32). Stained glass was added in the seventeenth century. Even by 1625 the Company had no great store of movable furniture; at that date the 'Inventory of Goods in the Hall' comprised[31]

Inprimis 3 long tables, & 5 long formes, 8 ioyned stooles for the high table, one cesterne of pewter, and a laver of lead, a deske and bible chained to it, a rounde table to carve on, a table of the Kinges armes, a Table of the Kinges picture, a table of Prince Henryes picture, and 3 curteins of silk sarsenet for them. [Added, ?1629]. One table of Mr Portingtons Arms, 1 table of the 10 commandments given by Richard Thomlinson carpenter, the Pallgraves picture, Mr Portingtons picture, one clock and case.

The use of the word table both for what we call a table and for a portrait on board is a little confusing; the round table to carve on was bought for 26s 8d in 1606.[32] The last items are certainly additions. It will be noticed that there is no chair for the Master; those at the high table sat on a form, presumably with their back against the wall, or on joined stools. In the inventory of 1643[33] the carving table is marked as 'gone' and 'one table of Mr Wyatts' is added, presumably that recorded as 'brought to the hall' in 1638 for the sum of 4d. If we go further and assume that this is the octagonal table dated 1606 (No. 33) we can call this a carving table, as a very similar table at the Armourers and Braziers Company Hall is called, but it must surely have had a more substantial top as well as a cloth spread over it.

The 1625 Inventory of goods 'in the Parlor belowe' is more complicated owing to deletions. There was 'one long table with a frame, one small table, 8 joyned stooles, a green carpet [i.e. a table-cloth] and a greene chaire of cloth'; then comes a deleted entry of a wooden chair for a man, and two wooden chairs for women, reduced by deletion to one. 'One sett cupboard, one greene cupboard cloth and 16 green cushions' come next, and then a 'paire of brasse and irons, a paire of tongs and a paire of bellows', all deleted. 'An iron back in the chimney, 6 poyses of pewter, and a wainscot chest with 2 locks; also a piece of wainscot to stand before the chest', deleted. At the end of the list are items added in a different hand, 'one pair of creepers, 21 leather chaires, 1 new grene carpett and 12 newe greene cushions, one faire paire of brasse and irons, tonges, fireshovel, bellows tipped with brasse and a brasse cappe pann'. This indicates a new standard of parlour luxury. If the list is accurate in its final form, that is to say, if no other furniture of the Company's was in the Clerk's or Beadle's houses, then the last surviving 'wooden chair for a woman' might be No. 36; the other given by Robert Maskall in 1590 had his wife's initials E. M.[34] The wainscot chest with two locks appears to have been bought in 1636 for £3 9s 4d including materials.[35]

Other furniture of simple types, mainly frame and 'tressel' tables, joined 'stooles and formes', was in the high parlour, or stored in the long and cross galleries. Some of this was no doubt for the largely attended feasts on election day or when the poor were entertained in the Hall.[36]

After 1660, the extent of the refurnishing is not clear: in 1667 a new Spanish table was bought for the Company's use for 8s 6d;[37] other expenditure is on wainscoting. Anthony Williamson Limner received 45s for 'James Palmer's picture new drawne and done and set into a frame'.[38] He was the son of a carpenter, a Reed's exhibitioner at Magdalene College, Cambridge, and later a benefactor of the Company. Possibly the furniture came to be completely neglected as the Company took to letting its Hall, using it only for elections. The iron chests for the Company's money, plate and documents were kept in the smaller rooms; a new iron chest was bought in 1734 for £2 1s 0d.[39]

In September 1713 a new Russia leathern chair was to be provided for the Master's use in the Court of Assistants,[40] and on July 30, 1733, the Court ordered—

'that the Renter Warden do buy of Mr Fordham the Companys Tenant for the Hall, Eight Chairs and a Masters Chair to stand in the Compting House. . .'.[41]

The cost seems to have been £11 16s 6d which, even though Mr Fordham was an upholsterer, sounds cheap if the present Master's Chair (No. 37) was included, unless it was secondhand. Mr Fordham also supplied cushions and six new chairs in 1745–6. In 1741 the inventory of Mr Vestille, the Beadle, shows that he had a 'great chair'[42] probably a watchman's chair with a canopy, but by 1744 he is charged with only one old elbow chair which could be the Russian leather one in decay.[43]

In 1760 there was a large bill for upholstery work, and the Court ordered payment to Mr Ellicott of his bill of £35 14s 0d for the 'Clock and Bracket'.[44] This is difficult to equate with the long case clock by Ellicott (No. 36); the firm thereafter continued to be paid for clock repairs and cleaning until 1835, without any indication of the type or number of clocks.

Subsequent accounts and minutes hardly refer at all to new furniture; perhaps there was some arrangement with the Company's tenants, latterly Messrs Fordham and Luck. Court room chairs were repaired at regular intervals. In 1818 a large screen was to be placed about a bed to give a room a parlour-like appearance[45] and hat and umbrella-stands were bought in 1822.[46] The furniture, portraits, and looking-glasses were rearranged in 1824 and the bill for gilding the picture- and glass-frames came to £30 3s 6d.[47]

32, 33, 34. THREE OAK PANELS FROM THE OLD HALL 1578–9.

32.   H. 34 in.   W. 25 in.

Carved from a single piece of wood with the Company's Arms on a shield surrounded by a floreated cartouche with ribbons and dated 1579. The 'planke' cost three shillings and the joiner was paid two shillings 'for his paynes and the carving thereof'.[48]

33.   H. 34 in.   W. 20 in.
Carpenter's mark of Thomas Harper, on a rectangular cartouche.
Inscription: 'I. 5. 7. 9. (a harp) THOMAS HARPER MASTER.[49]

34.   H. 34 in.   W. 20 in.
Wardens' names on a rectangular cartouche. ANTHONIE
BEAR (mark) LAWRENCE PVDDLLE ROBERT CAWSEY
BEING WARDENS.
The pre-1939 arrangement of these panels illustrated in the
Royal Commission of Historical Monuments Report.[50]

35. OCTAGONAL TABLE.
Dated 1606.   H. 31 in.   W. 40 in.
Oak with carved baluster legs and semicircular arched panels.
In the spandrels of the arches are the initials R. W. (for Richard
Wyatt, Master), W. W. (for William Wilson), G. I. (for George
Isack), I. R. (for John Reeve, wardens) and 1606. The top and
feet have been restored.
V. & A.M., 1927, No. 417.
A similar table, also dated 1606, belongs to the Armourers and
Braziers Company, and is described as a Carving Table.[51]

36. ARM CHAIR.
Early seventeenth century.   H. 42 in.
Oak, with carved back panel, turned front legs and supports to arms.
V. & A.M., 1927, No. 418.

37. MASTER'S CHAIR.
Mid-eighteenth century.   H. 72 in.
Mahogany, with high back, padded and surmounted by acanthus
carving with the Company's Arms. The arms end in lion masks;
square legs with fret pattern.
V. & A.M., 1927, No. 419.
Alterations to back and legs.

38. LONG CASE CLOCK.
Mid-eighteenth century.   H. 8 ft. 9 in.
By John Ellicott, FRS, of Cornhill (1706–72).
Ebony case with ormolu mounts.

39. LONG CASE CLOCK.
Early eighteenth century.   H. 8 ft. 11 in.
By Edward Bagshaw (admitted to the Clockmakers Company, 1691).
Marquetry case.
Presented by the Rosher family, 1960.

40. BRACKET CLOCK.
Late eighteenth century.   H. 20 in.
By Eardley Norton of 42 St John Street, Clerkenwell (fl. 1760–94), a well-known maker of musical and astronomical clocks.
Ebony case; the movement shows carpenters at work.
Presented by Lt-Col. William W. Dove, CBE.

41. WALL MIRRORS, pair.
Mid-eighteenth century.   H. 9 ft. 2 in.   W. 4 ft. 7 in.
Carved and gilt wood, with figures of Diana and Apollo (?).
From Charleville Castle, Ireland.

42. WALL MIRRORS, pair.
About 1765.   H. 6 ft. 9 in.   W. 46 in.
Carved and gilt wood.
V. & A.M., 1927, No. 421.

43. PIER TABLES, three.
1780–1800.   H. $33\frac{1}{4}$ in.   W. $57\frac{1}{4}$ in.
Satinwood and inlay, Sheraton style.

44. SIDEBOARD TABLE.
Early nineteenth century.   H. 35 in.   W. 66 in.
Mahogany and satinwood, veneered; shaped drawers fitted as cellarette, brass ring drop-handles.

45. STAINED GLASS PANEL.
Dated 1634.   H. 6 in.   W. $5\frac{1}{2}$ in.
Shield of Arms (Jermyn) and carpenter's mark, 'A. I.' for Anthony Jarman, Master 1633.

Similar panels with the names of Masters were set in the windows of the old hall.[52]
Presented by Lt-Col. William W. Dove, CBE, Master 1954.

46. CAUDLE CUP.
Dated 1666. H. 4¼ in.
Tin-glazed earthenware (Lambeth Delft) with the Arms of the Company and initials T. H. in underglaze blue.
Another cup with Company's Arms, initials T. E. M. 1676 and floral decorations, has been on loan to the London Museum. (C. 2437; Mr F. A. Crisp).

47. BOWL.
About 1775. H. 3¼ in.
Bristol porcelain, with painted flowers and gilt decoration, and Arms of the Carpenters Company. Mark, a cross in blue.
Presented by Mr B. J. Nicholson, Master 1961.

NOTES

(*Abbreviations are the same as used in the previous Appendix—see p. 220.*)

1. C.B. 4329/6, f. 16.
2. Jupp and Pocock, op. cit., p. 214 quotes admission procedure in 1673.
3. W.A., MS. 4326/7, f. 146v.
4. Jupp and Pocock, op. cit., Pl. 4, p. 239.
5. Grocers Company, *Facsimiles of MSS. Archives* (1886), p. 10.
6. W. Dumville Smythe, *Historical Account . . .* (1905), pp. 164, 268.
7. Jupp and Pocock, op. cit., p. 212.
8. C.B., MS. 4329/16, f. 171.
9. W.A., MS. 4326/10, ff. 440, 498v.
10. W.A., MS. 4326/10, f. 347.
11. W.A., MS. 4326/3, p. 517.
12. W.A., MS. 4326/5, ff. 34, 36.
13. Jupp and Pocock, op. cit., Appendix S., p. 641
14. C.B., MS. 4329/4, f. 79v.
15. Ibid., f. 304.
16. Jupp and Pocock, op. cit., p. 591.

17. See in general E. Croft Murray, *Decorative Painting in England* (1962), I, pp. 178a, 186a.
18. W.A., MS. 4326/3, p. 81. Jupp and Pocock, op. cit., p. 223.
19. W.A., MS. 4326/3, p. 238.
20. Ibid., p. 281.
21. Ibid., pp. 376, 392.
22. Measured drawings given to RIBA in 1846 (Portfolio W 13/1).
23. Fairholt papers, British Museum, Prints and Drawings, 290, c. 6.
24. C.B., 4329/26, p. 28.
25. British Museum, Prints and Drawings, 5, 12, 207–10.
26. W.A., MS. 4326/15, 1846.
27. *Archaeological Journal*, I (1846), p. 275.
28. Illustration. Jupp and Pocock, op. cit., Pl. I, p. 236.
29. British Museum, Cotton, Ms. Julius C. III, 280.
30. For recent notes on paintings see W. Reader in *Archaeological Journal*, XCII (1935), pp. 252–4; *Country Life* (1964), p. 1,336.
31. Inventory C.B., MS. 4329/7 (at back).
32. W.A., MS. 4326/5, f. 103.
33. C.B., MS. 4329/7, f. 8.
34. W.A., MS. 4326/3, p. 491.
35. W.A., MS. 4326/7, f. 241.
36. W.A., MS. 4326/5, f. 163. Jupp, p. 252.
37. W.A., MS. 4326/10, f. 415.
38. Ibid., f. 463, 1669.
39. W.A., MS. 4326/11, f. 304.
40. C.B., MS. 4329/13.
41. C.B., MS. 4329/15.
42. C.B., MS. 4329/17 (fly-leaf), Jupp, Appendix T, p. 642.
43. C.B., MS. 4329/18 (fly-leaf).
44. C.B., MS. 4329/16, f. 172v.
45. C.B., MS. 4329/22, p. 190.
46. W.A., MS. 4326/12.
47. Ibid., 1824.
48. Jupp and Pocock, op. cit., p. 224. Illustration. W.A., MS. 4326/3, p. 358.
49. Jupp and Pocock, op. cit., p.225. Illustration.
50. RCHM, London, City (1929), Plate 17(5).
51. Macquoid and Edwards, *Dictionary of English Furniture* (1954), III, p. 307.
52. Jupp and Pocock, op. cit., p. 235.

ABBREVIATIONS

Apprentices' Entry Books 1654–94 *Records of the Carpenters' Company*, edited by Bower Marsh (1913), Vol. I, Apprentices' Entry Books 1654–94.

Wardens' Accounts 1438–1516 *Records of the Carpenters' Company*, edited by Bower Marsh (1914), Vol. II, Wardens' Accounts 1438–1516.

Court Book 1533–73 *Records of the Carpenters' Company*, edited by Bower Marsh (1915), Vol. III, Court Book 1533–73.

Wardens' Accounts 1546–71 *Records of the Carpenters' Company*, edited by Bower Marsh (1916), Vol. IV, Wardens' Accounts 1546–71.

Wardens' Accounts 1571–91 *Records of the Carpenters' Company*, transcribed by Bower Marsh and edited by John Ainsworth (1937), Vol. V, Wardens' Accounts 1571–91.

Court Book 1573–93 *Records of the Carpenters' Company*, transcribed by Bower Marsh and edited by John Ainsworth (1930), Vol. VI, Court Book 1573–93.

Cal. Letter Book *Calendar of Letter Books Preserved Among the Archives of the Corporation of the City of London at Guildhall*, edited by Reginald R. Sharpe (12 vols., 1894–1912).

Guildhall Library Library of the Corporation of the City of London.

P.C.C. Prerogative Court of Canterbury.

Journal Journal of the Court of Common Council of the City of London.

Repertory Repertory of the Court of Aldermen of the City of London.

Abstract of Deeds An Abstract of Deeds and Other Documents relating to the Carpenters Company Estates, Guildhall Library, MS. 4346.

NOTES

1. For a discussion of the fraternities see, George Unwin, *The Guilds and Companies of London* (1925), pp. 93–127.
2. Details of these regulations are given by H. T. Riley (ed.), *Liber Albus* (1859), pp. xxix–xxxvii, 321 et seq.; H. T. Riley (ed.), *Liber Custumarum* (1849–62), Vol. I, pp. xxxi–xxxiv, 86–8; Philip E. Jones (ed.), *Calendar of Plea and Memoranda Rolls 1437–57* (1854), pp. viii–ix.
3. *Liber Custumarum*, op. cit., Vol. I, p. 86—the daily wage was fixed at 3d with food and 4½d without; cf., L. F. Salzman, *Building in England down to 1540* (Oxford, 1952), p. 68, who misquotes the rate as 4d without food.
4. These developments are investigated by G. A. Williams, *Medieval London: From Commune to Capital* (1963).
5. Ibid., pp. 20, 315–17.
6. C. J. Eltringham, 'Building Control and the Carpenters Company of London, 1588–1600' (1954), typescript in Guildhall Library.
7. *Cal. Letter Book A*, p. 184.
8. *Liber Custumarum*, op. cit., Vol. I, p. 100.
9. *Cal. Letter Book B*, p. 241.
10. A. H. Thomas (ed.), *Calendar of Early Mayor's Court Rolls 1298–1307* (1924), p. 25.
11. E. Ekwall, *Two Early London Subsidy Rolls* (Lund, 1951), pp. 101–11, 160, 203, 204. Galfr' de Kent paid 2s 4d, John de Westewoode 2s, John Oskyn 20s, John de Writele 3s. John Oskyn was probably the brother of Robert Osekyn (or Oskyn), Sworn City Carpenter, as both these names are mentioned in the will of Roger Oskyn, carpenter, proved in 1311. R. R. Sharpe (ed.), *Calendar of Wills proved and Enrolled in the Court of Husting, London—Part I* (1884), p. 223.
12. In particular see the wills of John de Writele and John de Westwoode, Sharpe, op. cit., pp. 177, 224. For other carpenters' wills during this period see ibid., pp. 100, 154, 155, 202, 229, 246, 250, 289, 450, 511.
13. A. H. Thomas (ed.), *Calendar of Plea and Memoranda Rolls, 1364–81* (1929), p. 1; redemption meant the purchase of the freedom of the City.

14. Williams, op. cit., pp. 157–95.
15. Ibid., p. 193. From henceforth, men could obtain the freedom of the City by a seven-year apprenticeship or by nomination by their fathers, being known as patrimony.
16. *Cal. Letter Book D*, pp. 35 et seq. These carpenters purchased their freedom for amounts varying from 10s to 22s 6d.
17. Ekwall, op. cit., pp. 226, 230, 231, 254, 258, 311, 331, 341; and George Unwin, *Finance and Trade under Edward III* (1918), pp. 35–60.
18. See note 12.
19. Public Record Office, *Chancery Miscellanea*, Bundle 46, No. 465. This was transcribed by Charles Welch and printed by the Carpenters Company in 1928 (reprinted 1953).
20. A. H. Thomas (ed.), *Calendar of Plea and Memoranda Rolls 1326–64* (1926), p. 108. The carpenters charged were Reginald de Cornwall, Richard Bene, Henry le Yonge, Roger de Arderne, and John de Essex.
21. Henry S. Lucas, 'The Great European Famine of 1315, 1316 and 1317', *Essays in Economic History* (ed. E. M. Carus-Wilson), Vol. II (1962), pp. 49 et seq.; J. M. W. Bean, 'Plague, Population and Economic Decline in England in the later Middle Ages', *Economic History Review*, April 1963.
22. See note 2; also Salzman, op. cit., pp. 68 et seq.
23. For a lively and interesting discussion of this period see A. R. Bridbury, *Economic Growth: England in the Later Middle Ages* (1962).
24. S. Kramer, *The English Craft Gilds* (1927), pp. 12 et seq.
25. Abstract of the Deeds, Indenture dated January 22, 1428/9.
26. Ibid., Deed Poll dated February 18, 1429/30.
27. Unwin, *Gilds* . . ., op. cit., pp. 176 et seq.
28. *Wardens' Accounts 1438–1516*, p. viii.
29. *Letter Book H*, pp. 41–4; see also pp. 76–7, 96–7, 132–3, etc., for similar examples.
30. *Wardens' Accounts 1438–1516.*
31. A. H. Thomas (ed.), *Calendar of Plea and Memoranda Rolls 1413–37* (1943), pp. vii, xii–xiii, 23, 57, 58, 68, 69, 75, 86, 97, 127, 151–2, 154–7.
32. Guildhall Library, MS. 8353.
33. Guildhall Library, MS. 4339.
34. *Wardens' Accounts 1438–1516*, p. 46.
35. Ibid., p. 49.

36. *Wardens' Accounts 1438–1516*, p. 52.
37. Ibid., p. 53.
38. Ibid., p. 55.
39. A full transcription from Archives of the Corporation of London *Letter Book L*, fos. 228–31, is to be found in *Wardens' Accounts 1438–1516*, pp. 247–53.
40. *Wardens' Accounts 1438–1516*, p. 247.
41. See chapter II.
42. *Wardens' Accounts 1438–1516*, p. 251.
43. *Acts of the Court of the Mercers Company 1453–1527* (1936), with an introduction by Laetitia Lyell, pp. 280–2.
44. *Wardens' Accounts 1438–1516*, p. xi.
45. C. Welch, *History of the Pewterers' Company* (1902), Vol. I, p. 282.
46. *Wardens' Accounts 1438–1516*, p. viii.
47. Ibid., pp. 64, 262.
48. Ibid.
49. *Court Book 1533–73*, the editor points out that there are a number of indications of the incompleteness of the records, p. viii.
50. The following details are drawn from *Court Book 1533–73, Court Book 1573–94*, and from the excellent introductions by the respective editors.
51. *Court Book 1573–94*, pp. xv–xvi.
52. *Wardens' Accounts 1438–1516*; *Wardens' Accounts 1546–71*; *Wardens' Accounts 1571–91*. The amount paid by freemen in the fifteenth century was 3d, this was raised to 4d in the sixteenth century, but through lack of records it is not possible to say exactly when this change was made. For the short period 1556 to 1560, quarterage was raised to 6d, and from 1589 Assistants paid a differential rate of 8d, *Court Book 1573–94*, p. 260.
53. *Court Book 1533–73*, pp. x–xi, 109–10, 121, 140.
54. Ibid., pp. 140–1.
55. *Wardens' Accounts 1571–91*.
56. *Wardens' Accounts 1546–71*, p. 59.
57. *Wardens' Accounts 1438–1516*, p. 41.
58. For a fuller discussion of this point see chapter II; cf., T. C. Barker, *The Girdlers Company* (1957), pp. 53 et seq.
59. For a list of typical gifts see *Wardens' Accounts 1438–1516*, pp. 243–4. For full details see Appendix 4.
60. Sharpe, op. cit., Vol. II, pp. 583–4. See chapter III for further discussion of this bequest.

NOTES

CHAPTER II (PAGES 27 TO 31)

1. See G. A. Williams, *Medieval London: From Commune to Capital* (1963); Ruth Bird, *The Turbulent London of Richard II* (1949).
2. Subsequent details in this respect are drawn generally from the following works: H. M. Colvin (ed.), *The History of the King's Works: The Middle Ages* (2 vols., 1963); L. F. Salzman, *Building in England Down to 1540* (Oxford, 1952); D. Knoop and G. P. Jones, *The Medieval Mason* (1933); M. Postan and E. E. Rich (eds.), *The Cambridge Economic History of Europe* (Cambridge, 1952), Vol. II, chapter VIII, Gwilym Peredur Jones, 'Building in Stone in Medieval Western Europe'; E. M. Jope (ed.), *Studies in Building History* (1961).
3. Knoop and Jones, op. cit., p. 93; Colvin, op. cit. pp. 191–2.
4. A. W. Goodman, 'The Choir Stalls, Winchester Cathedral', in *Archaeological Journal*, 1927. We are indebted to Mr M. Q. Smith for this reference.
5. Salzman, op. cit., pp. 355–594.
6. *Wardens' Accounts 1438–1516*, p. xi note.
7. Salzman, op. cit., pp. 575–7.
8. Cf., *Wardens' Accounts 1438–1516*, *Wardens' Accounts 1546–71*, *Wardens' Accounts 1571–91*.
9. *Court Book 1533–73*; *Court Book 1573–94*.
10. Op. cit.
11. This is clearly deducible from the details of bindings and admissions to the freedom, given in *Court Book 1573–94*.
12. *Court Book 1533–73*, p. 120.
13. Edward Basil Jupp and William Willmer Pocock, *An Historical Account of the Worshipful Company of Carpenters of the City of London* (1887).
14. *Wardens' Accounts 1438–1516*, p. 250.
15. Ibid., p. 252.
16. *Court Book 1533–73*, pp. 187–207; *Court Book 1573–94*, p. vii. Bower Marsh suggested that separate apprenticeship registers were probably kept at this time, *Wardens' Accounts 1546–71*, p. v.
17. G. T. Eltringham, 'Notes on Apprenticeship in the Carpenters Company of London in the Sixteenth and Seventeenth Centuries' (1954) (typescript in Guildhall Library).

18. Cf., *Court Book 1573–94.*
19. A. J. Tawney and R. H. Tawney, 'An Occupational Census of the Seventeenth Century', in *Economic History Review*, 1934.
20. Williams, op. cit., p. 317; Norman G. Brett-James, *The Growth of Stuart London* (1935), pp. 495–515.
21. *Wardens' Accounts 1438–1516*; *Wardens' Accounts 1546–71*; *Wardens' Accounts 1571–91.* The Company regularly employed carpenters and other building labour to work on its properties, and the prevailing wage rates for each year show up very plainly. If anything, these rates were probably lower than those for London carpenters in general, as the Company was almost certainly a very shrewd purchaser of labour. The provincial wage rate is taken from E. H. Phelps Brown and S. W. Hopkins, 'Seven Centuries of Building Wages', in *Economica* 1955. The comparison reveals a London differential rate of 33 per cent higher for the period between the mid-fifteenth and the mid-sixteenth centuries, widening to 50 per cent higher for the remainder of the period down to 1600.
22. *Court Book 1533–73*, p. xiv.
23. See chapter I.
24. H. T. Riley (ed.), *Memorials of London and London Life* (1867), p. 253.
25. *Letter Book G*, p. 301.
26. Salzman, op. cit., pp. 73, 75, 76.
27. Journal, 12 fo. 154b.
28. Repertory, 12 (2) fo. 390/396b.
29. See note 21.
30. The exact nature of this inflation has been the subject of a great deal of discussion, with the result that its effects on real wages are, to say the least, very uncertain: see, for example, Y. S. Brenner, 'The Inflation of Prices in Early Sixteenth Century England', in *Economic History Review*, December 1961, and 'The Inflation of Prices in England, 1551–60', in *Economic History Review*, December 1962; J. D. Gould, 'The Price Revolution Reconsidered', in *Economic History Review*, December 1964; F. J. Fisher, 'Influenza and Inflation in Tudor England', in *Economic History Review*, August 1965 (Essays in Economic History Presented to Professor M. M. Postan); Y. S. Brenner, 'The Price Revolution Reconsidered: A Reply', in *Economic History Review*, August 1965.
31. *Wardens' Accounts 1438–1516*, p. 252.

32. These and subsequent details are drawn from Journal, 12 fo. 155–155b.
33. Journal, 13 fol. 154–5.
34. Ibid.
35. Journal, 16 fo. 221b.
36. Salzman, op. cit. pp. 195 et seq.
37. *Court Book 1533–73*, p. 15.
38. Ibid., pp. 175–6.
39. *Court Book 1573–94*, p. 195.
40. Ibid., p. 123.
41. C. T. Eltringham, 'Building Control and the Carpenters Company of London, 1588–1600' (1954) (Typescript in Guildhall Library). See also the book recording building licences issued by the Company, Guildhall Library MS. 7783.
42. *Remembrancia* (Index to a series of records preserved among the archives of the City of London, 1878), p. 43.
43. Repertory, 20 fo. 449.
44. Peter Ramsey, *Tudor Economic Problems* (1963), p. 111.
45. Salzman, op. cit., p. 576.
46. Ibid., p. 560.
47. See E. H. Phelps Brown and S. V. Hopkins, 'Seven Centuries of the Prices of Consumables, Compared with Builders' Wage Rates', in the *Economica*, 1956.
48. See chapter I.
49. *Letter Book G*, p. 267.
50. The following details are derived from Colvin, op. cit., Vol. I, pp. 216–22.
51. Ibid., pp. 174, 175n, 218, 506n. Osekyn was first employed in 1298.
52. Ibid., Vol. II, p. 1,050. For biographical details of Goldyng see John Harvey, *English Medieval Architects* (1954), p. 116.
53. Colvin, op. cit., Vol. II, p. 1,050; Harvey, op. cit., p. 59.
54. Colvin, op. cit., Vol. II, p. 1,050; Harvey, op. cit., p. 118.
55. Harvey, op. cit., p. 184. It is not possible to establish the exact dates of Mauncey's tenure of this office, but we have followed the earlier historians of the Company in assuming that he was the only appointee between Graveley and Coke; Jupp and Pocock, op.cit., pp. 165–6.
56. Colvin, op. cit., Vol. I, p. 291; Harvey, op. cit., pp. 69–70.
57. Harvey, op. cit., pp. 189–192. On being appointed to this post Nedam took over a number of duties which had previously been

performed by permanent royal officials. There are a number of ways of spelling this name, but we have followed that used in the Company's records.

58. Ibid., pp. 59, 231–2.
59. Jupp and Pocock, op. cit., pp. 169–73.
60. Harvey, op. cit., p. 41.
61. Jupp and Pocock, op. cit., pp. 180–3; *Court Book 1533–73*, p. 212.
62. Ibid., p. 172.
63. Colvin, op. cit., Vol. II, p. 1,054; *Court Book 1533–73*, p. xx.
64. Colvin, op. cit., Vol. II, p. 1,059.
65. The following account is drawn from Harvey, op. cit., pp. 69–70.
66. Ibid., pp. 189–92.
67. J. W. Kirby, 'Building Work at Placentia, 1543–44', in *Transactions of the Greenwich and Lewisham Antiquarian Society*, Vol. IV, No. 6.
68. Ibid., pp. 231–2.
69. *Court Book 1533–73*, p. xix.
70. Ibid.

NOTES

1. *Wardens' Accounts 1438–1516*, p. viii.
2. *Wardens' Accounts 1438–1516*; *Wardens' Accounts 1546–71*; *Wardens' Accounts 1571–91*.
3. *Wardens' Accounts 1438–1516*, p. 2.
4. Ibid., p. 42.
5. Ibid., p. 55.
6. Ibid., p. 152.
7. See chapter II.
8. The will is dated September 3, 1478, and was proved November 8, 1481 (P.C.C. 4 Legge).
9. 15° Ric. 11.C.5–7. By their charter the Carpenters were empowered to hold land to an annual value of 20s free of the law of mortmain.
10. *Letter Book L*, p. 192, no. 2.
11. *Letter Book K*, p. 181.
12. *Letter Book L*, p. 192.
13. W. Archer-Thomas, *Drapers Company: History of the Company's Properties and Trusts* (1939–40), Vol. I, p. 52.
14. Abstract of Deeds.
15. Ibid., p. 55.
16. *Wardens' Accounts 1438–1516*, pp. 21–3, 25–6.
17. Ibid., p. 27.
18. *Wardens' Accounts 1438–1516*, p. 38.
19. Ibid., p. 25.
20. Ibid., pp. 57, 59.
21. See note 8.
22. *Wardens' Accounts 1438–1516*, pp. 77, 78, 79, 129, etc.
23. Will dated September 1, 1517, and enrolled in the Court of Husting, November 20, 1573.
24. See Abstract of Deeds, for this and subsequent documents.
25. *Wardens' Accounts 1438–1516*, p. 246. Cony died shortly after drawing up his will.
26. Will dated March 17, 1519/20, enrolled in the Court of Husting, November 30, 1575.
27. Abstract of Deeds.
28. See Jupp and Pocock, op. cit., pp. 341, 410, 437, 572.

29. P.C.C. 2 Rutland.
30. Abstract of Deeds; *Wardens' Accounts 1571–91*, p. 219.
31. *Court Book 1533–73*, p. 77; *Wardens' Accounts 1546–71*, pp. 43, 59, 87.
32. *Court Book 1533–73*, pp. 61–2; *Wardens' Accounts 1571–91*, pp. 68–9, 82.
33. *Wardens' Accounts 1571–91*, p. 219.
34. Cf., W. K. Jordan, *The Charities of London 1480–1660* (1960), p. 361, where Jordan draws his information on the Carpenters from Jupp and Pocock, who give an incorrect account of bequests made to the Company. A much bigger error occurs in the case of the Drapers Company where Jordan appears to have overlooked the very detailed analysis of the Company's estates by W. Archer-Thomson, op. cit.; on p. v the author lists twenty-nine cases of testamentary devise, which can be compared with Jordan, op. cit., pp. 140, 200, 353–4, 379–80.
35. Cf., W. K. Jordan, op. cit., and also his *Philanthropy in England 1480–1660* (1959).
36. *Wardens' Accounts 1438–1516*.
37. *Court Book 1533–73*, p. 29.
38. *Wardens' Accounts 1546–71*, p. vii.
39. *Wardens' Accounts 1438–1516*, p. 51.
40. *Court Book 1533–73*, p. 63.
41. *Court Book 1573–94*, p. 292.
42. Ibid., p. 289.
43. Cf., ibid., p. 282.
44. *Court Book 1533–73*, p. 89.
45. Ibid., pp. 97, 103.
46. Ibid., p. 138.
47. *Court Book 1573–94*, p. 80.
48. For example, the Drapers Company seems to have been especially deficient in this respect during this period; the rapid growth in its estates over-strained its administrative machinery, see Tom Girtin, *The Triple Crowns* (1964).
49. P.C.C. 29 Lyon 1570.
50. P.C.C. 21 Babington 1568.
51. The index of prices used is that given in E. H. Phelps Brown and Sheila V. Hopkins, 'Seven Centuries of the Prices of Consumables Compared with Builders' Wage Rates', in *Economica*, 1956.
52. *Wardens' Accounts 1571–91*, p. 211.
53. Sometimes it was necessary to suspend feasts. In the summer of

1597 an act of the Privy Council forbade all dinners 'while the present scarcity lasts', *Repertory*, 24 fo. 606–661.
54. *Wardens' Accounts 1438–1516*; *Wardens' Accounts 1546–71*; *Wardens' Accounts 1571–91.*
55. *Court Book 1533–73*, p. 61.
56. *Wardens' Accounts 1571–91*, p. 14. For full details see Appendix 5.
57. Ibid., p. 26.
58. Jupp and Pocock, op. cit., pp. 235–42. For full details see Appendix 5, pp. 225–8.
59. *Wardens' Accounts 1571–91*, pp. 200–1. For a full description of the Company's plate see Appendix 4.
60. *Wardens' Accounts 1438–1516*, pp. 138–9.
61. *Wardens' Accounts 1544–71*, pp. 138–40.
62. Ibid., p. 133.
63. Ibid., p. 219.
64. *Wardens' Accounts 1571–91*, pp. 22, 24–32.
65. Ibid., pp. 101, 104–9, 117–18, 122–4.
66. Ibid., pp. 183–5.
67. Ibid., pp. 196–8.
68. Ibid., pp. 228–32.
69. Guildhall Library, MS. 4326/5, Wardens' Accounts.
70. *Wardens' Accounts 1571–91*, pp. 150–1.
71. *Court Book 1573–94*, p. 209.
72. *Wardens' Accounts 1571–91*, pp. 150–1, 160, 169.
73. *Court Book 1573–94*, p. 243.
74. S. T. Bindoff, *Tudor England* (1950), p. 197.
75. Ibid., p. 284.
76. *Wardens' Accounts 1438–1516*, pp. 80–1.
77. *Wardens' Accounts 1546–71*, p. 91.
78. Ibid., pp. 104–5, 110.
79. *Wardens' Accounts 1546–71*; *Wardens' Accounts 1571–91*; MS. 4326/5, Wardens' Accounts.
80 *Wardens' Accounts 1571–91*, p. 43.
81. MS. 4326/5, Wardens' Accounts, 1597/8.
82. *Wardens' Accounts 1546–71*, p. 110.
83. Cf., Tom Girtin, op. cit.
84. See chapter II.
85. Journal, 23 fo. 44b.

NOTES

1. Guildhall Library, MS. 4329/3, Court Minutes, February 25, 26, 1606/7.
2. Ibid., December 7, 1607.
3. MS. 4329/3, Court Minutes, May 6, 1607.
5. See Norman G. Brett-James, *The Growth of Stuart London* (1935).
6. MS. 4329/3, Court Minutes, April 28, 1608.
7. MS. 4329/3, Court Minutes; MS. 4326/5, Wardens' Accounts.
8. MS. 4329/3, Court Minutes, December 22, 1607, July 5, 1608.
9. Ibid., October 10, 1609.
10. MS. 4329/3, Court Minutes; MS. 4326/5, Wardens' Accounts.
11. See George Unwin, *The Gilds and Companies of London* (1925), especially chapter XVII, pp. 329–51.
12. MS. 4329/3, Court Minutes, October 31, 1609.
13. Ibid., February 7, 1609/10.
14. Ibid., September 6, 1610.
15. Ibid.
16. Ibid.
17. Ibid., December 18, 1628.
18. These figures are based on quarterage returns.
19. *Apprentices' Entry Books 1654–94.*
20. See. G. J. Eltringham, 'Notes on Apprenticeship in the Carpenters Company of London in the Sixteenth and Seventeenth Centuries' (1954, typescript in Guildhall Library).
21. Guildhall Library, MS. 4339.
22. Once again, the figures used in this calculation are only very broad estimates, but the magnitude of the results obtained leaves no doubt that they are perfectly adequate for our purposes. It has been assumed that the population of London and the suburbs was 500,000 at the mid-century, showing a doubling since 1600; see Brett-James, op. cit., pp. 495–517.
23. See C. J. Eltringham, loc. cit.
24. MS. 4329/3–5, Court Minutes; MS 4326/5–8, Wardens' Accounts.
25. Brett-James, op. cit., pp. 105, 295.
26. *Apprentices' Entry Books 1654–94*, p. ix.
27. MS. 4326/10, Wardens' Accounts, 1663–4.

28. MS. 4329/3, Court Minutes, October 30, 1605.
29. Ibid.
30. Repertory, 30 fo. 333–333b.
31. MS. 4329/3, Court Books, May 7, 1616.
32. Ibid., 4, October 30, 1619.
33. Ibid.
34. Ibid., February 8, 1621/2.
35. Ibid., March 31, 1624/5.
36. The Court became so heavily committed financially that for a number of years it was troubled with the business of renewing loans.
37. *Liber Custumarum*, Vol. I, p. 80; at this time joiners were employed mainly on making saddle-bows, and were a subordinate craft to the Saddlers.
38. Journal, 23 fo. 44b.
39. MS. 4329/4, Court Minutes, April 24, 1621.
40. MS. 4326/7–8, Wardens' Accounts, 1623–4, 1624–5.
41. MS. 4329/4, Court Minutes, November 13, 1628.
42. Repertory, 43 fo. 270b.
43. Repertory, 46 fo. 361–82b, 385b.
44. MS. 4329/4, Court Minutes, January 28, 1632/3.
45. Repertory, 77 fo. 128.
46. MS. 4329/5, Court Minutes; MS. 4326/7–10, Wardens' Accounts.
47. Repertory, 77 fo. 208b–209.
48. See chapter II.
49. Repertory, 59 fo. 189b.
50. See George Unwin, *Industrial Organization in the Sixteenth and Seventeenth Centuries* (Oxford, 1904), pp. 212–13.
51. MS. 4329/5, Court Minutes, December 4, 1651.
52. Ibid., April 5, 1655.
53. Edward Basil Jupp and William Willmer Pocock, *An Historical Account of the Worshipful Company of Carpenters* (1887), pp. 309–11.
54. Ibid., p. 635.
55. Repertory, 64 fo. 145b.
56. Unwin, *Industrial Organization*, loc. cit.
57. MS. 4329/4, Court Minutes, August 1631.
58. See C. J. Eltringham, 'Building, Control and the Carpenters Company of London, 1588–1600' (1954, typescript in Guildhall Library); also Brett-James, op. cit., pp. 67–127.
59. Brett-James, op. cit., pp. 107, 116.

60. Charles Wilson, *England's Apprenticeship 1603–1763* (1965), p. 48.
61. Brett-James, op. cit., p. 117.
62. Brett-James, loc. cit.
63. MS. 4329/4, Court Minutes, February 9, 1620/1.
64. MS. 4326/7–8, Wardens' Accounts, 1640–1.
65. MS. 4329/6, Court Minutes, April 27, 1659.
66. For an excellent account of these events see T. F. Reddaway, *The Rebuilding of London After the Great Fire* (1940). The following section relies heavily on this authoritative work.
67. Jupp and Pocock, op. cit., pp. 278–9.
68. Jupp and Pocock, loc. cit.; Reddaway, op. cit., p. 117.
69. Repertory, 75 fo. 88b–89.
70. Jupp and Pocock, op. cit., p. 308.
71. MS. 4329/6–7, Court Books, February 1, 1669/70, March 1, 1669/70, April 5, 1670, etc.
72. Reddaway, op. cit., pp. 80–1, 112–36.
73. Ibid., pp. 130–6.
74. MS. 4329/4, Court Minutes, December 8, 1624.
75. John Wildgoose was Lower Warden in 1652, Middle Warden in 1656, Upper Warden in 1658, and Master in 1660.
76. J. Steven Watson, *A History of the Salters Company* (1963), pp. 71, 81–2.
77. Sir William Foster, *A Short History of the Worshipful Company of Coopers of London* (Cambridge, 1944), p. 76.
78. Ibid.
79. Jupp and Pocock, op. cit., pp. 229, 231, 232; Wildgoose was able to advance the Company a loan of £600 towards the cost of these operations.
80. Reddaway, op. cit., pp. 56, 206–7, 214–18.
81. See chapter V.
82. Reddaway, op. cit., p. 254, n. 1.
83. See chapter II.
84. The King's Carpenters was regularly visited, consulted and dined; cf., MS. 4326/7–8, Wardens' Accounts.
85. Jupp and Pocock, op. cit., p. 171.
86. Ibid., p. 172.
87. MS. 4326/8–10, Wardens' Accounts.
88. See Unwin, *Gilds . . .*, op.cit., pp. 329–51, for a general account of these developments.
89. This was part of a general movement among the minor crafts, but

it was successfully opposed by the 'Great Twelve' Companies who wanted to retain their freedom to recruit the most successful members of the minor Companies; ibid., p. 341.

90. See E. H. Phelps Brown and Sheila V. Hopkins, 'Seven Centuries of the Prices of Consumables, compared with Builders' Wage-rates', in *Economica*, 1956. For the seventeenth century, the Company's records contain only a few details of wage payments.

91. Cf., MS. 4329/5, Court Minutes, May 15, 1645.

92. Jupp and Pocock, op. cit., p. 316.

NOTES

CHAPTER V (PAGES 93 TO 96)

1. Guildhall Library, MS. 4329/4, Court Minutes, February 8, 1621/2.
2. Edward Basil Jupp and William Willmer Pocock, *An Historical Account of the Worshipful Company of Carpenters* (1887), p. 444; MS. 4329/4, Court Minutes, September 15, 1623.
3. MS. 4329/4, Court Minutes, March 31, 1624, April 15, 22, 28, 1624, June 9, 1625, July 7, 1625, etc.
4. Ibid., February 14, 1623/4, June 17, 1625.
5. Ibid., April 28, 1624, April 3, 1626; Petley was granted the lease of the house adjoining the wharf when he took over as manager in 1624.
6. Ibid., May 18, 1626.
7. Ibid., October 11, 1629, November 20, 1629.
8. Abstract of Deeds.
9. Ibid.
10. MS. 4329/4, Court Minutes, November 16, 1630.
11. Ibid., August 9, 1631.
12. Abstract of Deeds.
13. Loc. cit.
14. MS. 4329/4, Court Minutes, May 13, 1634.
15. Abstract of Deeds.
16. See below chapter VI.
17. MS. 4329/5, Court Minutes, April 30, 1651; Abstract of Deeds.
18. John Venn and J. A. Venn, *Alumni Cantabrigienses* (Cambridge, 1924), Part I, Vol. III, p. 300; Court Minutes, op. cit., Vol. 3, August 17, 1602. On a number of occasions Palmer preached the Election Day sermon. See also Appendix 5, p. 229.
19. Ibid., January 11, 1652/3.
20. Abstract of Deeds.
21. MS. 4329/6, Court Minutes, November 24, 1656, January 27, 1656/7.
22. Ibid., 5, November 13, 1654, December 14, 1654.
23. Ibid., 4, August 16, 1620.
24. MS. 4326/7, Wardens' Accounts.

25. MS. 4329/5, Court Minutes, September 28, 1636.
26. MS. 4326/10, Wardens' Accounts, 1660–4.
27. MS. 4329/3, Court Minutes.
28. MS. 4326/3, Wardens' Accounts, 1603–4.
29. MS. 4329/3, Court Minutes, April 17, 1604, August 3, 1604.
30. MS. 4326/3, Wardens' Accounts, 1603–4.
31. MS. 4329/3, Court Minutes, June 12, 1607.
32. Op. cit.
33. MS. 4329/5, Court Minutes, July 29, 1653.
34. Ibid., 3, August 1, 1603.
35. Ibid., May 17/18, 1613.
36. MS. 4326/6–7, Wardens' Accounts, 1618–19.
37. Jupp and Pocock, op. cit., pp. 73–4.
38. MS. 4329/4, Court Minutes, June 2, 1630.
39. MS. 4326/7–8, Wardens' Accounts, 1643–4.
40. MS. 4329/5, Court Minutes, October 31, 1656; part of the cost of this was borne by Richard Sanderson the retiring Master.
41. Ibid., 6, September 29, 1664.
42. Ibid., October 7, 1664.
43. Ibid., March 7, 1664/5.
44. MS. 4326/10, Wardens' Accounts, 1663–4, 1664–5, 1665–6; subsequent details are drawn from the same source.
45. MS. 4329/3, Court Minutes, January 22, 1604/5.
46. Ibid.
47. Ibid., June 12, 1607.
48. Jupp and Pocock, op. cit., p. 429.
49. MS. 4329/3, Court Minutes, January 22, 1615/16.
50. MS. 4326/6–7, Wardens' Accounts, 1615–16.
51. Ibid.
52. MS. 4329/3, Court Minutes, July 31, 1618.
53. Ibid., 4, September 11, 1619.
54. MS. 4326/7–8, Wardens' Accounts, 1640–1.
55. MS. 4329/5, Court Minutes, February 6, 1654/5.
56. For a detailed account of this episode see T. W. Moody, *The Londonderry Plantation 1609–41* (Belfast, 1939).
57. MS. 4329/3, Court Minutes, July 5, 1609, March 20, 1609/10, etc.
58. Ibid., October 31, 1615, May 7, 1616, October 30, 1616, etc.
59. MS. 4326/6–7, Wardens' Accounts.
60. See Jupp and Pocock, op. cit., pp. 251–4.
61. *Court Books 1573–94*, p. 92.
62. It has proved impossible to trace a will of Richard Sheres.

63. Edmund Basil Jupp, *Genealogical Memoranda Relating to Richard Wyatt*, etc. (private, no date).
64. MS. 4326/7, Wardens' Accounts.
65. MS. 4329/4, Court Minutes, August 31, 1626.
66. Ibid., June 16, 1626.
67. Ibid., July 28, 1628.
68. Ibid., November 10, 1628.
69. MS. 4329/4, Court Minutes, November 30, 1633.
70. Jupp and Pocock, op. cit., p. 255.
71. MS. 4326, Wardens' Accounts.
72. The following details are drawn from MS. 4326, Wardens' Accounts.
73. MS. 4329/3, Court Minutes, August 30, 1604.
74. Guildhall Library, MS. 4339.
75. MS. 4329/3, Court Minutes, April 5, 1609.
76. Moody, op. cit., p. 98.
77. MS. 4329/4, Court Minutes, January 18, 1620/1; MS. 4326/7–8, Wardens' Accounts, 1626–7. See also Appendix 4, pp. 205–7.
78. MS. 4329/4, Court Minutes, July 1, 1628.
79. Ibid., September 11, 1627, January 1, 1627/8.
80. Ibid., 5, January 21, 1635/6.
81. The original is at Carpenters' Hall.
82. See T. F. Reddaway, *The Rebuilding of London After the Great Fire* (1940), pp. 250–1.
83. MS. 4326/8, Wardens' Accounts, 1640–1, 1641–2, 1642–3; MS. 4329/5, Court Minutes, March 4, 1640/1, May 1, 1643, etc. See also Appendix 4, p. 207.
84. MS. 4329/5, Court Minutes, December 8, 1648. See also Appendix 4, pp. 207–8.
85. Ibid., April 11, 1649.
86. For full details see MS. 4326/7–10, Wardens' Accounts, and MS. 4329/5–7, Court Minutes.
87. MS. 4329/5, Court Minutes, March 25, 1644/5.
88. Ibid., November 20, 1652.
89. Ibid., 6, September 13, 1659. See also Appendix 4, p. 208.
90. Ibid., May 5, 1654.
91. Ibid., October 6, 1654.
92. MS. 4326/10, Wardens' Accounts.
93. Ibid., 1663/4. In addition some plate was sold; see Appendix 4, p. 208.
94. Ibid., 1665/6.

95. Ibid., 5, 1602/3.
96. Ibid., 6–7, 1621/2.
97. Ibid., 7–8, 1643/4.
98. Ibid., 6, 1621/2.
99. MS. 4329/4, Court Minutes, op. cit., October 21, 1623/4.
100. MS. 4326/5, Wardens' Accounts, 1604–5.
101. Jupp and Pocock, op. cit., p. 215. See Appendix 5, pp. 9–10.
102. MS. 4329/5–6, Court Minutes, December 15, 1648. For full descriptions of more possessions see Appendices 4 and 5.
103. Ibid., October 11, 1652.
104. Ibid., 6, February 1, 1658/9.
105. MS. 4329/5, Court Minutes, August 30, 1644.
106. Ibid., September 28, 1653.
107. Guildhall Library, MS. 4332, Register of Wills and Leases, Relating to the Carpenters Company, No. 5.
108. Ibid., No. 6.
109. MS. 4329/5, Court Minutes, October 6, 1654.
110. Ibid., 4, June 28, 1619.
111. Ibid., October 31, 1620.
112. The index of prices used is that of E. H. Phelps Brown and Sheila V. Hopkins, 'Seven Centuries of the Prices of Consumables, Compared with Builders' Wage-rates', in *Economica*, November 1956.
113. MS. 4329/3, Court Minutes, September 9, 1605.
114. MS. 4329/5, Court Minutes, August 15, 1644.
115. Ibid., May 15, 1650, September 10, 1650.
116. See Jupp and Pocock, op. cit., p. 453.
117. Cf. Chapter III, notes 50, 88.

NOTES

CHAPTER VI (PAGES 114 TO 118)

1. T. F. Reddaway, *The Rebuilding of London after the Great Fire* (1940), p. 120.
2. W. A. D. Englefield, *The History of the Painter-Stainers Company of London* (1923), p. 133.
3. Guildhall Library, MS. 4329/7, Court Minutes, February 1, 1669/70.
4. See chapter IV.
5. MS. 4329/8, December 6, 1670, June 6, 1671, etc.
6. Ibid., 7, February 1, 1669/70.
7. Ibid., May 3, 1670, June 2, 1670.
8. Repertory, 80 fo. 29.
9. Ibid., 80 fo. 40b–41.
10. See E. H. Phelps Brown and Sheila V. Hopkins, 'Seven Centuries of the Prices of Consumables, Compared with Builders' Wage-Rates', in *Economica*, 1956.
11. Reddaway, op. cit., pp. 300, et seq.
12. See chapter IV.
13. MS. 4329/8, Court Minutes, January 16, 1681/2, February 7, 1681/2.
14. Ibid., 10, February 7, 1687/8.
15. Ibid.
16. Repertory, 98 fo. 19–20, 64–5.
17. The following details are drawn from *Apprentices' Entry Books 1654–94*, pp. x–xi.
18. See G. J. Eltringham, 'Notes on Apprenticeship in the Carpenters Company London in the Sixteenth and Seventeenth Centuries' (1954, typescript in Guildhall Library), for this and similar details.
19. MS. 4329/11, Court Minutes, April 4, 1693.
20. *Apprentices' Entry Books 1654–94*, op. cit.
21. Edward Basil Jupp and William Willmer Pocock, *An Historical Account of the Worshipful Company of Carpenters* (1887), p. 268.
22. See John E. N. Hearsey, *London and the Great Fire* (1965), map showing the spread of the fire.
23. MS. 4329/6, Court Minutes, October 6, 1668.
24. Ibid., September 18, 1666.

25. MS. 4329/6, Court Minutes, October 2, 1666.
26. Ibid.
27. Ibid., October 12, 1666.
28. Ibid., October 7, 1670.
29. Ibid., 8, December 14, 1670.
30. Hearsey, op. cit., p. 169.
31. MS. 4326/10, Wardens' Accounts, 1664–5.
32. MS. 4329/8, Court Minutes, December 14, 1670.
33. Ibid., March 9, 1670/1.
34. Jupp and Pocock, op. cit., p. 231.
35. The accounts for these years are missing.
36. MS. 4329/8, Court Minutes, September 20, 1671.
37. Ibid., September 28, 1671.
38. Ibid., August 13, 1672.
39. Ibid., September 10, 1672.
40. Ibid., December 5, 1671.
41. Ibid., August 13, 1672.
42. Ibid., December 6, 1672.
43. Ibid., July 1, 1673.
44. Ibid., February 4, 1672/3.
45. Ibid., February 6, 1676/7.
46. Ibid., March 6, 1676/7.
47. Ibid., July 3, 1677.
48. Ibid., August 7, 1677.
49. Ibid., January 15, 1676/7.
50. Ibid., August 7, 1677.
51. Ibid.
52. Ibid.
53. Ibid., August 14, 1677.
54. See chapter V.
55. MS. 4329/8, Court Minutes, May 16, 1673.
56. Ibid., February 4, 1672/3.
57. Ibid., March 18, 1673/4.
58. Ibid., February 6, 1676/7.
59. Abstract of Deeds.
60. Ibid.
61. MS. 4329/8, Court Minutes, August 10, 1680.
62. MS. 4326/11, Wardens' Accounts.
63. MS. 4329/8, Court Minutes, October 5, 1680.
64. Cf., ibid., September 4, 1677, August 5, 1679.
65. Ibid., March 24, 1680/1, for this and following details.

66. MS. 4326/11, Wardens' Accounts, 1680–1.
67. MS. 4329/8, Court Minutes, April 15, 1682.
68. Ibid., May 2, 1682.
69. Ibid., August 5, 1679.
70. Ibid., September 12, 1681.
71. Ibid., June 19, 1684.
72. Ibid.
73. Ibid., August 11, 1684.
74. Ibid.
75. Ibid., Vol. 10, March 2, 1684/5.
76. Ibid., June 1, 1686; the original is at Carpenters' Hall.
77. Ibid., September 25, October 11, October 18, 1687.
78. Ibid., February 5, 1688/9.
79. Charles Wilson, *England's Apprenticeship 1603–1763* (1965), pp. 216–25.
80. MS. 4326/11, Wardens' Accounts, 1699/1700.
81. Ibid.
82. Ibid.
83. MS. 4329/11, Court Minutes, March 11, 1694/5. See also Appendix 4, p. 210.
84. MS. 4326/11, Wardens' Accounts, 1693–4.
85. MS. 4329/11, Court Minutes, October 5, 1697.
86. Ibid., October 20, 1697.
87. MS. 4326/11, Wardens' Accounts.
88. MS. 4329/10, Court Minutes, December 4, 1688, April 10, 1689.
89. Ibid., 11, November 7, 1693.
90. Tom Girtin, *The Triple Crowns* (1964), pp. 273–87.
91. Based on the quarterage returns.
92. See H. M. Colvin, *A Biographical Dictionary of English Architects 1600–1840* (1954), p. 57.

NOTES

CHAPTER VII (PAGES 129 TO 136)

1. Guildhall Library, MS. 4326/11, Wardens' Accounts, 1673–1740; MS. 4326/12, Wardens' Accounts, 1740–1828.
2. MS. 4329/13, Court Minutes, 5, April 29, 1720; Wardens' Accounts.
3. Wardens' Accounts.
4. MS. 4329/16. Note pasted on first page. The dates have been inserted by us.
5. MS. 4329/15, Court Minutes, February 2, 1724/5.
6. *New Complete Guide to London* (1772); *London Directory* 1780.
7. The Court at its meeting on November 7, 1738, had decided to put an end to breakfasts, which had been customary 'for many years past', but this decision had evidently not been acted upon. (MS. 4329/17.)
8. T. S. Ashton, *Economic Fluctuations in England, 1700–1800* (Oxford, 1959), pp. 19–20.
9. MS. 4329/16, Court Minutes, June 7, 1743.
10. MS. 4329/15, Court Minutes, July 5, 1737.
11. Ibid.
12. MS. 4329/16, Court Minutes, December 4, 1744.
13. Ibid., July 2, 1752.
14. MS. 4329/20, Court Minutes, July 3, 1764.
15. Ibid., September 4, 1764.
16. Ibid., February 4, 1766.
17. MS. 4329/15, Court Minutes, June 7, 1737.
18. MS. 4329/20, Court Minutes, April 4, 1775.
19. MS. 4329/15, Court Minutes, January 1, 1733/4; April 2, 1734.
20. With meticulous care. An enquiry into the accounts between 1685 and 1760 showed that income totalled £3,782 and expenditure £3,733 (MS. 4329/20, Court Minutes, June 2, 1761).
21. MS. 4329/15, Court Minutes, December 7, 1736. MS. 4326/11, Wardens' Accounts, 1735–6.
22. Ibid.
23. MS. 4326/12, Wardens' Accounts, 1799–1800.
24. MS. 4329/13, Court Minutes, September 5, December 5, 1721; January 2, 1721/2.

25. MS. 4329/20, Court Minutes.
26. MS. 4329/20, Court Minutes, May 2, 1769.
27. MS. 4329/12, Court Minutes, May 18, 1722.
28. MS. 4329/20, Court Minutes, June 3, October 7, 1777; March 3, April 7, 1778; February 5, 1779.
29. Ibid., 4, May 18, 1779. For William Jupp, see also below, pp. 143–4.
30. MS. 4329/20, Court Minutes, October 5, 1779; February 6, April 3, 1781; November 5, 1782.
31. MS. 3429/13, Court Minutes, January 3, 1720/1.
32. MS. 4329/15, Court Minutes, July 3, 1733.
33. Ibid., May 4, 1736.
34. MS. 4329/17, Court Minutes, July 3, 1739.
35. MS. 4335, Freedom Admission Books.
36. MS. 4329/15, Court Minutes.
37. MS. 4335, Court Minutes.
38. The twenty-four included the Master and Wardens (MS. 4329/16, Court Minutes, May 15, 1746).
39. MS. 4329/17, Court Minutes, August 1, 1738; MS. 4329/16, Court Minutes, March 17, 1758.
40. MS. 4329/17, Memorandum on first page of Court Minutes, 1737–57.
41. MS. 4329/20, Court Minutes, January 4, 1791.
42. Ibid., February 4, 1772. On February 3, 1795, the Court ordered that not more than twenty-four silver gilt medals should be bought for the Court and not more than 120 silver medals for the Livery (MS. 4329/22).
43. MS. 4329/16, Court Minutes, June 24, 1751.
44. Ibid. (This Minute also includes a summary of the Clerk's income from 1688). MS 4326/12, Wardens' Accounts, 1750–1, and MS. 4329/15, Court Minutes, July 2, 1751.
45. Ibid., October 7, 1760.
46. MS. 4329/13, Court Minutes, November 4, December 2, 1712.
47. MS. 4329/15, Court Minutes, October 3, 1732.
48. MS. 4329/17, Court Minutes, March 7, 1737/8.
49. MS. 4329/20, Court Minutes, November 5, 1782.
50. The total number of Liverymen was limited to 100 in 1736 (MS. 4329/15, Court Minutes, June 1, 1736).
51. MS. 4326/11, Wardens' Accounts, 1699–1700; MS. 4329/20, Court Minutes, March 6, 1772, December 5, 1780, November 5, 1782.
52. Sir Henry Clay, Lord Norman (1957), p. 2.
53. MS. 4329/20; MS. 4329/22: See also the supplement to the British

Directory (1793), which gives a list of Liverymen, their companies and the professions to which each belonged.

54. MS. 4329/13, Court Minutes, August 14, 1711, December 7, 1713; *Dictionary of National Biography* (Supplement 1909).

55. H. M. Colvin, *A Biographical Dictionary of English Architects, 1660–1840* (1954), pp. 7, 8.

56. Alfred B. Beaven, *The Aldermen of the City of London* (1913), Vol. II, p. 138; William Hone, *The Year Book of Daily Recreation and Information* (1832), pp. 669–70; *City Biography* (2nd ed. 1800); cuttings at Guildhall Library, C78, including copies of monumental inscriptions at St Giles, Cripplegate.

57. *Gentleman's Magazine*, Vol. 4 (1734), p. 572.

58. Colvin, op. cit., 314–16; *Dictionary of National Biography*.

59. Colvin, op. cit., 18, 330–1; *Dictionary of National Biography*.

60. Colvin, op. cit., p. 331. For R. W. Jupp's election as Clerk, see MS. 4329/22, Court Minutes, June 19, 1798.

NOTES

1. Guildhall Library, MS. 4326/12, Wardens' Accounts, 1740–1828.
2. MS. 4329/23, Court Minutes, February 2, June 7, 1830.
3. MS. 4326/15, Wardens' Accounts, 1828–80.
4. MS. 4329/22, Court Minutes, January 1, 1805.
5. MS. 4334/2, Livery Lists, 1823–76.
6. MS. 4329/23, Court Minutes, September 1, 1835. Not to be confused with Thomas Cubitt, the famous contractor.
7. MS. 4329/22, Court Minutes, August 2, 1803. The date 1801 given in more recent printed lists would appear to be incorrect.
8. Ibid., September 7, 1819.
9. Ibid., November 2, 1819.
10. *A Letter to the Liverymen of the Worshipful Company of Carpenters* (1825). A copy is to be found in Guildhall Library.
11. MS. 4329/23, Court Minutes, February 7, 1826.
12. Ibid., March 2, October 5, 1830.
13. Ibid., October 5, 1830.
14. Ibid., September 3, October 7, 1833; July 7, 1834; September 6, October 4, 1836.
15. Ibid., June 6, July 4, 1837.
16. Ibid., October 3, 1837; Edward Basil Jupp and William Willmer Pocock, *An Historical Account of the Worshipful Company of Carpenters of the City of London* (1887), p. 598.
17. MS. 4329/23, Court Minutes, November 5, 1839.
18. Ibid., December 3, 1839; January 7, 1840; May 4, 1841.
19. Ibid., June 24, 1841.
20. Ibid., August 3, 1841.
21. Ibid., July 5, October 4, 1842.
22. Ibid., November 7, 1843; MS 4329/26, Court Minutes, May 6, 1845.
23. MS. 4329/23, Court Minutes, January 3, 1843.
24. Ibid., January 2, 1844.
25. MS. 4329/26, Court Minutes, January 6, 1846.
26. Ibid.
27. Jupp and Pocock, op.cit., pp. 236–8.
28. Jupp and Pocock, op.cit., pp. 240–1. See also chapter III, p. 63.

29. Ibid., p. ix.
30. MS. 4329/26, Court Minutes, February 1, 1848.
31. By 1871, the Clerk received a basic salary of £400 and a total income of £555. The basic salary was raised to £500 in October of that year (Court Minutes, October 3, 1871).
32. Ibid., September 5, 1848.
33. Ibid., October 5, 1852.
34. *London and Its Environs* (1820), p. 32
35. Cecil J. Allen, *The Great Eastern Railway* (3rd ed. 1961), pp. 17–18.
36. MS. 4329/26, Court Minutes, December 1, 1846; January 5, 1847.
37. Ibid., December 7, 1847.
38. Ibid., September 1, 1846, January 5, February 2, 1847.
39. MS. 4329/23, Court Minutes, July 5, 1842.
40. MS. 4329/26, Court Minutes, July 4, August 1, 1848.
41. Ibid., September 3, 1850.
42. Ibid., July 5, August 2, September 5, 1853; November 7, 1854; March 6, April 3, 1855.
43. Ibid., April 6, 1852; December 7, 1853; December 2, 1856.
44. Ibid., January 1, 1856.
45. Ibid., July 3, 1855; February 5, 1856.
46. Carpenters' Hall, Court Minutes (1859–72), November 5, December 3, 1861; December 1, 1863.
47. Ibid., September 1, 1862.
48. Ibid., December 1, 1863.
49. Ibid., August 2, 1864.
50. Ibid., May 3, July 5, 1864.
51. Ibid., July 5, 1864.
52. Ibid., May 5, 1868; November 2, 1869.
53. Ibid., May 2, 1871.
54. Ibid., March 6, June 3, 1862; January 6, October 6, 1863.
55. Ibid., May 2, July 4, 1865; November 27, 1866; February 2, 1869.
56. Ibid., May 3, 1870; September 5, 1871; June 4, 1872; Court Minutes (1872–82), July 2, 1872. Report of the City of London Livery Companies Commission, 1884, c. 4073–II XXXIX Pt. 3, p. 225.
57. Court Minutes (1872–82), March 3, December 1, 1874; August, 10 1875; February 1, March 7, April 4, November 7, 1876.
58. Ibid., March 4, November 4, 1873; June 6, 1874; January 4, 1876.
59. *The Builder*, January 23, 1920.

60. MS. 4329/26, Court Minutes, October 7, 1845.
61. Ibid., August 1, 1848.
62. Ibid., December 17, 1850.
63. Ibid., November 2, 1853.
64. Carpenters' Hall, Court Minutes (1859–72), March 1, 1859.
65. Ibid., March 6, April 10, 1860.
66. MS. 4326/15, Wardens' Accounts 1828–80; Report of the City of London Livery Companies Commission, 1884, C.4073–II XXXIX, Pt. 3, p. 237. In 1857 the Company sold land in Bramshot and bought ground rents and some property in Victoria Grove, Chelsea (Court Minutes, December 2, 1856; December 9, 1857).
67. Report of the City of London Livery Companies Commission, 1884 [C. 4073–I & II] XXXIX, Pts. 2 & 3.
68. Guildhall Library, Noble Collection C. 78, news-cuttings, October 2, 1849; November 25, 1855.
69. Ibid., *Penny Illustrated Paper*, November 14, 1863; *Illustrated London News*, November 21, 1863; news-cuttings, December 8, 1855; obit., *The Times*, April 19, 1897.
70. Ibid., *Illustrated London News*, November 7, 1868; obit., *The Times*, May 22, 1897.
71. Report of London Livery Companies Commission, p. 228. In 1877 freedom fines were increased to £3 for admission by patrimony or servitude and £15 15s od for admission by redemption. The former were to be fined a further £35 on admission to the Livery and the redemptioners a further £52 10s od (Court Minutes, July 3, 1877).
72. Carpenters' Hall, Court Minutes (1872–82), August 4, 1874; June 1, August 3, 1875.
73. The son of William F. Pocock, Master in 1840, he was admitted to the Livery on August 1, 1843. He was concerned with the purchase of ground rents in 1857 (above, fn. 66) and was to be responsible for a new edition of Jupp's History which was published in 1887.
74. Court Minutes, June 23, 1876.
75. *The Builder*, August 12, 1876.
76. Court Minutes, November 17, 1876.
77. Ibid., June 5, 1877.
78. Ibid., November 5, 1878.
79. Ibid., March 4, 1879.
80. Ibid., November 4, 1879.
81. Ibid., December 2, 1879; January 27, 1880.

82. *The Times*, November 26, 1880.
83. For plans of the two storeys and photographs of the exterior and Livery Hall, see *The Builder*, January 23, 1920.
84. *The Builder*, December 4, 1880.
85. *The Builder*, February 9, 1878.
86. Ibid.

NOTES

1. D. S. L. Cardwell, *The Organization of Science in England* (1957) pp. 98–103.
2. Carpenters' Hall, Court Minutes (1883–92), August 7, 1883; May 6, 1884; October 6, 1885; August 2, 1887.
3. Ibid., November 4, December 15, 1884.
4. Ibid., January 3, 1886.
5. Ibid., May 25, 1886.
6. Ibid., February 2, 1886.
7. Carpenters' Hall, Court Minutes (1872–82), November 4, 1879.
8. Ibid., June 7, 1881.
9. Court Minutes (1883–92), July 1, 1884; January 6, 1885.
10. Ibid., February 16, 1886.
11. Ibid., May 4, 1886.
12. Ibid., May 25, 1886.
13. Ibid., October 19, 1886.
14. Ibid., November 2, 1886.
15. Ibid., June 7, 1887.
16. Ibid., February 5, March 5, July 23, 1889; May 6, June 2, 1890; May 5, 1891.
17. Ibid., May 3, 1892.
18. Much of this paragraph is based upon *The Story of the Carpenters' Technical School (1891–1905) and of the Old Carpentarians*, a duplicated booklet produced privately by the committee of the Old Carpentarians' Association, 1964.
19. Carpenters' Hall, Court Minutes (1893–1904), August 7, 1894; August 3, 1897.
20. Ibid., April 4, June 20, 1893; February 27, 1894.
21. Ibid.
22. Court Minutes (1883–92), July 1, 1884.
23. Ibid., July 3, 1888. A third exhibition was held in 1892 (ibid., June 7, 1892).
24. Ibid., July 3, 1888.
25. Ibid., August 5, 1890.
26. H. Westbury Preston, *The Worshipful Company of Carpenters* (privately printed by the Company, 1955), p. 35; Court Minutes, July 24, November 6, 1888.

27. Court Minutes (1883–92), July 3, 1883.
28. Ibid., February 4, 1890.
29. Ibid., July 7, 1896; April 6, 1897; June 7, 1898; Preston, op. cit., p. 35. We are grateful to Cdr. A. W. Preston for information about the relationship between Sir Henry Harben and S. W. Preston. For the Harben and Chamberlain families, see J. L. Garvin, *The Life of Joseph Chamberlain*, Vol. I (1932), pp. 16–19.
30. Court Minutes (1883–92), October 7, 1884.
31. Ibid., November 3, 1885; January 18, March 1, 1887.
32. For instance, see Court Minutes, January 2, 1883; December 2, 1884; May 4, 1886 and *Story of Carpenters' Technical School*, p. 2.
33. Court Minutes, August 3, 1897.
34. Ibid., March 31, 1885.
35. Ibid., March 4, 1890.
36. Ibid., August 7, 1888.
37. Ibid., March 4, 1890; April 2, 1895.
38. The rest of this chapter is based upon H. Westbury Preston, *The Worshipful Company of Carpenters* (London: The Carpenters Company, 1953), certain annual reports to the Livery, and information from Captain Barstow, Mr A. W. Powell and Cdr A. W. Preston.
39. The President of the IBICC has always been a member of the Court of the Carpenters Company. The London branch used to hold its meetings at Carpenters' Hall and resumed the practice after the new Hall was opened in 1960. The Joinery Managers Association, formed in 1950, has also met at the Hall since 1960. We are grateful to Capt. Barstow for this information.
40. A list of honorary members is to be found in Appendix 6. In 1960 the Court made a distinction between honorary Liverymen (in honour and appreciation of services rendered to the country) and honorary freemen (in honour and appreciation of services rendered to the Company). Mr H. A. Hall, the architect of the new Carpenters' Hall, was the first person to be elected to the new category of honorary freemen.
41. Charles E. Peterson, 'Carpenter's Hall', *Transactions of the American Philosophical Society*, Vol. 43, pt. 1. We are grateful to Cdr A. W. Preston for drawing our attention to this paper.
42. A search through the London apprenticeship lists from 1660 to 1720 produced the names of John Nichols and John Harrison (men of the same name were founders of the Philadelphia Company) and William Clark and William Coleman (men of the same

name were among its early members). There were no fewer than three separate William Clarks apprenticed in London between 1693 and 1704. The names of the Philadelphia members are contained in a letter from T. S. Keefer, Jr, to K. M. Roberts, dated May 1, 1963, a copy of which is preserved among the records at Carpenters' Hall.

43. This information is based upon Cdr Preston's account of his visit to Philadelphia in October 1957 during his term of office as Master. The Philadelphia Company in that year resolved that the Master of the London Carpenters Company for the time being should in future be one of its honorary members.

INDEX

Ackroyd, Sir Cuthbert, 169
Aldridge, 87
allied crafts, *see* demarcation, etc., *also* various companies
Ambrose, Richard, 43, 45
apprenticeship:
   regulations and effectiveness, 29, 30–4, 39–40, 47, 69, 70–1, 72, 73, 74–5, 85, 86, 90–1, 104, 116–17, 137–8, 237 No. 15; *see also* Carpenters Company
architects, 89, 142, 143, 144
Architects' Club, The, 143
Armourers and Braziers, 155

Bakers, 155
Banks (or Banckes), Mathew, 89, 127–8
Benkes (or Bynckes), Thomas, 52
Barbers, 101
Bartlett School of Architecture, 164
Beadle, 23, 62, 108, 110, 112, 117, 140–1
Bird, John, 43
Black Death, 17, 18, 35
Bland, John, 92
Blinkhorne, John 76, 77, 92, 93
Blinkhorne, Margaret, 92
boardmen, 36
Boxmakers, 86
Boyce, Sir Leslie, 169
Bradshaw, Lawrence, 43
Brewers, 101, 155
Bricklayers, 82, 83, 85, 86, 114, 115, 160
Brixton School of Building, 164
building:
   contractors, 33, 40, 41, 83, 87, 88, 89, 142
   contracts, 28–9, 41
   construction, 37, 61, 77
   licences, 48
   materials, 22, 30, 36–8, 70, 76, 84, 86, 88
   regulations, 13, 14, 36, 38–9, 40, 69, 70, 72, 73–4, 81, 83–4
Butchers, 23

carpenters:
   craft, 27, 73–4, 83–4
   total number of, 31–3, 39, 73
   wills, 15, 16, 19

Carpenters Company:
   accounts, 19
   apprentices, geographical origins, 31, 73, 116–17
   apprenticeship, *see* separate heading
   arms, 20–1
   Assistants, 22, 25, 34, 40, 71, 73, 81, 112, 117, 121, 122
   avoidance of office, 90, 124
   bequests, *see* separate heading
   black box (or chest), 46, 63, 99, 126
   borrowing by, 119–20, 123
   capital, 46, 67, 92, 96, 111, 145
   charities and pensions, 61, 110, 127, 132–3, 147, 158–9; *see also* gifts and bequests
   charter, (1477) 13, 20–1, 50; (1606) 104–5; (1640) 105; (1673) 121; (1686) 124–5
   Court, 23–4, 121, 139
   economy campaigns, 107, 119, 122, 131–2, 133
   estates, *see* property
   expenditure, 61, 63, 67, 104, 120, 159
   fines for trade offences, *see* separate heading
   freedom, 30–1, 47, 61, 73, 138–9
   Hall, *see* separate heading
   income, 46, 48, 58, 60, 92, 104, 107, 110–11, 113, 122, 126, 127, 129, 131, 145, 155, 158–9, 163, 164
   levies on, 66, 105, 106, 126, 131
   Livery or Clothing, 22, 24–5, 47, 62, 70, 92, 104, 106, 112, 126, 139, 141, 145–6, 163, 166, 169
   loans by, 66, 104, 105, 106–8, 126
   membership, 24, 26, 31, 72–3, 89, 127
   ordinances, (1333) 16–17, 170; (1455–87) 21–3, 29–30, 33–4, 41; (1606/7) 69–70, 82
   patrimony, 30, 112–13, 117, 155, 237 No. 15
   procedure, 24–5, 65, 112
   quarterage, 24, 46–7, 61, 62
   redemption, 15, 30, 114, 117, 139, 155, 163, 236 No. 13

INDEX

Philadelphia Carpenters Company, 169–70
philanthropy, apparent rise in the sixteenth
    century, 58, 244 No. 34
Plasterers, 82, 85, 86, 114, 115
plate, 25, 62, 109, 129–30, appendix 4
Plumbers, 19, 23, 114
Pocock, W. F., 149
Pocock, W. W., 156, 162
poor workmanship, 84; *see also* fines for
    trade offences
Pope, William, 122
Portington, William, 71, 89, 128
Preston, Alfred, 162
Preston, H. Westbury, 164, 165, 166
Preston, Stanton W., 156, 161, 162–3
property (Carpenters Company's estates):
    Lime Street, 25, 48, 49–50, 51, 52, 56,
        58, 63, 64, 95, 99, 100, 118, 153, 167
    London Wall, 48, 50, 52, 53, 54, 56, 57,
        63, 95, 96, 97, 119, 135–6
    Hall Almshouses, 50
    Whitefriars Wharf, 77, 92–3, 94, 97
    Norton Folgate, 94, 100, 105, 153
    Crutched Friars, 94, 95, 96, 100, 105,
        120–1, 122, 126
    Southwark (Bermondsey Street), 94,
        123, 152
    Great Almonry (Westminster), 95, 96,
        97 152
    Godalming Almshouses, 102–4
    Coleman Street, 122
    Fenchurch Street, 122, 123, 126, 127
    Carpenters Buildings, 135–6
    Stratford, 135, 136, 145, 151–3, 159,
        167, 168
    Twickenham Almshouses, 149, 163
    Rustington Convalescent Home, 162,
        166; *see also* leases, rents, sales of
        property to railway companies,
        tenants, view day

quo warranto proceedings, 124–5

railways, *see* sales of property to
'railway mania', 154
Read, John, 94
Redebourne, Stephen de, 15
redemption, *see under* Carpenters
    Company
Regent Street Polytechnic, 164
rents, 48, 58, 92, 118, 126, 127, 129, 145

Revell, John, 43
Rich, Sir Robert, 40
Royal Commission on The City Com-
    panies, 158–9
royal demands for loans, *see* Carpenters
    Company, loans by,
Russell, John, 42–3, 44

Saddlers, 155
sales of property to railway companies,
    148, 151–3
Salters Hall, 87
sawyards, 37, 81
sawyers, 81, 82, 83, 85–6, 116; *see also*
    opposite wage rates
Scott, John, 128
Scriveners, 101
Serle, William, 29, 41
Sheres, Roger, 102
Sheres, Thomas, 45
Shipwrights, 81, 83, 86
Simmons, John, published attack on the
    Company, 147–8
Skinners, 23, 142
Smart, Thomas, 52, 53, 56, 57
Smiths, 114
South Eastern Railway, 152
South Sea Company, 129
Staines, Sir William, 142
Stationers, 23
Statute of Apprentices, 32
Stockdale, Sir Edmund, 169
Stodeye, William, 19
Street, William, 19
subsidy rolls, 15, 16
Surveyor of the King's Works, 42, 43, 89
Surveyor of the Fabric of St Paul's
    Cathedral, 143
Surveyor of the Fabric of Westminster
    Abbey, 143
Sworn Masons and Carpenters of the City
    of London, 13–14, 16, 18, 20, 36, 38,
    40, 42, 44, 68, 69, 89, 236 No. 11

Taylor, William, 98
technical education, 158–61, 162, 164
tenants, 95–6
testamentary devise, 49, 50, 51, 52, 57–8
timber, *see* building materials
timber-frame houses, 37
timbermen, 36

270

271